# THE LOVE YOU FIGHT FOR

A NEXT LIFE NOVEL

BRIT BENSON

# THE LOVE YOU FIGHT FOR

Copyright© 2024 by Brit Benson

All rights reserved.

No part of this book may be reproduced, distributed, or transmitted in any form or by any electronic or mechanical means, including information storage and retrieval systems, without written permission from the author, except for the use of brief quotations in a book review and certain other noncommercial use permitted by copyright law.

Any use of this publication to "train" generative artificial intelligence (AI) technologies to generate text is expressly prohibited. No generative AI was used in the writing of this work. The author expressly prohibits any entity from using this publication for purposes of training AI technologies to generate text, including without limitation technologies that are capable of generating works in the same style or genre as this publication.

This book is a work of fiction. Names, characters, places, and incidents are either the product of the author's imagination or are used fictitiously. Any resemblance to actual persons and things living or dead, locales, or events is entirely coincidental. Except for the original material written by the author, all mention of films, television shows and songs, song titles, and lyrics mentioned in the novel are the property of the songwriters and copyright holders.

**Cover Design:** Murphy Rae

**Editing:** Rebecca at Fairest Reviews Editing Services, Emily Lawrence at Lawrence Editing, Sarah Plotcher at All Encompassing Books

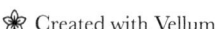 Created with Vellum

## PLAYLIST

Matilda – Harry Styles
Little Girl Gone – CHINCHILLA
Talk – Hozier
Devil is a Woman – Cloudy June
Breakfast – Dove Cameron
don't break my... – Kenzie Cait
I Did Something Bad – Taylor Swift
Rescue – James Bay
Figure You Out – VIOLÀ
Spin You Around – Morgan Wallen
Heartbroken – Diplo, Jessie Murph, Polo G
Afterglow – Taylor Swift
Feels Like – Gracie Abrams
Would That I – Hozier
Your Bones – Chelsea Cutler
Power Over Me – Dermot Kennedy
Vigilante Shit – Taylor Swift
Paper Rings – Taylor Swift
I Hate Love Songs – Kelsea Ballerini
Work Song – Hozier
All Of The Girls You Loved Before – Taylor Swift

**For the extended playlist, please visit my website,** https://authorbritbenson.com/playlists/

## CONTENT WARNING

**Please be aware,** *The Love You Fight For* contains some difficult topics that could be upsetting for some readers.

**Topics that take place on page are:** vulgar language, sexually explicit content, sexual harassment, physical violence*, sexual assault and attempted rape*

**Topics that are referenced but do not take place on page are:** rape, sexual abuse of a minor, overdose, abortion, traumatic car accident resulting in severe bodily injury

*If you require a content-specific chapter guide for these topics, you can find one on my website at https://authorbritbenson.com/contentwarnings/

## NOTE FROM THE AUTHOR

While *The Love You Fight For* can be read as a standalone, it is recommended that you first read the *Next Life* duet to best understand the depth of the character relationships, as well as to get a more complete picture of the main characters' backstories.

For reference, *The Love You Fight For* takes place approximately eight years after the ending of *The Love of My Next Life*, and approximately one and a half years years after the end of *This Life and All the Rest*.

*The Love You Fight For* **does** contain spoilers for the *Next Life* duet.

*To the mask-wearers and role-players,
May the part you love most be that of your true self.*

## PROLOGUE

Past

IT'S QUIET IN THE HALLWAY OUTSIDE MY BEDROOM DOOR, BUT WHEN I twist the knob and pull it open a few inches, I can hear them.

The deep laughter and the clinking of rocks glasses.

The smell of cigar smoke wafts up the stairs, tainting the air.

My skin crawls, and slowly, I push the door shut again with a soft *click*.

I check the clock on my nightstand: 11:57 p.m.

If this party is anything like the others, it won't wind down for another few hours. They'll stay here, drinking my father's expensive bourbon and smoking his imported cigars until their eyes cross and their drivers have to cart them home just before dawn. They'll grow rowdier, their refined façades fading along with their good sense. Along with their decency. Or at least, the decency they fake in public.

I know the truth, though.

Those men downstairs? They're no better than boys. Reckless, spoiled boys who aren't used to hearing the word no. Who think the very rules they make don't apply to them.

I check the clock on my nightstand again: 12:01 a.m.

I was sent to bed over an hour ago, my dutiful daughter routine deemed fulfilled for the evening, and the security guard won't be by again for another thirty minutes. If I have any chance of making it, it has to be now.

*Almost ready?* I type into my phone.

My friend responds immediately.

*Pulling up now.*

Without overthinking it, I slip my phone into my back pocket and sling my backpack over my shoulder. It's heavy despite being filled with the bare minimum. The makeup, the designer bags and shoes, the jewelry. I don't need any of it. I don't want it. I hate it all, really. Pretty trinkets meant to buy me. Not my love—my father couldn't care less about that—but my loyalty. My *silence*.

I cross the floor to my window and push it open. It slides up without a sound. I toss my backpack out the window and listen as it thuds on the grass below, then slide the window shut again. I go over my plan as I hurry back to my bedroom door.

Down the back stairwell and through the kitchen. Disarm the alarm, then out the side door near the garage, and around the front to grab the backpack. Haul ass to the street, climb the fence, and slide into the waiting car.

I smile a little, though I know I shouldn't. I shouldn't jinx it by getting my hopes up. But if this works. If I can do it...

"Almost there," I whisper to myself, then I twist the knob and poke my head into the hallway. I check up and down the dark corridor before taking a quiet step out of my room. I move to turn left, toward the back staircase, when a shuffling sound draws my attention back to the right.

A familiar head of salt-and-pepper hair emerges slowly as he ascends the main staircase, and before he can look up and see me, I step back into my bedroom and shut the door.

*No.*

My heart pounds in my chest, and I glance at the clock on my nightstand once more. This isn't right. It's too early for his visit, and now I'm running out of time. I turn the lock on my doorknob and take a step backward. It won't keep anyone out, but it might buy me some time.

The knob jiggles, and my breath catches in my throat. There's a pause—he's undoubtedly stunned—before he jiggles the handle again. When it doesn't open, he knocks.

"Samantha," his deep voice rasps, and it chills my blood. "Wake up, honey. It's me."

I'm frozen, eyes flicking between the door and the clock on my nightstand. He's early. He's *hours* early. I timed everything up perfectly. I was supposed to be long gone before he even set foot on the staircase.

"Samantha," he says, louder this time. More urgent. Irritated. "Be a good girl and let me in."

My phone buzzes in my pocket, and I know it's my friend asking where I am. I should have been at the car by now. We should be turning off my street and heading to the interstate. When another knock sounds through my bedroom, I start to move.

Back to the window, I slide it open and take a seat on the sill before swinging my legs out, dangling from the second story opening. I can still do this. It can still work.

I glance down where my backpack lies twelve feet below. The distance seems farther in the darkness, but the grass looks deceptively soft.

This is a terrible, terrible idea.

"Samantha, open this door."

My stomach churns at the authority in his tone. He's not even trying to keep his voice down now—apparently, he's over pretending like this needs to be kept a secret. As if anyone would care. As if anyone would do anything to stop it.

A heated discussion starts in the hallway. Two male voices. Both familiar.

My father has arrived.

I turn my body and grip the windowsill with shaky hands. Slowly, too slowly, I lower myself down. My shoulders and biceps ache with the movement. Sweat coats my palms, and I tighten my grip. My head pounds. I'm hanging now, stretched out as far as I can, and all that's left is to drop.

"Oh, god, please let this work. Please. Please, please, please."

When I hear my door swing open, I release my grip on the windowsill and let myself fall—

—I SIT UP WITH A GASP.

The bedsheet falls to my waist, the air-conditioning calming my sweat-slicked skin, and I take deep gulps of cool air into my lungs. My eyes burn, and my hands press on my chest to feel the rapid thrumming of my panicked heartbeat.

The dream.

It was just the dream.

It's okay. I'm okay. It was just the dream.

I squeeze my eyes shut and fist my fingers in my hair, tugging at the root, willing myself to feel something else—to focus on *anything* else—but flashes of memory still paint the darkness behind my closed lids.

The sudden drop. The crunch of bone. The chase. The fear. The desperation. The pain.

My gut roils and my head throbs.

I kick off the bedsheet and climb out of bed, hurrying my way through the darkness toward my en suite bathroom. I don't bother turning on the light. I just rush to the toilet, drop to my knees, and empty the meager contents of my stomach into the bowl. I heave until sparks dance before my eyes. Until my throat feels raw and my face is wet with sweat. Then I flush the toilet and stand, forcing myself to face my reflection in the mirror.

I reach over and flip the light switch, wincing at the shock of the sudden brightness, then look at myself in the mirror. My skin is red-splotched and shining. My blond hair sticks to my forehead and neck. I stare into my own bloodshot eyes, the blue stark against the red tint, and I don't like what I see.

A scared, vulnerable little girl. A damaged woman. A *victim*.

My lip curls in a snarl of disgust. This is who I promised myself I'd never become.

I open the cabinet under the sink.

With practiced movements, I pull out the bottle and the shot glass, then uncap the bottle and pour some of the amber liquid into the glass. I will my fingers to stop trembling as I bring the shot glass to my lips and swallow back its contents.

The bourbon burns, and I welcome it, breathing through my nose to try to calm my still racing heart. But when I close my eyes, I still see it. I'm right back there, picking up where it left off before I jolted awake.

I pour another shot and choke it down, gritting my teeth against the desire to cry.

When my eyes start to well anyway, I slam my fist on the quartz countertop. Once. Twice. I relish the vibration that shoots up my wrist and forearm. I pound once more just to feel the ache in my shoulder.

I swore I wouldn't let them take up any more space in my head. That I wouldn't spend another second feeling scared. I force myself to feel anger instead, then will that anger to swallow my fear, and thoughts of revenge, of getting even, fight through the haze. I latch onto them.

I pour a third shot and swallow it as a single tear breaks past my lashes. It rolls down my cheek and falls onto my chest. With the back of my hand, I wipe it away, then meet my own eyes in the mirror once more. I glare at my reflection until the panic starts to fade. Until the scared, vulnerable child I've outgrown is gone. Until she's tucked back safely where she belongs.

I return the bottle and shot glass to the shelf under the sink, then slip on the silk robe hanging next to my shower. Back in my bedroom, I turn on the light. The guy in my bed flinches but doesn't wake, so I round the bed and pull the blanket off him, giving the mattress a shove in the process.

"Get up. Time to go."

He cracks open a confused eye. "What?"

"I said it's time for you to leave. I've got a schedule to keep."

I don't give him a chance to question me, and truly, it's not too far out of the realm of possibility for someone to be starting their day at 4 a.m. on a Sunday. Especially not in this city. As he sits up, I gather his clothes from where they've been discarded on the floor and hand them to him one by one. Designer boxer briefs. Perfectly pressed button-down. Bespoke navy-blue slacks and jacket. Brown Italian leather belt. No tie, though. He was too trendy for that.

The metal bracelet jangles as he slips on his Cartier watch. His eight-hundred-dollar cap toe Oxfords are downstairs by the front door where he took them off. The shoes are what caught my eye last night. I'm a sucker for a stylish shoe.

"There will be a car waiting for you downstairs," I say flatly as he stands and starts to dress. I grab my phone off the charger and head to my walk-in closet. "Turn the lights off when you leave, please, but don't worry about locking up. Security will take care of it."

"Can I call you?" he asks my back, and I pause.

My hand flexes on the knob of my closet door and my lips purse before I force my face into a soft smile and glance at him over my shoulder.

"I'd rather you didn't."

I push open the door and step inside, then shut it tightly behind me. With my ear trained to the noise coming from my bedroom, I listen to him dress. The bedroom door opens. The soft click of the wall switch is paired with the disappearance of the light beam seeping under the closet door, plunging me back into darkness.

I send my security detail a text, telling him to let the gentleman out of the building, then wait for the *all clear* before I use my app to relock my door and reset the alarm.

In the comfortable darkness, I make my way to the back of my closet, to the section of racks that hold cocktail and evening gowns. Hundreds of thousands of dollars hang delicately on display, but I don't bother looking at them. Instead, I drop to my knees and crawl through them until I'm nestled in the corner behind a wall of long protective garment bags. Then I put my phone on speaker and dial my only emergency contact.

"Hey," my best friend answers, and her knowing voice is warm with concern.

It's around 9 a.m. in Paris, so I close my eyes and picture her sitting at the window in her small apartment with a croissant and a coffee surrounded by painting supplies.

"Hey," I reply. "What are you working on?"

"A commission piece. Landscape. I'm almost done."

I hum in response and listen to her soft movements on the other end of the phone. Clinking of what could be a coffee cup or a pastry plate. Rustling of fabric. Shuffling of papers. The faint music that I heard when she answered gets louder, then shuts off completely.

"Where are you?" she asks, and I smile grimly to myself.

"Hanging out with my friends, Oscar de la Renta and Tom Ford." I sigh and force a weak laugh as I run my fingers over one of the garment bags hanging next to me. "Donatella and Vera are here somewhere, too."

I hear pages of a book, then, and the tension in my neck and shoulders loosens. Tears of relief prickle the backs of my eyelids, and I inhale deeply through my nose.

"I think we were on chapter fourteen," she says smoothly, her voice low but free of pity.

All I hear is love and unwavering support.

Her tone suggests that there is absolutely nothing wrong or shameful about me calling her up at 4 a.m. my time while cowering in the back of my luxury walk-in closet. I don't need to be embarrassed or sorry for interrupting her painting. I know she knows about the shots of bourbon that came before this phone call and the vomiting before that. She knows about the nightmare. She doesn't ask, but she doesn't have to.

And anyway, none of it matters anymore.

"Chapter fourteen is perfect."

I rest my head against the wall as she inhales smoothly, then starts to read out loud from *Pride and Prejudice*, picking up exactly where we left off the last time.

In only takes a few sentences for my muscles to relax, a couple paragraphs for the threat of tears to abate completely. As she ends the chapter and begins a new one, my body sags with exhaustion, but the panic and fear are gone.

"Hey, Len," I interrupt.

"Yeah?"

"I love you."

I can't see it, but I can feel her soft smile. I hear her sniffle, then chuckle lightly before she responds.

"I love you too, Sam."

# ONE

Present Day

"Good morning."

I force a grin that I'm certain no one believes as I push my way through my father's D.C. office space.

"Good morning, Ms. Harper," one of the volunteers greets with mock cheeriness.

I don't acknowledge them.

Instead, I set my empty latte cup on the table in front of them and walk past without a word. Everyone knows I hate being called Ms. Harper. That's why they do it. But honestly, I don't blame them. Why should they be nice to me? I'm horrible to them.

I breeze through the glass doors into the full conference room and plaster on a more believable smile. It's what's expected, of course. I'm the doting, supportive daughter. A Harper through and through. I don't bother surveying the room. It's always the same faces. Instead, I zero in on my father and bat my eyelashes in a shitty display of contrition.

"I'm so sorry I'm late," I lie sweetly. "I was helping an elderly man with his groceries."

My father's eye twitches. It's the only sign on his grinning face that he's irritated, and I doubt anyone notices it but me. I saunter up to the head of the table where he's standing and take my seat to the left of him.

"Quite all right, Samantha," he says smoothly. "Now we can get started."

After one last imperceptible glare in my direction, my father faces the room with his megawatt, slimy politician smile. I still don't understand how it fools anyone, but I suppose that's the power of carefully curated talking points, bleached white teeth, and conservative Botox injections.

"Thank you so much for coming in early today, everyone."

He claps his hands in front of his chest and makes intentional eye contact with every person in the room. The excitement in his expression is so convincing, even I almost believe it. I have to hand it to him. He's a brilliant actor. If career politicians could win Oscars, he'd give Hollywood a run for its money. I have to actively fight to suppress my grimace.

"I have an announcement that I'm sure won't surprise anyone" —*rehearsed chuckle, perfectly positioned pause for dramatic effect*—"but after discussing it with my family"—*theatrical loving glance at me*—"we've decided that the time has finally arrived"—*another dramatic pause as the energy in the room pulses*—"to make my presidential bid."

The room erupts, and though I was expecting it, I still startle at the noise. My smile is immediate. My applause doesn't falter. I stand and embrace my father in a Hallmark-worthy hug, then I sit back in my seat and attempt to ignore the chorus of congratulations that fills the conference room. I work to maintain my innocent smile. I keep it from reflecting the way I actually feel.

Of course, I knew this announcement was coming, though the "discussion" my father mentioned was actually only a single declarative statement spoken *at* my mother and me two nights ago. He'd summoned us to the house in Franklin for it, and while I was irritated to have to drive back from D.C. on short notice, my anger was nothing in comparison to my mother's. She was forced to leave her lover in Saint-Tropez for something that could have easily been handled via text message for all the care my father put into it. I'm guessing he sent my brother a text, though, since Chase hasn't returned from his "sabbatical and missionary work" in South Africa.

"Thank you, thank you," my father says jovially, then waves his hands, gesturing for everyone to sit back down. They do. Like obedient little dogs. "I'm so glad to see you're all just as passionate and excited as I am about this next step."

I tune out as he continues to prattle on about the work *we* have to do. The ground *we* have to cover. The "good" *we* will accomplish. Blah blah blah campaign promises blah blah blah. My eyes start to glaze over the longer he grandstands, but then movement on the opposite end of the table catches my attention. It takes a breath for my brain to register what my eyes are seeing, but when it finally clicks, the scowl I've been fighting breaks through.

Ashton Cartwright.

Son of the Honorable Andrew Cartwright. Pruitt Boys Prep School valedictorian. Former fraternity vice president. Princeton University graduate. Slimeball.

What the fuck is he doing here? Well, right now he seems to be trying to peer down the front of the finance manager's blouse, but *why* the fuck is he here?

Ashton and my older brother were friends, but Chase is in South Africa, and last I heard, Ashton was clerking for some judge in New York with hopes of following in his daddy's footsteps. Ashton is six years older than me—thirty-two to my twenty-six—and he used to visit our house when he was on breaks from school. He and Chase would attend parties together. More than once, I stole cocaine from him—*after* he bought it from Chase—just because I could. Once I walked in on him fucking our housekeeper. He saw me but didn't stop. Just winked at me as he pounded into her. I almost vomited on the spot.

Objectively speaking, Ashton Cartwright is attractive. Perfectly coiffed blond hair. Crystal blue eyes. Straight white teeth. Flawless skin. He's conventionally hot. A trust fund daughter's wet dream.

But once he starts talking, he automatically becomes a face only a mother's Facebook friends could love.

When he catches me sneering, I swear his eyes twinkle with predatory glee. I narrow mine back when he drops his gaze to my chest. He's so fucking gross. Then my father's hand comes down on his shoulder, so I turn my attention to the devil in charge.

"I'd like you all to meet my new campaign manager, Ashton Cartwright."

My jaw drops before I can stop it, and I know Ashton sees by the way his lip twitches with humor. I scan the room for the first time since arriving and, sure enough, my father's former campaign manager is nowhere to be found. I bet her husband found out about the affair and my father paid him off. Tying up loose ends before the presidential run, I guess.

Is Ashton even *qualified* for this job? I know he went to an Ivy League law school, but I had no idea he was into politics now. He's been off my radar for *years*, and I feel off-kilter that I could have missed this. My father never lets me in on his plans—he attempts to hide everything from me—but usually, I'm pretty good at keeping myself informed. This development has more than caught me off guard. I don't like that I am missing things. It makes me worry about what other bigger things I'm not seeing.

My father drones on, and I school my face back into placidity. I keep my eyes on his chin, on the small scar there from a bicycle accident when he was a child. It's one of the few human things about him. Proof he can feel pain. Proof he's just as breakable as the rest of us.

When he stops talking and everyone begins to stand, I follow suit. They all file out of the conference room to "get to work," and I close the distance between myself and my father. And Ashton Cartwright.

I smile pleasantly and stick out a limp hand. Instead of giving it a weak shake like I expected, Ashton takes my hand between both of his and holds it hostage while he grins down at me. He wants me to be uncomfortable, to pull away in disgust, so I don't.

"Ashton. So wonderful to see you."

He knows I'm lying.

"Looking beautiful as always, Samantha."

When he finally drops my hand, I resist the urge to rub it on my skirt. I don't want his grime to stain it.

"I thought you were clerking for a judge in Manhattan, Ashton. Isn't being Daddy's campaign manager considered a conflict of interest? Challenging the integrity and impartiality of the judiciary, and all that?"

His grin doesn't falter. He just nods and grins as if he's talking to a child.

"Samantha, that was years ago. I've decided my particular talents would be better suited here, helping Senator Harper make a difference in the world. This is my true calling." Ashton turns his smarmy grin onto my father. "Working as your campaign manager is the opportunity of a lifetime, sir. I won't let you down."

*Barf.* I want to gag him with the crimson-red tie around his neck.

"I know you won't, son. And with Samantha as your assistant, you should have all you need to help manage a successful campaign."

My brow furrows slightly as I bounce my eyes between Ashton and my father. I clear my throat, but I don't let my smile drop.

"Assistant? I thought I would be canvassing the college campuses again and running your social media."

That was what we'd discussed. That's what I did on his last two reelection campaigns for senator. That's why he was able to pull so much of the youth vote. He'll never admit it, but it's a big part of why he won.

Because of me.

I try not to think too much on it; otherwise, I'll start to feel guilty, and guilt is a useless emotion.

"You're not in college anymore, Samantha, and I've decided your talents would be better suited as Ashton's assistant."

My father's voice is upbeat—kind, even—but I can tell he wants to smirk at me. He relishes any opportunity to assert his dominance over me. To make me feel disposable. A pawn in his dangerous game.

I swallow my pride, smile brightly, and bat my eyelashes at Ashton.

"I think we'll be a great team," I say cheerily. "Daddy is sure to win with you managing the campaign, Ashton."

His eyelid twitches. I think he wants to laugh. Instead, he smiles.

"Especially with you as my *assistant*," he drawls, putting emphasis on the last word.

As my *subordinate*, he implies.

I hate him.

My father slaps his hand on Ashton's shoulder, then places his other hand on my back. To anyone standing outside the conference room, it would look like a jovial moment. I just feel trapped.

"I'm sure you'll both make me proud." My father turns his attention to me.

There's a warning in his eyes. I know it well. It's the one he'd give me when I was a child and he commanded me to behave. To not embarrass him. If I thought I could get away with sneering at him right now, I'd do it.

"I won't let you down, Daddy."

There's a warm smile on my lips, my voice smooth as honey, but my eyes are frigid. He doesn't seem to care.

Ashton and I stay rooted to the spot as my father leaves us in the conference room, and it's not until he turns the corner that I finally let the rigidity in my spine loosen.

"Are you ready to get started?" Ashton asks, turning his fake smile on me. "I've got some plans I'm sure you'll need to see, and I should probably share my calendar with you so you're aware of all upcoming events."

I cock my head to the side and wait. When the faux kindness in his smile vanishes, I almost sigh in relief.

"My dry cleaning needs to be dropped off at seven a.m. on Thursdays and picked up at seven a.m. on Mondays, and I have a very specific coffee order that you'll probably want to memorize."

He's so damn smug. It's the same expression he gave me when I caught him banging the housekeeper. I don't let my mask falter. My smile never fades. My tone is all business, respectful and to the point, but with a hint of feigned sweetness.

"Do share the plans with me, Ashton. I'll review your strategy and get back to you on Monday with suggestions for improvement."

I reach out and smooth the lapels of Ashton's expensive suit jacket as I speak, fussing a little over a nonexistent stain.

"I'll also provide you with a comprehensive list of everything we've done in the past that's worked so you know exactly what the community is expecting from us. After all, Senator Harper's track record is strong, and we will want to use it to our advantage. If you've checked the files from the previous campaign manager, I'm sure you've found them lacking. Martha was always too busy being bent over office surfaces and trying to hide her affair with my father from her husband to worry about thorough records. Luckily, you have me, and I keep meticulous records."

I move my fingers to Ashton's crimson-red tie. He probably thinks it looks like a symbol of his patriotism. I think it looks like blood. I run my fingers over the smooth material, then take hold of the perfect double Windsor.

"If you think for one second that my position on this campaign team means I will be picking up your dry cleaning or going on latte runs, you should think again. I am committed to my role here, and I will do what is required of me, but I am not your errand girl."

I grab the Windsor knot and slide it higher, tightening his tie until he has to swallow back a cough and grit his teeth.

"I am not at your beck and call. I am not your personal assistant. I will play nice until it no longer suits my needs. Remember that."

I take a step back and remove my hands from his torso, then drag my eyes over his polished, flawless appearance before meeting his gaze once more. I smile bigger. I laugh lightly.

And then I let it all drop.

"And lose the South Carolina old money accent, Cartwright. You're from fucking Richmond. You're not fooling anyone."

I leave before he has a chance to say anything else, laughing a little on my way out the door. Ashton Cartwright is such an idiot.

I find a nameless volunteer and tell them I'll be out of the office for the rest of the day, then I leave without bothering to find my father. He'll be angry, but I don't care. Working on this campaign might kill the last shreds of dignity I have left. Kissing his ass. Pretending I care, all while being an accomplice in deceiving the public. If I could, I'd tell him to fuck off. Hightail it out of town and never look back.

God, how I wish I could.

When I get to my car, I double-check our shared "family calendar" to make sure no one is planning to be at the house in Franklin. When I see that it's free, I put my name in red for the weekend. Then I send our housekeeper a text to tell her that though I'm on the calendar, I'll be "staying at a friend's," so she doesn't have to prepare the house for me.

I never stay at the house anymore, but I doubt anyone outside of the staff has noticed. My mom only returns to Virginia when summoned, my father will occasionally stay for a week or two to keep up appearances around election times, and Chase is...well, it's better for everyone if he just stays wherever my father has sent him to dry out. The story this time is South Africa, but I never can be sure. All I care is that none of them are actually in Franklin when I'm there.

I close the text with the housekeeper and open my thread with Lennon.

ME

On the road to you. What are we doing this weekend?

# TWO

## *Chris*

I take Old Courthouse Highway out of town toward the county fairgrounds.

We used to hang out there back in high school—trespass to get drunk and high—but I haven't set foot on the fairgrounds in years. Not even when the fair is actually in town. I might feel a bit more nostalgic if it weren't for my shitty mood, but looking back now, nothing good ever happened at the fairgrounds. It's probably why Macon wanted to do it here.

When I turn down a familiar gravel road, I notice a white 4Runner parked about half a mile down, right next to a section of fence that I know has been cut and bent just enough that an average-sized high school kid could crawl through. I know because I was with Macon when he cut it our junior year.

I pull my truck to a stop on the other side of the road and watch as Macon hops out of his driver side door and rounds to the back before opening the trunk and pulling out a bright red gas can. Despite my mood, I grin.

I climb out of my truck, then grab the big cardboard box from the back seat before turning to face Macon. A stick of red licorice hangs from his mouth, a habit he's picked up since quitting smoking, and a USMC baseball cap sits backward on his head. The smudges of dried clay on his jeans and forearms tell me he was probably hard at work in his studio when I called.

He still came, though.

Dropped everything without question.

"You don't think we could just drive through the front entrance now?" I ask, flicking my eyes to the hole in the fence. I don't know if I'll fit through it. I'm a few inches taller and about twenty pounds heavier than I was in high school. "It's not like we're carrying illegal substances or drunk off our asses."

Macon chuckles. "Where's the fun in that?"

I laugh and shrug, then follow him to the fence. I hold up a section of it as he drops down and crawls through first, effectively covering his jeans and Run DMC band tee in dirt. Once he's on his knees, I pass the gas can through to him, followed by the cardboard box, and then I finally crawl under last.

"I'm too old for this shit," Macon grumbles as if this wasn't his fucking idea.

I roll my eyes and hoist the box under my arm. He picks up the gas can, and I follow him silently through the grassy open field toward what's usually the livestock barn when the fair is going on. We spent a lot of time back here as teenagers. It's weird to see it in the daylight and not high as fuck.

We walk a safe distance from the barn, then stop on a large, empty patch of dirt.

I wordlessly drop the box, then watch as it lands on the ground and topples over. I don't tear my eyes from the contents as they spill onto the ground, but Macon whistles, low and slow.

"So, she said no, then?" He kicks a pink stuffed animal back toward the box from where it fell.

I stare at that stuffed animal, my jaw tensing as I study it. It's a little teddy bear, about twelve inches tall, and it's holding a red sparkly heart. I won it at a carnival in Virginia Beach last summer. We'd only been dating a few months at that point, but it was the first time I told Sable I loved her. It took her three weeks to say it back, and even then, it only came after I'd given her a bracelet worth more than two paychecks from Franklin Auto Body. I probably should have known then.

I narrow my eyes at the bear. I hope that fucker is flammable.

"She said no," I confirm with a sharp nod, then flash him a sardonic grin. "She's got ambition, you know? High standards and goals. Apparently, I was just a detour. Little bit of fun before getting serious with someone more *suitable*."

"She said that?" he asks, anger in his voice.

He's nothing if not fiercely protective of his people. I nod once in response, and Macon curses under his breath.

"When?"

I sigh.

"'Bout two weeks."

He goes quiet at my answer, and I can feel his eyes on my face, but I don't take mine from the pile of Sable paraphernalia. He's probably wondering why I didn't tell him sooner. I shrug and give him the explanation he didn't ask for.

"I needed to process."

He nods in my peripheral, then bends down to right the box.

Slowly, Macon puts everything back inside of it. I try not to, but my brain catalogues each item, quickly cycling through every *when*, *why*, and *how* as Macon lifts it from the dirt and drops it into the box.

The cards from every holiday. The little "just because" gifts I'd given her. The picture book from our trip to Nashville. The corny shot glasses we'd started collecting. Crayon pictures that the twins drew and colored for her. Even the wool hunting socks her mother got me for my birthday last year (despite the fact that I don't hunt). Sable diligently collected all of it and dropped it at my house last week. Exactly one week after laughing in my face and telling me that the last thing she'd ever want is to be tethered to me for the rest of her life.

How *thoughtful*.

The box contains the story of us. Of me and Sable. Unsurprisingly, the expensive, flashy bracelet isn't in there, but the engagement ring is.

I called Macon this morning and asked him what he'd do if he had a box full of bad memories.

*Douse it in gasoline and strike a fucking match*, he said.

Now that I'm here, I have to admit that I agree with him.

Macon pushes himself to standing and I zero in on the black velvet box in his hands. He flips it open and the sunlight glints off the diamond. Makes me wish it were fucking thunderstorming instead of this sunny and sixty-five-degree weather. It would certainly fit the mood and the task at hand.

"You sure you want to torch this?" he asks, pulling the ring out and inspecting it more closely. "You could probably pawn it."

I huff a dry laugh.

"That's exactly what Sable said."

She also suggested I use the money to *invest in my future* so that I could *make something of myself*. I don't tell Macon that. He'd riot. He and Lennon never said it, but I could tell they didn't like Sable. They tried to like her because I liked her, but they never thought she appreciated me. Seems they were correct.

Macon tosses the ring box to me, and when I catch it, I swear I can almost feel it burn my palm.

"Pawn it and buy something she'd fucking hate," he says.

I put the ring box in my pocket without a word.

"Ready?" he asks, bending over and snatching the gas can before handing it off to me.

I guess I'm as ready as I'll ever be. I take a few steps forward and splash some gas on the stuff inside the cardboard box, making sure to soak that fucking pink teddy bear. When I hand Macon back the gas can, he gives me a booklet of matches, so I strike one and drop it into the box without thinking twice.

Everything is in flames within a second, the cardboard turning to ash before my eyes and the cheap pink teddy bear practically melting in the heat. Macon and I take a few cautionary steps backward, and then I fold my arms over my chest, content to watch the last year of my life burn.

I turn slightly to tell Macon as much, but a loud pop rings out from the box along with a spark of flames, making Macon and me both jump. When a second, louder pop sprays even more flames into the air, we yelp and take off running, stopping about twenty yards from the box before turning to stare at it warily.

"Shit." Macon pants. "The fuck else was in there?"

I squint at the flaming box, once again mentally running through the contents before barking out a loud laugh.

"Perfume," I say through my laughter. "I forgot about the fucking perfume."

"Fuck. Lennon told me to bring Benny." Macon laughs, pulls off his ball cap, and swipes sweat from his forehead before putting the cap back on. "Maybe I should have called him."

Benny's a kid we've known since middle school. He's a volunteer firefighter now. That just makes me laugh harder.

"It was just one bottle," I tell him with I grin. "I think we're good now."

We stay with our feet planted where we're standing, though. We don't approach the box again until the flames are dying down and all that's left of my relationship with Sable are charred remains and ashes.

Good fucking riddance.

---

I SET A DR. PEPPER WITH LIME AND A MOCK BLOODY MARY ON THE end of the bar, popping an extra pick full of green olives into the tomato juice.

Lennon grins at me, grabbing the garnish pick and eating one of the olives.

"Thanks, Casper," she says while chewing.

I screw up my face in feigned disgust. "You might as well be drinking pasta sauce."

She laughs like I knew she would, but she doesn't argue.

Even though booze was never Macon's vice of choice, and he says it doesn't bother him when other people drink, Lennon's still gone sober in solidarity. She misses brunch cocktails, though. It's something she picked up in France and hasn't lost. When they come into The Outpost, it's always mock Bloodies or mock Mimosas for her, and Dr. Pepper with lime for Macon.

"Can you keep an eye on the door for Sam?" Lennon says casually, and I hope she doesn't see how I freeze momentarily. "She's on the way here. Just tell her we're in the booth in the back."

I raise an eyebrow as I slide extra napkins in front of her before she can ask for them.

"The princess is coming down from her gilded tower?"

Lennon rolls her eyes. "Be nice, Casper. I don't want to play mediator."

"I'm always nice." I shrug, and she scoffs.

"No, you *used* to be nice. Now you're all snarky and antagonistic."

I don't say anything. I take an order and fill a draft beer, ignoring Lennon's eyes on me. When I slide the pint in front of the customer and drop the dollar bill in the tip jar, I turn back to face her. She takes a sip of her drink and pops a brow.

"I'll be nice," I tell her earnestly.

"Hmm." She hums, popping another olive in her mouth.

She looks me over once more, gives me a thin smile, then turns to leave, but I stop her.

"Don't bring up Sable, okay?" I say quickly, averting my eyes and grabbing my ballcap from beneath the bar. "I just don't want to talk about it."

Lennon cocks her head to the side and watches as I run my hand through my hair, pushing it back before putting the cap on my head backward. Lennon releases a slow, exasperated sigh.

"Real mature, Casper," she scolds, and I wink at her.

"I said I'd play nice. But you can't expect me not to defend myself, Lennon."

Lennon shakes her head, then switches both drinks to one hand so she can pick up the stack of extra bar napkins with the other. I grab her another garnish pick of olives.

"I won't bring up Sable," she says, and I drop the pick in her drink as a thank you. "I'll make sure Macon doesn't either."

I nod and she smiles once more—a genuine, not irritated smile—before heading to the back of the bar.

I try not to check the door every sixty seconds. I also don't second-guess the few glances I toss into the mirror behind the bar. My lips twitch with the need to smirk when I see the camo ballcap in my reflection, and then I go back to serving drinks.

Fifteen minutes later, I *feel* her.

I might be imagining it, but it seems like everyone else in the bar does too. People tend to take notice when town royalty graces us plebians with her presence. It's like the crowd parts for her, letting her pass freely. I don't have to look up from the drink I'm making to know that everyone is looking at her—whether through their periphery or blatantly staring—and she's not acknowledging anyone.

A bar stool opens to the right of me and a poised blond figure immediately fills the empty space. I ignore her for five minutes, chatting up some customers and making a few drinks, until I see her manicured nails drumming on the bar top.

I grab a pint glass as I step in front of her. It's been months since the last time I saw her, but she looks the same. Same straight, shiny, blond hair. Same dark, elegantly arched eyebrows. Same bright red lips. I don't know what I expected, but it still makes me want to sway a little on my feet.

"Sam," I greet.

I set the pint glass under the draft taps. Sam focuses her cold blue eyes on my backward camouflage ballcap and doesn't remove them until she speaks.

"You work here still." She drags her eyes from my ballcap to my face, her expression full of thinly veiled irritation. "Are you still at the garage?"

"I do work at the garage. I also work here. Not all of us have a trust fund, Samantha. Most of us actually have to work to make money."

She hums, then drops her gaze to my hand where it's propped on the bar top.

"At least there's no grease under your fingernails."

I slap both hands down in front of her for inspection. Her lips twitch at the corners, but she doesn't smile. Instead, she makes eye contact with me and raises one of those perfect eyebrows. I can practically hear her thoughts.

*You want an award for bathing, Christopher?*

"What can I get you?" I ask, moving the pint glass under the tap of a local IPA and pulling the handle.

Sam puts a fancy-looking clutch purse on the counter and opens it to retrieve her credit card. Every move is smooth and confident. Every inch of her is perfectly pressed and flawless, not a wrinkle to be seen, not a hair out of place.

It's like the girl I knew in high school doesn't exist anymore. Granted, that was eight years ago, but the way she acts now? It's like she's forgotten that I've seen her high off her ass and sneaking off to fuck Macon in the back seat of his car. The classy woman before me *would never.*

"I'll take a Boulevardier. Blanton's Single Barrel if you have it, but if not, Angel's Envy will do." She looks up from her wallet with a thick black credit card held delicately between her index and middle fingers like a cigarette. "Bourbon, of course, not rye. Two ice cubes and an extra orange twist."

I let the pint fill until the foamy head is running over into the drip tray and the ale is just below the lip of the glass. Then I drop a bar napkin down in front of Sam and set the pint on top of it. I don't bother wiping the glass off like I do for everyone else. Wouldn't kill the princess to get her hands a little dirty.

"On the house." I smirk at the way her nostrils flare.

She forces a sweet smile, flutters her eyelashes in a way that gives me unwelcomed flashbacks, then picks up the pint and drinks a quarter of it without breaking eye contact. I don't bother fighting the way my smirk grows into a full-fledged grin as she sets the glass back onto the napkin. Some beer dribbles from the side of her mouth and down her chin, drawing attention to her blood-red lips. Unfazed, she uses her perfectly manicured thumb to delicately wipe it away.

Samantha Harper is the only person I know who can make messy look regal. Her plump lips, her delicate fingers, her sharp attitude. It all screams opulent and unattainable. It only makes me want to dirty her up more. To see just how close to filthy I can take her until her ethereal shine is made human and she's back on level with the rest of us mere mortals.

"Thank you, Casper," she says, the picture of poise and grace. "I assume Lennon and Macon are in the back."

Hearing Sam use my last name just like everyone else is a bit of a slap to the face. I'd gotten used to her calling me by my first name, and even though I know I shouldn't, I comment on it. I can't help it.

"So I'm *Casper*, again? What happened to Chris or Christopher?"

She shrugs casually, then gives me a fake, serene smile.

"Is there something wrong with that? I thought your first name required a level of familiarity. Last I heard, *Christopher* was reserved for family members and significant others."

She flicks her eyes to her free hand, making a show of checking her nails.

"How would Sheena feel if I took such an act of audacious liberty?"

She pins me with a dead stare, and it's her only tell. The *lack* of tells. That's what gives her away, and it fucking thrills me. I smirk.

"You mean Sable," I correct, just to piss her off.

She rolls her eyes and waves her hand in the air as if Sable's name doesn't matter. Sam has no idea how spot-on she is, but I'm enjoying her act. I could tell her Sable and I broke up, but why would I? I like having the upper hand right now. It doesn't happen often with the princess. She likes to play with her food, but this time, I'm not on the menu.

I fold my arms across my chest once more and nod.

"Lennon and Macon are in back," I confirm.

I don't miss the way Sam's eyes flick to my biceps. I've added more ink to my sleeves since I saw her last. She stands from the stool and turns to leave with the pint of beer in one hand and her clutch in the other.

"Be careful, princess," I call out. "This floor tends to get sticky on Friday nights. Wouldn't want to ruin those red bottoms."

She pauses and glances over her shoulder at me, brow arched.

"What do you know about red bottoms?"

I snag a cherry from the garnish tray and toss it in my mouth then speak to her while chewing.

"I'm a multifaceted guy, Sam. My knowledge is vast and plentiful. You'd be surprised at what all I know."

Her crimson lips curve up on the side, then she rolls her eyes and turns back around without another word. Despite my better judgment, I watch her leave. The bar crowd parts once again for her, like she's something biblical and prophesied, and my eyes don't move from her pert ass encased in those skin-tight designer dress pants until she's past the pool tables and out of my sight.

"How someone so fucking hot can be so fucking cold, I'll never know," Benny says, and I turn to find him leaning on the bar across from me, staring in the same direction I just was. "It's a damn shame."

I grab a pint glass and pour him a draft.

"I didn't see you standing there." I slide the beer in front of him.

He snorts a laugh. "You had better things to catch your attention."

*If only that were true.*

# THREE

## *Sam*

Lennon waves as soon as she sees me, and it's like a ton of bricks has been lifted off my chest.

I want to put on sweats, kick off my heels, and pull my hair up into a messy bun, but I'll have to save that for after I'm out of the public eye. I return her smile as I slide into the booth next to her, nodding a hello in Macon's direction just before Lennon throws her arms around me and tugs me into a hug.

I melt into her instantly. God, I want to cry. I've missed my best friend.

I've had a shit day—a shit few months, really—and having to see Chris at the bar has only exacerbated my anxious mood. I can't help but flit my eyes around the crowd in search of *her*. That's the last thing I need. To have to deal with my father, Ashton Cartwright, and Chris Casper's bitchy, smug, pain-in-the-ass girlfriend all in one day.

"I'm so glad you came down," Lennon says into my hair before ending the hug. "I've missed your face."

"You video chat almost every day," Macon drawls, and when I flick my eyes toward him, he's smirking over the top of his soda glass while chewing on a stick of licorice.

It makes him look younger, like we're sixteen again and skipping school to hang out in Chris Casper's garage. Only back then, the licorice would have been a joint and the soda would have been expensive liquor we stole from my father.

"Can you blame her?" I say to Macon. "She has to see your ugly face every day. She deserves a respite with someone more aesthetically pleasing."

Macon grins, chewing his licorice with his mouth open, and Lennon laughs from her spot beside me. I glower jokingly at him, then turn to face my best friend.

"Thanks again for letting me stay with you." I don't have to tell her how much I hate sleeping at my parents' house. It's cold, haunting, and full of memories I'd rather banish from my mind. "I just needed to get out of D.C. for a few days, and I feel like we haven't hung out in forever."

"Three months since my last gallery show." She nods.

Lennon is a very talented artist. So talented, in fact, that her watercolor paintings are displayed at a gallery in D.C., and the gallery regularly features her new pieces in artist spotlight events. Usually when she's in town for gallery-related things, she'll stay at my place, and when I'm in Franklin, which isn't very often anymore, I'll stay with her and Macon.

I look back at my best friend's boyfriend.

"You're sure you're cool with me crashing?" I ask, and he arches an eyebrow.

I hold my breath even though I know what he's going to say. It's been eight years since we graduated high school, even longer since our "relationship" died a violent death, but the dynamic between Macon and me will probably always be a little weird. We've always cared for each other. There will always be love there, but we weren't kind to each other. We used each other. And despite the fact that he's now in an epic love, soulmate sort of relationship with my best friend, he'll always be another man who let me down.

It's times like this—where I'm left feeling vulnerable and at his mercy—that I have to remind myself just how badly I also let him down.

Macon and I were terrible friends to each other. We were even worse lovers. We were young and selfish and fucking stupid.

But Macon and Lennon?

They're perfect together and seeing their love flourish gives me hope. If Macon and Lennon can heal each other's broken hearts and grow together, there could be someone out there for me. Eventually.

"Would it matter if I wasn't?" Macon smirks.

"Nope." Lennon's grin is playful, and he huffs a laugh.

"I'm going to go play darts." He pushes himself up to stand beside the booth. "You're always welcome at our place, Harper. You know that. Even if I do end up exiled to the couch so you and my girl can have sleepovers like you're twelve years old."

Macon locks eyes with Lennon and bends over so he's leaning into her space. Gripping her chin lightly between his thumb and forefinger, he brings his mouth down to hers, kissing her softly in the middle of the bar. I don't look away. Instead, my grin grows as Lennon's face flushes and her ears turn pink.

When he breaks the kiss, her chest is rising and falling more rapidly than before, and I have to stifle a laugh at the way her hands fist in her lap. No doubt, to keep from reaching for him. Macon is smirking when he straightens to his full height, then he waggles his index finger between me and Lennon.

"You two be good."

Lennon salutes him with a serious nod, trying and failing to act like he didn't just light a fire under her with that kiss, and he winks at her before heading off to the dart boards. She stares at his back until he disappears, and then I release a teasing laugh, bumping her shoulder with mine.

"Jesus, Len, take a breath already."

She squirms a little and rolls her eyes.

"Shut up. I can't help it. When he does stuff like that, it makes my brain go all fuzzy." She takes a few sips of her drink, then flares her eyes at me sheepishly. "Sorry."

"I'm kidding." I bring my own glass up to clink it with hers.

"You know I love seeing you in love. It sure as hell beats when you were mopey and pissy all the time. Though I'll admit, I liked not having to share you."

Lennon's smile falls a bit, and she purses her lips. I know what she's thinking. Our relationship has taken a hit in the last year or so, and that's on me. I haven't been around much. She moved back to the States, yet the distance between us has grown. I've either been busy, or I've been avoiding this town. Usually, it's a little of both.

"How are you? How have you been?" Her voice is lower this time, and she lets her eyes scan over my face. "Are you sleeping? You look tired."

I laugh her off.

"That's a nice way of telling me I look like shit, Lennon."

She shrugs and takes a sip of her drink.

"You apply a damn good face, Sam, but you forget that I know your secrets. I know the flawless concealer and highlighter just means you need to hide the circles under your eyes. I know the overlining of your lips is because you need a confidence boost, and if I were a betting woman, my money would be that you're wearing waterproof mascara and eyeliner, too."

My jaw drops, and I blink at her.

"I hate you."

She lets out a laugh and shakes her head.

"Well, I love you, and I'm just being a concerned friend. My phone is never on silent, but it hasn't rung lately..."

I sigh and take a sip of my disgusting beer. Fucking Chris. I hate IPAs. He gave me this to fuck with me. I take another sip and pretend it's a cocktail.

"I'm fine, Len. I'll be fine, I promise. I just need to get laid. I'm all wound up and Pilates isn't doing it right now."

She snorts a laugh.

"Yes, because fucking some rich wanker whom you abhor is so much better than therapy."

I smirk at her.

"It sure doesn't hurt."

She shakes her head and rolls her eyes, then scans me again. I smile brightly and move through some flash poses. I give her a kissy face. I wink comically. I vogue. She giggles and throws a bar napkin at me.

"Are you really here just to hang out?" she asks finally. I furrow my brow and shrug. She sighs. "Well, I guess I'll take what I can get."

She doesn't press. She won't. Not here, anyway. But tonight, when we're in the privacy of her bedroom, just the two of us, I'll probably have to tell her the truth.

Most of it, at least.

---

"Spill."

Lennon throws herself next to me onto her freshly made bed. She's wearing pajama shorts and a too large The Black Keys shirt that must be Macon's. I heard him shuffling about in the apartment a few minutes ago, but it's quiet out there now. He's probably retired to his studio for the night since Lennon kicked him out of the bedroom.

I drop my head back on the pillow and sigh.

"I have a meeting tomorrow."

I don't tell her more than that. I want to—god, do I want to—but I can't. She nods in understanding before pivoting topics.

"Saw the senator's announcement. How's it feel to be the future first daughter of the United States?"

I roll my eyes. My father put out an official announcement regarding his presidential bid on social media this afternoon. It wasn't really a surprise to anyone, but I'm glad I'm not in D.C. this weekend so I can avoid the fanfare. He's sure to be strutting about like an insufferable peacock.

"Riveting," I deadpan, and Lennon snorts a laugh. "He's summoned all of us for a press conference on Tuesday. My mother and Chase will be flying in on Monday for it. We are to behave like a happy and supportive family, et cetera."

Lennon hums. "When was the last time you saw Chase?"

I have to think about it for a moment. I count back the months, bypassing every holiday and family gathering from which Chase was absent until I find a memory that includes him.

"I think it's been over three years," I say finally. "He was back in the States for a few months, staying in D.C., but then he did something stupid that my father probably had buried, and Chase was sent to 'do mission work' in South Africa. Allegedly."

Lennon scoffs. She knows it's all a big farce. My older brother is a fucking disaster. As toxic and problematic as they come. He's always getting himself involved in unsavory and reprehensible things, and my father is always cleaning up his messes.

"I hate all of them," I say pointedly.

There's not even any venom in my statement. I've uttered it so many times that it's lost its bite. At this point, it's just a matter of fact. An undeniable subset of my reality. I *hate* every member of my immediate family. It just is what it is.

Lennon grabs my hand and gives it a squeeze.

"I know. Me too."

We fall back into silence for a few moments, just the sounds of our breathing and the distant hum of music filtering from the art studio in the next room. I could easily fall asleep. I always sleep soundly here. Being in a little Lennon-made cocoon is my happy place. It's like the only time my body can fully relax.

"So where was what's-her-face tonight?" I ask randomly, breaking through the quiet. "Sarah? Serena? Siobhan?"

I try to sound casual, only mildly curious, but I'm sure I fail. Mercifully, Lennon doesn't call me out on it. Instead, she releases my hand and rolls onto her stomach, propping her body up on her arm and resting her chin on her palm. She narrows her eyes at me.

"I'm not supposed to bring her up," she says slowly, and my head jerks back.

"What? Why?"

"Casper asked me not to." Lennon gives me a little one-shoulder shrug. "But since we're here now and technically *you* brought her up, not me...Sable and Casper broke up."

My jaw drops. Not many things can shock me. But this? This shocks me.

"Damn." I let my eyes drift from Lennon's and stare blankly at the light switch on the wall. Chris and Sable were together for about a year. I was prepared for news of an engagement, not a breakup. "I thought they were going to get married."

"I did, too. I mean, don't get me wrong, I never liked them together, but I thought Sable was *it* for him."

I nod because I thought the exact same thing.

"I'm not exactly sure what happened," she continues. "Macon hasn't said much. You know how those two are. Casper just called him up the other day and the next thing I knew, Macon was filling up a gas can to go burn a box of Sable's stuff at the fairgrounds."

"Wow." That's all I can say. *Wow*.

"He *did* propose." Lennon's words are said softly, like she knows the information is delicate, and this time I don't hide the way I wince. "She said no. And now it's over."

I swallow a few times and let it all set in. I try to sift through my emotions, to decide how the news makes me feel, and I don't like what I find.

"How is he?" I ask, and Lennon gives me another small shrug in my periphery.

"As fine as can be expected, I guess. He's been boxing with Macon at the rec center a lot more, but other than that, he seems fine. He seems normal."

When I don't respond right away, the weight of Lennon's attention grows heavier. Her eyes stay on me until I can't ignore them anymore. Until the only thing I can do is tear my gaze away from the light switch and meet hers.

"What happened with you two?" she asks like I knew she would. "You seemed close for a while. Why'd it change?"

I blow a harsh breath through my nose, then push myself up so

I'm sitting cross-legged on the bedspread. I twirl the ring on my middle finger so I don't have to focus on Lennon's face.

"We were hanging out for a bit. Then we weren't. That's all."

"Did you ever..."

She waggles her brows, and I huff a laugh with a shake of my head.

"No, definitely not. It never got that far."

"How far *did* it get?" she asks on a gasp, a grin spreading wide across her face, and suddenly, we're just two girls at a sleepover swapping hookup stories about our crushes.

Not that I have a crush on Chris Casper. But if I did, this is probably what it would feel like.

I roll my eyes, but I don't fight my smile. I should have told her as soon as it started, but she had just gotten back with Macon, and after all the bullshit they'd been through, I didn't want anything to interrupt it.

And then after...

Well, I guess after, I just didn't feel like sharing anymore.

"Not far. Very PG-13."

Lennon frowns like she was expecting something juicier, and I scoff playfully.

"Sorry to disappoint. It just never got past that. And then a few weeks later, he was dating Selena."

"Sable," Lennon corrects, and I wave her off.

"*Anyway*. We were only hanging out because you and Macon were all loved up in your own little world and we felt abandoned."

Lennon's jaw drops, and I roll my eyes.

"Kidding! Kidding. Not abandoned, but maybe left out? Definitely bored. The point is, it was never anything serious. It was never much of anything at all, actually."

She's quiet for a minute, then she sighs.

"Maybe it could have been." Her voice is wistful, and I groan.

"God, no. Could you imagine? His idea of a date is probably a fried food basket at The Outpost and then beers from a Styrofoam cooler in the bed of his beloved truck." I fake a gag, and Lennon laughs. "I have heartburn just thinking about it."

"The horror," she says flatly, then studies me with her eyes narrowed and her lips pursed. I'm about to tell her to stop analyzing me like I'm one of her paintings, but then she smiles and perks up. "I almost forgot. Are you still thinking about getting a place here?"

I blink a few times at the rapid subject change. I mentioned finding a place near Franklin months ago and haven't said a word about it since. With the shitstorm that's sure to come with my father's presidential bid, though, it's probably best I make it a priority.

"Yeah, I think I am. Something away from D.C. that doesn't require me to stay at my parents' house. Why? You know somewhere?"

"Maybe." Lennon shrugs. "The apartment above The Outpost has been renovated, and the owner is renting it out. It's actually really nice. The music will probably filter through on weekends, but it's worth looking into."

I think about it for all of five seconds before I make up my mind. Living above a bar might not be the best for optics, but I have to be smart, and right now, any place in Franklin is better than my condo in D.C. or the house I grew up in.

"Do you have the owner's contact information?"

# FOUR

## *Sam*

It's weird seeing The Outpost at 9 a.m. on a Saturday.

The parking lot is empty. The sidewalk in front of the building is missing its trademark cigarette break crowd. The neon OPEN sign isn't buzzing brightly in the window, and there's no pulsing sound of music or loud rumble of conversation emanating from the building like its very own heartbeat. In fact, it's quiet in a way I didn't think possible when it comes to the popular Franklin watering hole. As I stand beside my car in the gravel lot behind the dive bar, the only sounds I hear are my own breathing and the breeze.

It certainly won't stay like this. Come 4 p.m., the lot will be packed, the music will be loud, and the cloud of cigarette smoke covering the sidewalk out front will be suffocatingly thick. But right now, it's almost peaceful.

I look up at the windows on the second floor of the building. Someone hung generic navy-blue curtains over them, but I can tell they're new. Probably energy efficient and easy to open. There are stairs that lead down to the parking lot and a cute little porch light at the top of them. Enough space for a chair and maybe some plants, if I were the type to keep plants alive for longer than a few weeks. I've never tried, but I'd wager I'm not.

I try my best to picture myself climbing up and down those

stairs, entering and exiting through that door on the porch, parking my car in this gravel lot. I try to imagine what it would be like to pull back those drab curtains and look out the window into the parking lot while taking in the view of the brick building next door.

Every attempt I make at envisioning myself living in the apartment above The Outpost only makes me dislike it more, and I haven't even seen it yet. I want a place in Franklin. I need a place of *my own* that is close to the only person in my life who matters. But this sure-to-be dingy, loud, stuffy little flat above the town's diviest dive bar? This place might not be it.

My hand is wrapping around the handle of my car door when a loud rumbling catches my attention, and the sound of truck tires crunching gravel has me turning around. I almost laugh out loud, but I don't. I fold my arms across my chest and wait. When Chris puts his truck in park and hops out, I make a show of checking my watch.

"You're late."

At the sound of my voice, his head shoots up and he stops walking. I'm grateful for my dark sunglasses because that means he can't see the way my eyes scan his body. Dirty jeans. Dirty boots. A plain white, grease-stained T-shirt, the sleeves of which are tightly hugging thick, tattooed biceps.

He must have come here straight from the garage.

I stop myself from checking out his hands and instead glance at the ballcap sitting backward on his head. Black, not camo. I'm almost disappointed that I don't have an excuse to scowl. He must not have known it was me he was meeting. Good. That means I'm not the only one caught off guard.

"The fuck are you doing here, Harper?" He stalks toward me slowly. Unlike me, he brazenly lets his eyes roam over my body. "I know you're not here for the apartment."

"I am." I pop a hand on my hip. His gaze brushes over my skin like a phantom caress. I have to fight back a shiver. "Why are you the one here to show it to me? I thought I was supposed to be meeting Alan."

"Alan moved to Kentucky. Been there for about six months. I own half the bar now since Mackie's dad passed."

I blink twice, but I don't let him see my surprise. Mackie used to bartend at The Outpost, and then he bought into the bar a year or so ago. Last I heard, his dad was diagnosed with lung cancer, but I didn't realize he'd died. Mackie must have moved to be with his mom.

"Congrats," I say and mean it. "Will you be my landlord, then?"

Chris chuckles. "You're not going to move in here, Sam."

I raise an eyebrow at the surety in his voice. "Oh, no?"

"This isn't the kind of penthouse you're used to."

He kicks a bit of gravel with his scuffed-up boots, making a show of the puff of dust that follows.

"This ain't good for your custom paint job." He nods to my car, then raises his hand and points to the rooftops. "No security cams on that door, either. We just got the one that points at the main parking lot. This place isn't cut out for royalty."

I don't react. I make a show of checking my nails, so he thinks his attitude is boring me.

"Just show me the apartment," I say curtly.

He doesn't move an inch except for his eyes, dropping down my body and back up once more. I swear, it takes forever for him to complete his survey. I almost want to sass him, ask him if I've passed inspection, but I don't. I just let him look and ignore how much I like it. Then, after a few deep breaths, he walks silently past me and toward the staircase that leads to the second-floor apartment. I follow.

"This staircase was just redone, so it's sturdy," he says as we climb the stairs. When his feet reach the porch, he gestures to the railings. "But this isn't big enough for hosting brunch parties or high teas. Probably not a good backdrop for campaign videos either."

Asshole. When I don't respond, he pulls a key out of his pocket and unlocks the door. He swings it open wide, then gestures for me to enter.

"Ladies first," he says, so I push past him and step into the apartment.

It's not terrible. There's not much natural light, but it's actually larger than it looks from outside. Though that could just be because it's empty. It's not very wide, but it's deep. It must run the length of the bar. I walk to the windows and open the ugly blue curtains, noting the dust motes that puff up around me when I disturb them.

"This is the living room," Chris says. "Like I said. Not big enough for hosting parties." He stomps his foot on the floor. "This isn't real wood, either." He moves to the kitchen and knocks on the white countertop. "Laminate. Not marble or granite or whatever natural stone you'd probably prefer."

I sigh loudly.

"Cut the bullshit, Casper."

"Just bein' helpful, princess." He smirks, throwing his palms up. I clench my teeth and breathe through my nose, and he hooks a thumb to the plain white fridge. "That's new, but it's open box from the floor. Dented on the side. All new plumbing under the sinks, though."

I check out the kitchen. For as much as he's trying to point out the negative, the kitchen is stylish. White subway tile backsplash, white cabinets, white counters. It works to brighten up the otherwise dark space. I follow him as he walks through a small hallway, gesturing to two doors on either side.

"Full bathroom. Only one. And laundry."

I glance inside the bathroom. It's like the kitchen. It's nothing special, but it's neat and stylish. Everything looks new.

"Whoever did the renovations did a good job picking the finishes. I assume it was a tight budget, but everything looks good," I say honestly as I run my fingers over the sliding door that encloses the small washer and dryer. "It all looks high-end." *Ish.*

"I know," Chris says. "Thank you for noticing."

I turn to face him, realizing for the first time just how narrow this hallway is. I can smell him. It's familiar in a way I wish it wasn't, and my heart speeds up in a way I wish it wouldn't. Pine trees and motor oil, a hint of laundry detergent and deodorant. I don't hate it. In fact, I have to resist the urge to lean in closer and sniff. When he smirks, I know he knows.

"Thank you?" I repeat with a raised brow, and he nods.

"I did the renovations, Sam. All of 'em. And it was my idea to rent out the apartment."

His confidence is sexy. I can't deny that. And though I don't want to be, I'm impressed.

"Multifaceted indeed," I say after a moment, and he smiles proudly.

I don't move back right away even though I know I should. When he reaches up and fingers the ends of a strand of my hair, I don't swat him away. Instead, I tilt my head toward him a fraction of an inch and my eyes flutter shut against my will. The touch is so gentle, so comforting, that for a moment, I imagine it lulling me back to sleep after a nightmare.

"I'll show you the bedroom."

I might have imagined the way his voice dropped around the word *bedroom*. I might have imagined the suggestive curve of his lips, too. I tell myself I did and follow him through the door. The bedroom, like the rest of the apartment, is small and dull. There aren't even any features to dress it up. It's just an empty, neutral-toned box with two windows.

I'm extremely underwhelmed.

"As you can see," Chris starts, his tone patronizing in a way that sets my teeth on edge, "this isn't big enough for a canopied bed. You probably sleep in, what? California king? Probably only comfortably fit a full in here. A queen if you squeeze. And the closet? Small. Not a walk-in. It could accommodate maybe a tenth of your wardrobe."

I wait stone-faced until he's done listing all the reasons the apartment is not a good fit for me. And while it's *not* a good fit for me, it's for none of the superficial bullshit he's been throwing at me since he arrived. My mood requires more natural light. My job performance and creativity require a quiet atmosphere that surely won't come between the hours of 8 p.m. to 2 a.m., which is peak work time for me.

And, okay, fine, he's right. I need more space for my shoes.

I have every intention of bowing out gracefully, walking away with class, but then he goes and sets fire to my composure.

"See, princess? This place isn't fit for a Harper. You're probably better off moving back into the senator's McMansion or one of the luxury condos at the beach. That's more your style."

I *hate* being compared to my family.

"I'll take it," I say before I think twice, and the way his jaw literally drops fills me with enough joy to get me through half the coming week of campaign torture.

"We don't take Amex Black Cards," he says after a moment, and I smile.

"Of course not. I prefer to write a check, anyway." I reach into my handbag and pull out my personal checkbook, then wave it with a flourish between us. "First and last, I assume? I assure you I'm good for it, but I can go get cash from the bank if that makes you more comfortable."

He narrows his eyes and folds his arms over his chest.

I flutter my eyelashes, the picture of innocence.

"You're going to hate it. It's loud every night. The lot gets crowded. The internet is shitty. At least once a week, I have to call the cops."

I lift a shoulder in dismissal and don't take my eyes off him. It feels good, watching him concede. It feels good to win, even if I know he's right. I likely *am* going to hate living here, even if it will only be for the occasional weekend when I can get away from D.C. I'll probably loathe it, but I will drown myself in a vat of that disgusting local IPA before I ever let him know it. I drank that pint he gave me last night and asked for another out of spite. My pettiness knows no bounds, and annoying Chris Casper has become something of a personal interest of mine recently.

"Okay, Harper. I've got the lease in my truck."

I follow him back out of the apartment, down the stairs, and into the gravel lot. I sign the lease, write the check, then stick my hand out to shake his. When he takes it, his warm, calloused hand almost swallowing mine, I have to fight back the urge to rub my palm against his. It surprises me enough that I don't shake right away. I just stand there with his hand encasing mine until he smirks. I roll my eyes, pump his arm twice, then let go of him.

"Thanks for showing me the apartment. I'll move in next weekend."

He doesn't say anything. He just nods and steps back, but his eyes don't leave me until I'm in my car and pulling out of the parking lot. I know because I checked the rearview before I drove off.

As soon as I'm out of town, I turn on an audiobook and attempt to calm my nerves. I have an appointment in North Carolina this afternoon, and I'm going to need the entire drive to get my head on straight.

# FIVE

## *Chris*

"Uncle Chris!"

My niece and nephew launch themselves at me the moment I step through my sister's front door. I hitch at the waist and wrap them in my arms, hauling Lucy over my shoulder and scooping Luke under my arm. Their giggles fill the foyer, but they turn to shrieks when I start to spin us in circles.

"Oh no, I'm getting dizzy," I shout, making myself wobble dramatically. "I might fall!"

Lucy and Luke's laughter becomes interspersed with playful cries for help as I weave my way through the hallway and into the living room, then I drop them both onto the couch before throwing myself down next to them.

"Man, I am so tired now." I fake a yawn, then close my eyes and pretend to snore. Immediately, the twins start to climb on me.

"Wake up! Wake up, Uncle Chris!"

"Wake up! We want to play!"

I snore louder, which they find hilarious, and it's hard for me not to laugh right along with them. I swear, nothing is cuter than a five-year-old's laughter, and I get double the cuteness with my niece and nephew.

"You make more racket than the kids."

My sister's voice cuts through the giggles, and I pop open one eye to find her leaning on the doorway between the living room and the kitchen. She's trying to look annoyed, but she's failing. I grin.

"And here I thought you'd be happy that I was early."

Tiff glances at the clock above the couch and laughs.

"Three minutes early is nothing to brag about."

I take a couch pillow and whack Luke over the head with it, setting him and Lucy off with the giggles again.

"Better than three minutes late."

My sister rolls her eyes, and I scramble out from under the twins so I can stand up from the couch.

"Where's the punk?"

"She's in her bedroom. Michael is outside at the grill. I'm finishing up in the kitchen, so if you want to help, you can set the table. Dad should be here soon."

I nod, then close the distance between us and plant a kiss on the top of her head.

"You should sit down," I call over my shoulder as I make my way to the stairs. "You look like you're about to pop. You sure it's not twins again?"

I hear her groan, then something hits my back before I disappear behind the stair railing.

A dishtowel.

My big sister threw a dishtowel at me.

I deserved it. She's not very far along, and she looks nothing like she did with the twins.

I laugh, then walk down the hall to Chy's room. I stop at the closed door and grin at the STAY OUT sign taped to it. I'm sure having five-year-old siblings has been taking a toll on her. Those kids are a handful, the exact opposite of Cheyenne. She's quiet and observant. The twins are chaos.

I knock three times, then wait.

"Who is it?" Cheyenne calls from inside.

"Your favorite uncle."

"Come in," she says, so I open the door and step into her room.

It looks exactly how you'd expect an eight-year-old's room to look. Kind of on the precipice of "big kid" interests, but still holding on tightly to those "little kid" favorites.

The books on her bookshelf are getting thicker, no longer showcasing the thin spines of picture books and short stories. She's reading chapter books and comic books now. Her favorite stuffed animals still line her bed, but they're slowly being replaced with things like Barbies and superhero action figures. She used to have posters of unicorns all over the walls, but they're gone now, and in their place are several large posters of a popular band, the silver-haired lead singer smirking front and center in every single one.

I'm not ready for Cheyenne to be a big kid. The thought actually makes me sad.

"You're my only uncle," she says without looking at me.

She's kneeling in front of a cage, watching her hamster run on its wheel, so I step toward her and sit down on the floor beside her.

"Whatchya doin', Punk?"

"Watching Puma exercise." She finally tears her eyes from the rodent and turns her smile on me. "He's getting faster."

"He is." I sit in silence with her for a moment, watching Puma run. His little legs are just a blur. I think she's right. He *is* getting faster. "Your mom is putting me to work, but I thought I'd see if you wanted to help me."

Cheyenne thinks it over for a moment, then shakes her head.

"Mom says I can't bring Puma downstairs, and I don't want him to be lonely."

"I get it." I nod. "Will you sit by me at dinner?"

She smiles bigger. "Yes."

I ruffle her hair, and she squeaks a little, batting me away with a laugh, then I look at the hamster.

"Later, Pumba."

Cheyenne laughs some more. "It's *Puma*, Uncle Chris. P-u-m-a."

"Oh, right." I tap my head with a shrug. "I always forget. See you in a bit, Punk."

She's already turned away from me, attention back on the

hamster, and I'm forgotten. I pull her door shut behind me. On the way back downstairs, I peek into the twins' room, and unsurprisingly, it's a disaster. I don't know what Tiff and Michael's plan is for when the new baby gets here in a few months because there is no way they can put it in here, and I don't know how Cheyenne will feel about having to share a room with an infant.

Instead of stopping in the kitchen, I head straight to the backyard where my brother-in-law is manning the grill. As soon as I see him, I whistle and drag my eyes down the length of his body, taking time to survey his legs.

"Look at you showin' off," I joke as I sidle up next to him. "They look good. How do they feel?"

Michael lifts the leg of his shorts and knocks on his left prosthetic with a smile.

"They feel good. Fit good. Train better."

"Nice." I lean my hip on the deck railing next to the grill. "Boston won't know what hit them."

"Eventually," Michael says, casually flipping hamburger patties like he's not a total badass.

He's gotten back into distance running in the last year, and the new prosthetics are a result of that. His plan is to run the Boston Marathon again, but this time in the para-athletics division. I have no doubt he's going to do it. Michael is one of the strongest, most determined people I know.

I watch him man the grill, and he side-eyes me.

"Stop judging my burgers," he grumbles.

"I wasn't." I laugh. "I swear."

"You're a shit liar," he says, and I shrug.

Technically, I hadn't judged his burgers. *Yet*. I was still assessing the setup. Guessing the charcoal temp, surveying the patty placement on the grates. I hadn't even had a chance to catalog the seasoning being used. He figured me out before I could get that far.

"You hanging in there?" he asks, changing the subject.

He gestures to a large serving platter on the table beside me. I grab it and hold it out so he can start putting the hamburger patties on it.

"Yeah, I guess. I'm more angry that I didn't see it coming than anything else," I confess. "When I think about it now, I just feel stupid about how much shit I missed."

Michael snorts a laugh, and I groan.

"Yes, I know. I'm sure I'll hear about it from Tiff. I don't need to get it from you, too."

"I'm staying out of it," he says innocently. He flips the last hamburger patty onto the platter, then closes the lid on the grill. "Can't make the same promise for your sister, though."

"Trust me, I know."

I follow Michael into the house and set the platter of burger patties on the counter. I can hear my dad laughing in the living room with the kids, but when I glance in there, I don't see Chy. She must still be upstairs in her room. I move to the pantry to pull out hamburger buns, chips, and paper plates so I can help set the table like Tiff asked. I'm allowed a mere three minutes before my sister brings up the breakup.

"So how are you feeling, then?" Tiff asks casually, and I flick my attention to my brother-in-law before answering. The way Michael flares his eyes at me tells me Tiff's feelings on the matter are anything but casual.

"I'm feeling good," I lie.

I'm not feeling *bad*, per se, but I'm definitely not *good*. Can't tell my big sister that, though. If she catches even a whiff of heartache, she'll put a hit out on my ex.

"We just wanted different things, and I respect that," I add.

This is the truth. Sable and I did want different things. *Very* different things. I just didn't realize it until I was hit upside the head with it.

Tiffany scoffs.

"You were the best thing that ever happened to that uppity brat. You're better off. People like her..." My sister huffs and shakes her head, turning to point a plastic spatula at me. "People like her don't deserve people like you. She puts too much worth on what's in a person's bank account and not nearly enough on what's on the inside. You have more heart in your pinky finger than she has in her whole body. You deserve someone like you. Someone who will appreciate your heart and match it with one of their own. You deserve someone so much better than her."

I smile softly as I watch her rant. My overprotective, passionate big sister. As much as it hurts to hear, I can't deny that I love seeing her come to my defense.

Now, anyway. I always shut her down before. I thought I was in love and didn't want to hear it. I had to learn for myself the hard way.

"I know, Tiffy," I say. "You were right, and I should have listened."

Tiffany sighs.

"You want to see the good in everyone, Chris, and that's a great quality. But sometimes... Well, sometimes you need to recognize the difference between authentic good and manufactured good, especially when you're the one manufacturing it."

"*Especially* when the manufactured good outweighs anything authentic," Michael adds.

I narrow my eyes in his direction, but he's conveniently not looking at me. So much for *I'm staying out of it*.

"I know you both care about me. Thank you. But it's over now. We can stop talking about it. Sable and I are done, and I'm moving on."

The subtle glance my sister and brother-in-law share makes all my defenses shoot up, and I immediately shake my head.

"No. You're not setting me up, Tiff. No."

"Chris," she says pointedly. "You'd really like her. She's a teacher in Suffolk. She's in my book club. And she's like us."

I cock my head to the side and raise an eyebrow.

"Like us?"

"Yeah, you know." She turns back to whatever it is she's cooking on the stovetop. "Down to earth. Focused on family and community. Cares about what's important."

"You mean in our tax bracket," I state, and she shrugs nonchalantly.

She's so full of shit. Tiff has always hated people with money, and she's not fooling me with the *cares about what's important* line. Tiffany hated that Sable was always wanting to trade out and up. Her biggest gripe about my ex was that Sable thought she was "too good for people like us." See also: people who don't make seven figures, drive fancy cars, or summer in the Hamptons.

It's a valid complaint, I'll admit, but Tiff has gotten to the point where she snarls at anything that even hints at wealth. I don't argue with her. I don't point out that she's being hypocritical, or that she's being prejudiced. Instead, I walk up behind her and pull her into a hug.

"I love you. You're a good big sister." I sway back and forth a little for levity. "I am fine, I promise, so please, for the love of God, do not try to set me up. I cannot handle it. I will run away."

She snorts a laugh and elbows me lightly in the stomach. When I was little, anytime Tiffany tried to assert authority over me, which was always because she's six years older than I am, I would threaten to run away. One time, Tiff tried to make me clean up my bedroom, and I actually did run away.

I didn't make it any farther than Macon's house, but I had everyone terrified for hours before my mom found me. I was eight. It's been a running joke ever since.

"Fine," she concedes, flipping another burger patty from the frying pan in front of her onto an empty plate by the stove. "Fine, Chris. Wouldn't want you to run away."

"Thank you."

Tiffany shouts "DINNER" into the house, and four tiny feet come running into the kitchen, followed shortly by my father. He pats me on the back as he ambles to the table. Michael shouts up the stairs for Cheyenne and she slides into the chair next to me just as I'm sitting down.

I give her a smile that quickly turns into a curious smirk when I notice the front pocket on her T-shirt is bulged and slightly moving. I raise a brow, and she shushes me, darting her eyes from me to her mother and back.

"You're breaking the rules again, Punk," I whisper, and she purses her lips.

"He's sleeping. He won't bother anyone," Cheyenne says as she stares at me. I stare right back until she narrows her eyes. "Don't tattle," she commands, and I scoff dramatically.

"I'm no snitch."

"Swear it," she urges.

My jaw drops.

"When have I ever snitched?"

There's no denying the offense in my whispered tone. I'm defending my honor to an eight-year-old over a smuggled hamster at the dinner table. But seriously. I. Don't. Snitch. Cheyenne just raises a brow and waits until I cave.

"I swear it," I say finally, and she grins.

My sister and Michael work to get the twins situated, so I start to make Cheyenne's burger, but she stops me just as I'm plopping a hamburger patty onto her plate.

"I can't eat that," she shouts, startling me enough that I jump.

"What? Why? What happened?" I examine the hamburger patty, flipping it over in case I missed something. "It looks fine."

"I'm a vegetarian now." Cheyenne nudges the plate with the patty away from her.

I look at my sister. Tiff is fighting a grin and gestures to the lone burger patty on a separate plate in the middle of the table.

"That one is for her," Tiffany says. "It's black bean."

"Since when?" I ask, glancing between Cheyenne and my sister. "She had pepperoni pizza at her birthday party a few weeks ago."

My sister cocks her head to the side and smirks.

"Since you got her that hamster."

My eyes flare. So this is *my* influence. Who would have thought such a tiny rodent could encourage such a big lifestyle change in an eight-year-old. Without saying anything else, I trade plates with Chy so she now has an empty one.

"You still like ketchup and mustard?" I ask Cheyenne, and she nods, so I grab the black bean burger and fix it up for her. I dump some chips on her plate, then ruffle her hair before sliding the finished plate in front of her. "Bon appétit, Punk."

After dinner, Cheyenne retreats back to her bedroom with her smuggled rodent and my sister gets the twins in a bath. I help Michael clean up the kitchen, then sit next to my dad on the couch in the living room. He's got the television on the nightly news and he's glaring at the screen. When I settle my eyes on the broadcast, I understand why.

It's a recap of a press conference from earlier in the day. Our very own Senator Thom Harper announced that he'll be running for president in the next election, and the whole Harper family is assembled behind a podium while the senator rambles.

My dad's hands are fisted tightly in his lap as he watches. He's always disliked the senator. It might seem excessive to some, but it's more than warranted.

"Thom Harper is no better than a backwater charlatan," my dad finally says, shaking his head slowly. "But he's got everyone snowed. I don't know how people don't see through his lies."

"Money," my sister chimes in.

I glance up and find her leaning on the wall in the hallway that leads to the bathroom. From where she's standing, she can see right into the bathroom with the tub where the twins are, and I can hear them giggling and splashing. Her eyes dart from the screen to the bathroom and back.

"The Harper family has money, and they use it as a smoke screen," she continues. "People see flashy things and want what they have. They buy into the lie that if Senator Harper is in charge, the wealth will be shared."

"It will be a cold day in hell if I ever have to call that man my president," Dad says. "I'd sooner move to the Amazon and join a family of spider monkeys."

I chuckle.

"You're not civilized enough for the spider monkeys," I say, but he doesn't acknowledge my joke.

My dad never takes his scathing eyes off the television where Senator Harper is still speaking. I glance at Tiff and find that she's still glaring, too. But when I look back at the screen, the only face I see is the one that belongs to the senator's daughter.

Sam is standing between her mother and her older brother, and she's smiling proudly at her father. She's looking at him like he hung the fucking moon, and anyone who doesn't know her would easily fall for the act. She's been playing the role of devoted daughter her whole life, so of course she plays it perfectly. I've known her since we were kids, though, so I know the truth.

Sam *hates* her dad.

She hates everyone in her family, but she hates her dad with a passion. If someone shot him dead right now, she would probably have to make herself cry while forcing herself not to cackle with glee. Hell, if someone shot him dead, I wouldn't be surprised to learn that Sam ordered the hit. I've never known anyone to hate a person as passionately as Samantha Harper hates her own father, which makes watching her at this press conference absolutely fascinating.

There are no cracks in her façade. No tells to belie her true feelings. It's almost scary, how easily she can fake it. How flawlessly she can sell the lie. My dad's words about the senator from moments before replay in my mind—*no better than a backwater charlatan*—and I wonder just how far Sam's apple fell from her family tree.

On the television screen, in her designer clothes and diamond stud earrings, her blond hair curled and her crimson lips smiling, she is nothing but the beautiful, poised, proud daughter of a presidential candidate, and everyone in the nation believes it. It's almost unfair that someone so cold and deceitful can be so beautiful.

It's even worse that she's *exactly* my type.

When I started dating Sable, I actively avoided anywhere Sam might be because I felt guilty as hell for being so attracted to someone who wasn't my girlfriend. Even when we were in high school, and Sam was in a toxic, fucked-up situation with my best friend, I couldn't deny her beauty. But now that we're older? She's a fucking knockout, and damn if it doesn't make me angry.

A memory flashes through my head.

Fogged windows and cheap wine. Hot breath. Desperate hands. Deep red lipstick stains on the collar of my white T-shirt.

"That family is bad news," Tiffany says, pulling me from my thoughts.

Her statement makes my stomach twist.

"Every one of them," my dad adds.

Michael hums in agreement.

All I can do is sit quietly and wait for the news segment to end.

# SIX
## *Sam*

"Good morning, Samantha."

"Ashton," I greet curtly, tossing a thick file folder on the table in front of him, then leaning my hip against it. "I took the liberty of printing everything out for you since you don't seem to know how to work a shared drive on the internet. That's the only possible explanation for why you haven't viewed my plans and suggestions. I know technology can be hard, Ashton, but it's in your best interest to figure it out. Daddy is trusting you, after all."

Ashton grins at me as he scoops the file folder up and drops it into a drawer in the desk. He never opens it. Never so much as glances at it. It makes my blood boil. I force a smile.

"Do you need assistance in opening file folders, too? Gosh, Ashton, I'm starting to think you might be in over your head as Daddy's campaign manager."

Ashton stands from his chair so he's towering over me, but I don't step away. He grins down his nose at me, and I make a mental note to wear higher heels tomorrow. And to find a way to remove the lifts from his loafers.

"I assure you, I am more than capable, Samantha. Your father has trusted me with this job, and I will not let him down."

He runs his eyes over my face, assessing and cataloguing.

Judging. Looking for flaws. Trying to read me. I don't flinch away despite the fact that I want to. Despite the fact that his cologne is too strong, and his closeness is giving me the creeps. I stand my ground and keep my voice calm.

"My experience on this campaign team is vital, and my plans sh—"

"Your experience on the previous *senate* campaigns is useless, Samantha. Small potatoes. This is a much bigger ballgame. The stakes are higher. What you've suggested...it just won't work again."

I cock my head to the side and raise an eyebrow.

"You didn't even look at it," I say slowly. "How do you know it won't work?"

Ashton's smile widens to show off all his perfectly straight, too white veneers. I want to punch him right in the mouth, but I don't want to ruin my fresh manicure.

"Samantha, I know you don't want to hear this, but Senator Harper gave you the role he believes you'll best serve. You are to be my *assistant*. Let the rest of us worry about the campaign strategies."

It takes all of my carefully crafted composure not to explode on him, with his smug grin and his pompous tone. He's lucky I'm still riding the high of my morning Pilates class endorphins. I should have choked him to death with his tie last week when I had the chance and let my father clean up my mess. Lord knows he does it enough for Chase.

I hate myself for what I'm about to say, but it's the only leverage I have right now. I straighten my shoulders and keep my breathing even, then give him a practiced smile.

"I'll have to speak to my father, then."

"You do that."

I walk away, keeping my steps leisurely. I put an extra sway in my hips because I can feel his beady little creeper eyes on me, and I don't want him to know just how irritated I am.

That man is insufferable.

To act as though my experience is worthless? The disrespectful way he shoved my folder into the drawer? The casual way he shot me down? It's enough to make me want to commit a felony.

I'm used to men treating me like I'm lesser. Like my big breasts and high heels automatically denote subpar intelligence. I'm used to it, yes, but that doesn't make it any easier to handle. Especially when it's coming from an immature neanderthal like Ashton fucking Cartwright. The man bought a copy of the SAT and still had to pay someone else to retake it for him when he tanked. He's old money nepotism to the highest degree, and I hate him for it.

I hate even more that, on the surface, I appear to be the same.

I don't bother knocking when I get to my father's office, and it calms my mood slightly to see his campaign finance manager jump back from where she'd been leaning on his desk. I narrow my eyes at her and smile.

"You may leave, Brenda." I gesture to the door.

She smooths her hands over her skirt and acts offended.

"It's Denise," she corrects.

I raise a brow dismissively and nod toward the door again, and she scurries out. I turn my smile at my father.

"Daddy, isn't it unwise to start flirting with the staff this early in the campaign? I would hate to lose Brenda the same way we lost Matilda. What would the media think?"

Both names I used were wrong, but my father doesn't bother correcting me. He ignores my statement entirely and barely glances in my direction as he flicks his eyes to his computer screen with a sigh.

"Good morning, Samantha. What can I do for you right now?"

"I'd like to discuss Ashton Cartwright with you," I say, getting right to the point. "Specifically, I'd like to discuss my task as Ashton's assistant when I believe my skills would be better suited for a more important role on the campaign team."

My father finally looks at me. His smile is patronizing. His eyes are cold. At times like this, I know he hates me just as much as I hate him. That isn't what bothers me, though. What bothers me is that he probably knows how much I hate him, and knowing he knows makes it harder to carry out the act. It also makes it more dangerous.

"Your job as Ashton's assistant is very important, Samantha. Helping my campaign manager is helping me, and you had no complaints about it last week."

"That was when I assumed Ashton and I would be working *together* to help you win, but he's shown no interest in what I have to say. My data from the previous senate campaigns is invaluable. The work I did to get you the youth vote should be proof enough that my suggestions are worthy of consideration. Ashton refuses to see me as little more than the hired help."

My father leans back in his desk chair and folds his hands in his lap, the movement too similar to the one Ashton carried out moments earlier. Men like them? They're all the same.

"Is there a reason you want so badly to be part of this campaign, Samantha?"

His question catches me off guard, and my skin crawls. I can only hope that he reads my shock as offense and not guilt.

"My only concern has always been helping you to succeed," I say firmly. "When you succeed, we all succeed."

The lie tastes bitter in my mouth, like bile, but I hold eye contact. I don't flinch.

My father takes a breath before speaking and implements a dramatic pause while he looks me over. I already know that I'm not going to like what he has to say.

"Samantha, I made Ashton my campaign manager for a reason. I trust him. You should, too. You were very helpful in my previous campaigns, I will admit, but you're older now, and politics is no place for a woman of your breeding. Harper women are not politicians. They are not made for working in these sorts of roles. I indulged your political science and business management follies while you were at Georgetown because a good education makes a woman like you more valuable, but you're nearly thirty. It's time you start prioritizing things more fitting for a woman of your social standing."

I barely hear him over the sound of my livid heartbeat in my head.

A woman of my *breeding*? Makes a woman *more valuable*?

I'm not fucking livestock, yet he's talking about me as if I were. I almost laugh in his face. I almost shout at him. *Nearly thirty*? I'm twenty-fucking-six, and I graduated at the top of my university class with honors, beating out hundreds of men of similar "social standing." That's not folly. That's fucking intelligence, determination, and hard work.

I want to throw a tantrum. I want to pick up his computer and bash it over his head. Instead, I take a subtle deep breath and force a smile.

"Daddy," I say coolly. "Forgive me if I've misunderstood your implications with my tiny woman brain. You can't possibly be suggesting you've demoted me on this campaign because you want me to start prioritizing more...*domestic*...tasks."

This time, his smile is full teeth.

"That's precisely what I'm saying, Samantha. And I think you should start with Ashton."

My eyebrows rise in shock, and not a lot shocks me when it comes to my father.

"Excuse me?" I bite out, and my father sighs.

"Ashton is perfectly suited for you, Samantha. His family is a good match for ours. Be more agreeable, would you? It wouldn't hurt you to appear more likable when he's around. And I think, if you stop being so bullheaded and submit to your role as his assistant, you might find that you enjoy it."

Oh, I hate him.

"And you're hoping that I, what? That I will love *submitting* so much that I'll decide to make a life out of it and marry him?"

My father shrugs, and I want to scream. That's *exactly* what he's hoping for.

"You can't be serious," I whisper.

I can't hide the disgust and, to my horror, the fear in my tone.

My father has probably already worked out the conditions of my marriage to Ashton with the Honorable Andrew Cartwright. Just the thought of that disgusting, vile man makes me want to vomit. But becoming legally tied to him? To that family? I cannot handle all the emotions roiling in my stomach.

"You want to help me, Samantha? You want to see me succeed? Joining the Harper and Cartwright families would be the most helpful thing you could do to ensure my success and the success of our family. Not to mention, I'm sure the media would love to see you two together. I know my voters would love it."

My father's words are spoken so casually, so matter-of-factly, that it might as well be a one-sided conversation. No matter how a relationship between a senator's daughter and a judge's son would look. It could already be seen as a conflict of interest with Ashton as his campaign manager, but he thinks he's untouchable. They all do. He's already made up his mind how this will go, my feelings be damned, and that only serves to make me angrier.

"So you're pimping me out?" I accuse through gritted teeth. My fresh manicure bites into the soft flesh of my palms as I squeeze my hands into tight fists. "You've relegated me to arm candy and ass kisser? *I* am the reason you got the youth vote in the last senate election, and if you remember, Father, the youth vote saved your seat. You wouldn't have been reelected if it weren't for me. *I* am the reason you got reelected. Me. But now I'm only worthy of being a chattel bride in your attempts to elevate our family status? Are you even hearing how archaic and ridiculous this is?"

My father sighs again, this time louder, like I'm a petulant child.

"Don't be so dramatic, Samantha."

"I'm not being dramatic," I argue. "I will not be—"

"Enough," he cuts me off. His nostrils flare as he flicks his eyes to the door and back to me. "You will not argue with me about this in front of my staff. If you want to be here, you will do as you're told. If you cannot do that, you can leave. But let me remind you that there are conditions to your trust fund, Samantha. You live comfortably on your allowance because I *allow* it, but my generosity is not infinite, and you do not want to violate the conditions of your trust."

His threat is about as subtle as a nuclear warhead.

I wince because I know he wants me to. I back down because pretending like I give two fucks about his money is the only safe and believable angle I have. But god, does it physically hurt to lose this one.

"Do you understand what I am saying, Samantha?"

I jerk out a nod.

"Loud and clear, Daddy."

"Perfect." His answering smile nearly burns my retinas. "How about you go see if there is anything you can do for Ashton to make his job easier, hm?"

I smile, nod once more, then leave without another word. The day I no longer have to kowtow to Thom Harper will be the day I finally know true and complete happiness.

I walk slowly toward Ashton's office space. I open the door and give him a radiant smile. The way he blinks in my direction tells me he was expecting my wrath. He doesn't know what to do with a smile.

"I'm taking an early lunch, Ashton, but I wanted to know if you had any tasks you needed me to complete for you while I'm out."

Every word is like chewing on thumbtacks, but I get them out. I say them, and I make it sound like I mean them. I'm a fucking gold star liar. Like father, like daughter.

I leave the building with a bulleted list of menial errands from the man-child whom I now serve, and I wait until I'm safely across town in my car before I pull to the side of the road and scream into my expensive designer handbag.

I scream so long that my voice cracks and my head starts to throb.

My eyes prickle with tears and the back of my neck dots with sweat.

I scream until I can't scream anymore.

Then, I rest my forehead on my steering wheel and breathe. I replay Lennon's voice reading *Persuasion* in my mind. I spell my name on my leg with my finger—S-a-m-S-a-m-S-a-m—over and over. I imagine the look on my father's face when he reaps what he's been sowing his whole life.

I tell myself that I can do this. Over and over and over.

I can do this. I can. I am strong enough. I am clever enough. I am *good* enough.

I repeat it until my mind clears, my chest no longer aches, and my eyes are dry.

I bring my head off the steering wheel and flip down my visor. Checking my reflection in the mirror, I use my fingers to clean up the places where my watery eyes smudged my mascara. I take my red lipstick out of my handbag and reapply a fresh coat to my lips.

Then I reach into my glove compartment and pull out my second cell phone. I power it on and send a single text to the only number in the contacts.

ME
SOS.

# SEVEN
## Chris

"I've got two hours before I have to be at the bar."

I strip off my grease-stained, standard-issue Franklin Auto Body work shirt, followed by my equally grease-stained white undershirt, and drop them both in a pile beside the boxing ring. My mood has been on a downward spiral since this morning. I need to blow off steam before my bar shift, or it's sure to be a fucking terrible night.

"Then we better get busy." Macon tosses a pair of boxing gloves at my feet. "You got shorts or anything? Going to be uncomfortable as hell to get your ass beat in those jeans."

"Who says you're going to beat my ass, Davis?"

"Always do, Casper."

He smirks as he pulls on his boxing gloves, and I shake my head. He's full of shit. Our record is about tied, and last time we boxed, I won.

I kick off my shoes, then take off my socks. I don't answer his question about my jeans. I didn't bring athletic shorts with me this morning. I didn't think I'd need them. It's just added to my irritation, and though I know I could borrow some from Macon's apartment upstairs, I figure I'll deal with the discomfort. Consider it self-punishment for being a fucking dumbass today.

I follow Macon into the ring and face him. I usually wear a

mouthguard and headgear anytime I'm in the ring with him, but I didn't grab them today. The way he sizes me up tells me he's already suspicious.

"Don't pull any punches today."

He arches a brow. "When do I ever?"

I arch a brow right back. "Every time you're in a shitty mood."

Macon is a former Marine and was a trained instructor in the Marine Corps Martial Arts program. I'm not stupid. I know he could do serious damage, even with his leg injury. I leave our sparring matches with some bruises, aches, and pains, but it's probably a far cry from what he's capable of, especially on days when he's pissed or anxious, or battling one of his many mental demons and craving a fix. He's been sober for years now, but I know every day is a battle.

Macon narrows his eyes at me, surveying my face. I know the moment he notices the tightness there. The frustration. The pain. His concern is evident, but he doesn't say anything about it. He just nods once, then pounds his gloves together.

"Two hours." He smirks. "Hit me, fucker."

---

"Fuck, dude." Macon huffs out a laugh as he prods at his swollen eye. "Lennon is going to fucking kill you."

I chuckle, but it's weak.

"I'll apologize to her for ruining her soulmate's face," I tell him.

I use my tongue to inspect my split lip. It's swollen and tastes like blood, and I can already tell a bruise is forming on my cheek, but Macon looks worse. I hear plastic rustling and look over my shoulder to see him opening a pack of red licorice. He pulls out a piece and pops it between his lips, and I take note of the way his fingers hold it as if it were a cigarette. Or a joint.

"For giving me shit about pulling punches, you sure proved you've been leavin' a lot in the tank during our sessions." He grins. "You've never busted me up so thoroughly."

"You're fucked in the head for enjoying it," I joke, and he snorts but doesn't argue.

"So what did it?" he asks finally. "Did you hear from Sable or something?"

I don't answer and he sighs.

"C'mon, Casper. Something's got you all keyed up. I know you, man. What happened?"

Fuck him for being so intuitive. I drop my head back, close my eyes against the harsh recess lighting, and speak to the ceiling.

"She *accidentally* tagged me in one of her pictures last night. I didn't know until this morning, and only because she sent me a message to apologize."

Macon scoffs. "Accident my ass."

I laugh. He's not wrong. I know she did it to fuck with me. Why not just remove the tag and leave it alone? Why tag me, leave it, and then message me to say *whoops, sorry, hope all is well*?

Because she wanted to rub something in my face. And like a fucking asshole, I took the bait.

"You scrolled, didn't you?" Macon says, and I nod.

"I scrolled."

It's been a little over a month since Sable and I broke up, and in that time, she's been living her best rich life up and down the East Coast. Bottle service at a club in New York City. Cocktails at some swim-up bar in Florida. New flashy jewelry. Thirst trap pictures in a burnt orange McLaren. Don't know whose. Don't care. But what the fuck? Scrolling through those pictures just hit home how fucking wrong I was about her. How completely clueless I was about the person I thought I loved.

"Was she always so..."

I let the question trail off. I don't have to finish it because Macon is already nodding, his face twisted up like he smells something rancid.

"Yes. She was. Always. Fucking insufferable. And rude. Shitty tipper, too."

I jerk my head back.

"How do you know she's a shitty tipper? I always paid."

He grins.

"Remember that time Lennon and her went out to lunch? That's how I know. Len said Sable was rude to the server, complained about everything, sent her food back twice, and then left a two-dollar tip. It was so bad that Lennon went back later that day just so she could apologize to the server and give her a hundred bucks."

*Fuck.*

No wonder Lennon never invited Sable out again. I scrub a hand down my face and groan.

"I'm an idiot."

Macon chuckles. "Nah. I mean, you *were* an idiot, but you're not anymore."

"Macon, I fucking proposed. The only reason I'm not engaged right now is because she said no. Not because I wised up and realized what a shitty person she was. She might be a bitch, but that doesn't change the fact that *she* dumped *me*." I sigh and shake my head. "I am an idiot."

Macon drops a hand on my shoulder and gives it a squeeze.

"Fine. You're right. You're an idiot."

I laugh and shove him off me.

"I gotta go," I tell him. I have just enough time to hit up my house for a change of clothes before I have to be at The Outpost for my shift. "You comin' by tonight?"

"Can't. We've got Evie tonight."

Macon's younger half-sister is absolutely adorable, and he and Lennon watch her one weekend every month. He's the proudest big brother. Between him and Lennon, Evie will never want for anything. She's not even five and she already has her own kiddy-sized pottery wheel and paint easel at their apartment.

"Oh, do me a favor," he says as he types something into his phone. "Check to make sure Harper hasn't injured or kidnapped my girlfriend when you get to work, would ya?"

I raise a brow.

"What?"

"Lennon is helping Sam move stuff into her apartment today, but I haven't heard from her in hours." He slides his phone into his back pocket and laughs. "Sam moving into The Outpost Penthouse was not something I saw coming."

"No shit." I didn't see it coming, either. "I'll check on them before I pull the chain. Later."

I wave over my shoulder as I leave the rec center gym, and I hear Macon call goodbye just as the doors close behind me. I nod my greeting to some of the volunteers milling about the building, then head straight to my truck. I drive to my house, shower and change clothes quickly, grab my camouflage baseball cap, then I rush to The Outpost.

Instead of parking in my regular spot in the lot, I pull behind the building and park next to Sam's BMW. The moment I open my truck door, I'm hit with screeching and laughter, so I bolt toward the sound, only to find Lennon and Sam on the staircase, standing on either side of what looks to be a brand-new full mattress.

"What the fuck are you guys doing?" I shout as I rush to them, and both their heads turn in my direction.

"Oh, thank god, Casper," Lennon says, though she's hard to understand through her incessant giggles. "Help. We're stuck."

"We're not *stuck*." Sam fights like hell to contain her own laughter. "We're...just...resting."

They both start laughing again, and I watch as the mattress slowly inches backward, down the staircase, and Lennon screeches again.

"Oh fuck, I'm losing it," she shouts between laughs. "Oh my god, I can't die because of a rogue mattress. This is so embarrassing!"

"Stop making me laugh," Sam shouts back. "Just...push it!"

"I can't push it," Lennon says. "I can't. I can't feel my arms."

Their giggling is contagious, and my cheeks hurt from grinning when I spring into action, rushing up the staircase and taking the back end from Lennon.

"Jesus Christ." I grunt as the weight of the thing pushes into my chest. "Fuck, Lennon, what the hell? You thought you guys could get this up there by yourselves?"

She's lucky this thing didn't slip and run her over on the way down. It probably weighs a hundred pounds, and it's awkward as fuck, all floppy and unevenly distributed.

"We got it halfway," Lennon says indignantly, panting to catch her breath.

"We can...get it the rest of the way...without you," Sam shouts from the other end of the mattress, but her statement is breathy and weak. "Shoo. Be gone, *man*. We have this...under control!"

Lennon busts up laughing behind me again and the mattress starts to shake as Sam falls back into laughter, too. All I can do is wait patiently, holding up my end of the mattress until Sam catches her breath.

"Are you done?" I ask, forcing seriousness into my tone. "I'm going to be late opening up the bar if you don't get your shit together."

"We don't need your help," Sam snaps again. "We were fine before you swooped in. We're not damsels in dist—"

"Oh, shut up, Sam. You were ten seconds from losing the mattress and letting it crush Lennon."

"I was not!"

"You *were*. Now, be quiet and listen," I say sternly, like I would if I were shouting orders to the guys at the garage, or giving some drunk asshole a warning to behave or he'd get booted from the bar. "I've got this end. I can hold the majority of the weight. I just need you to guide it up to the landing so we can lay it on its side and shove it through the door."

"That was already our plan," Lennon chirps.

"You shut up too, Len," I tease, sending her some side-eye.

She huffs and folds her arms, but she can't hide her little smirk.

"Ready, Harper?" I shout, and she growls.

I can picture the look of disdain on her face. She hates the idea of someone—of me—coming to her rescue. When she doesn't answer, I lift the mattress a little higher so more of the weight tips onto her, and I hear her squeak.

"I don't have all day, princess. I'm ten seconds from leaving and letting you two dummies get back to your suicide mission."

"Ugh, *fine*." She groans. I feel the mattress shift as she fixes her grip. "All right, let's go."

Slowly and steadily, I take the steps up to what Macon has dubbed "The Outpost Penthouse." Once the mattress is on its side on the landing, I watch Sam swing the door open and maneuver her end of the mattress through the doorframe.

"Okay," she calls from inside the apartment, popping her head out around the doorframe to look at me. "You can push it in."

I smirk at the innuendo, and she glowers, so I give the mattress a hard shove. She yelps and jumps backward.

"Asshole!" she shouts, and I'm biting back laughter as I shove the mattress the rest of the way into the apartment.

I don't look at her. I just slide the mattress all the way down the hallway, then prop it on one of the walls in the bedroom. I note a few LV suitcases and garment bags as I walk out, and I realize she's actually going through with this. I can't help but chuckle.

Sam's so fucking stubborn. I knew my comment about her family would piss her off, but this is next-level spiteful. She's going to hate it here, but she'll suffer through it just to make a point.

When I step back into the living room, Sam is checking her nails, and I bark out a laugh.

"Break a nail, princess?"

She looks up from inspecting her hand, smiles sweetly with her blood-red lips, then slowly brandishes her middle finger in my direction, displaying a pristinely manicured nail. Even the vulgar gesture is classy when she does it.

She raises a brow, and I lock my eyes with hers. I smirk, drop my gaze down to her middle finger, then bring it to her lips before finally looking back at her face.

"Thank goodness," I say playfully, and she rolls her eyes and looks away.

Then I notice the couch, end table, and television already set up in the living room.

"You got a couch up here?"

Lennon grins at my surprise. "It's Ikea, so it was in boxes. But the boxes were heavy, *and* we put it together." She puts her hands on her hips. "See? We could have done the mattress. I just got a cramp in my leg, and it messed up our momentum. And then we started laughing..."

I shake my head.

"I would never doubt what you ladies are capable of," I say honestly, then I turn my head to Sam. "But it's not beneath you to ask for help when you need it."

Sam sighs dramatically and turns her back to me.

"You may leave now," she says.

Lennon stifles a laugh, and I narrow my eyes at her before stalking slowly up to Sam. I feel her stiffen when I brush my chest against her back, but she doesn't flinch. When I lower my mouth to her ear, I think she even stops breathing.

"I'm right downstairs if you need me, princess." I keep my voice low. I wait a breath, just long enough that my pause is noticeable, then I straighten and make my way to the door. "See you later, Lennon. Try to stay out of trouble."

Lennon grins and tells me thank you for helping with the mattress, and I step out onto the landing. Just before I pull the door shut behind me, I hear Sam shout.

"I won't need you!"

I close the door without a response, but the smile I'm sporting carries me all through my bar shift.

# EIGHT

## Chris

THE LIGHTS FLICKER FOR THE THIRD TIME IN AN HOUR.

I check the clock. It's only midnight, but the storm outside is getting pretty bad. So bad that I'm surprised more people haven't fucked off to their own homes already. I even changed the bar televisions to the weather channel to stay informed. The high winds mean high potential for downed trees, and it's pouring, so some of the streets in town are probably already starting to flood.

The longer I watch the radar, the closer I come to kicking everyone out and closing early. A storm like this is dangerous at the best of times, but when you've got a bar full of drunk people who need to get home? I don't want that on my conscience.

I tell Paul, the other bartender working tonight, my decision, and we start closing out tabs without an announcement, handing people back their cards when we see them and doing the closing routine as we go. I've just locked up the register when the lights flicker for a fourth time. Then a fifth.

Then they go out completely.

Everyone yelps, some people start to laugh, and there's a smattering of applause when the emergency lights come on, but after thirty seconds, I realize something must be wrong with the backup generator because the rest of the lights in the bar stay dark.

I glance at Paul.

"How much you want to bet Alan didn't have the generator serviced before he skipped town?" I ask, and Paul flares his eyes.

"I doubt it's been serviced at all."

Fuck. I scrub a hand down my face.

"Work on getting everyone out," I say over the commotion. The murmuring of the customers is getting louder, and we have to get ahead of it. "Make sure people get rides who need them. Take keys and threaten a lifetime ban if you have to. No drunk assholes on the road, got it?"

Paul nods, and I feel around under the bar for the Maglite. The emergency floodlights at the exits give off enough light that we're not in a total blackout, but it's still hard as fuck to see anything clearly.

"I'll go out and see if I can figure out what's wrong with the generator. If I can't, we risk losing everything in the cooler."

Fucking Alan.

As Paul starts corralling customers out the door, I head out the back to look over the generator. I don't have a coat or an umbrella, so I'm soaked in seconds, but it doesn't take long to figure out that the battery is dead.

*What's the point of having this fucking fancy generator if you don't keep the battery serviced, Alan?*

I'm going to call him tomorrow and chew him out, then demand he foots the bill for everything in the cooler we'll need to replace.

I turn to head back inside, soaked from head to toe, and literally scream when I find someone standing next to me. I jump back, ready to throw a punch, but a cackle of glee stops me short.

"Sam, what the fuck?" I shout, and she grins, showing off bright white teeth in the semi-darkness.

"Sorry," she says, obviously not sorry.

She has to shout over the sound of pounding rain and wind. I catch my breath and take a moment to look her over. A flash of lightning illuminates the sky, making it easier to see the fine details, and I laugh at what I find.

"What the hell are you wearing?"

Sam Harper stands in front of me wearing a trash bag like a cape over a thin silk robe. Her hair is up in a sopping wet towel and sad, soaked, pink slippers that look like dicks are on her feet. And, to make it worse, her face is covered in some sort of brown goop.

She props her hand on her hip and scowls.

"I thought this shithole had a generator," she snaps, straight up ignoring my question. "Why the fuck is my apartment pitch black? There are only two windows in that cave. I can't see a damn thing."

There are five windows, but I don't correct her.

"Shithole?" I repeat, tilting my head to the side with a smirk. "I thought y—"

"Oh, shut up," she snarls.

I have to admit, I am fucking loving this. Seeing the princess all disheveled and worked up, looking like something straight out of a horror film. If I had my phone, I'd snap a picture.

"We do have a generator"—I gesture to the machine in question—"but the battery is dead."

"So get a new one."

"It's nearly one in the morning, Sam. The hardware store is closed, so the only way I can get a new one is if I call the owners and ask if they can open up shop for me, which I won't do because they're in their fucking eighties, and in case you haven't noticed, this weather is not safe for anyone, let alone the elderly."

The anger on her face flickers briefly.

"Shit," she mumbles. "Shit."

"What's all over your face?" I ask finally, and she sighs.

"A mud mask. And my hair is being deep conditioned, which I'm now going to have to shampoo it out or I'll look like a fucking greased pig."

She groans and drops her head back, the wet towel unraveling and falling into a puddle at her feet. Her makeshift raincoat was a valiant effort but completely worthless, and her dick slippers are little more than pink fuzzy blobs. She mumbles something like *bad fucking idea*, and she's such a pitiful sight that I take mercy on her.

"C'mon, princess." I put a hand on her shoulder and turn her around, shoving her toward the back entrance to the bar. "We'll get you fixed up."

I snatch her towel off the ground as I follow her through the door, and the moment she steps into the main bar, a yelp of fright comes from Paul, followed by a scoff from Sam.

"Sorry about the swamp monster, Paul." I pat Sam on the head. She swats my hand away with a growl. "Found her rummaging in the trash out back and felt bad. Couldn't leave her out in the storm."

"Ha-ha. You're hilarious," Sam says, stalking back out the way we came, but I step in front of her and grab her shoulders.

"I'm kidding. I'm kidding. Just give me a few minutes, okay?"

She scoffs again and folds her arms across her chest, but she doesn't move to leave. I hand her a stack of bar napkins and gesture to her face, then I turn back to Paul. He and I make sure the walk-in cooler and freezer are locked up tight and make plans to come back first thing in the morning to check the damage.

When Paul heads out the front door, I finally face Sam again. Most of the mud mask is gone, but her hair is a greasy, wet mess stuck to her face and neck, and her silk robe and slippers are in even worse shape. She's still wearing the trash bag cape, too.

"So I'm guessing you can't get ahold of Lennon since you're here and not there?"

She sighs. "They've got Evie tonight, and she hasn't responded to my text. I didn't want to call and disturb them if they were sleeping or dealing with a scared child."

The statement is more considerate than I would have expected from her, but I don't say that out loud. She and Lennon are extremely close, so I guess it makes sense that Sam would have Lennon's comfort in mind.

"Well, I can bring you to my house and you can use my shower —I have a generator that I know for a fact works—or I can take you to your dad's, but it's probably better for me to take you in my truck than you attempt it in your coupe. Some of these roads flood pretty bad."

She nods slowly and fixes her eyes on something over my shoulder. I watch her work out my offer as she chews on the inside of her lip a bit.

"You're sure you don't mind taking me to your place?" She sounds so defeated that I don't give her shit. I like to fuck with her, but not when she's vulnerable and obviously uncomfortable.

"It's fine, Sam. We can go back up and you can grab your stuff, and then we'll head out."

I double-check that the front door is locked, the neon sign is unplugged, and the lights are all flipped off before I trail Sam out the back and up the stairs. I keep the flashlight on and shining on her path, so she doesn't trip. She grabs a toiletry bag, shoves some clothes in an oversized designer tote, and grabs her phone and charger out of the living room.

I'm surprised to see that her coffee table is completely covered, and I shine the Maglite on it to get a better look. Books, an open spiral-bound notebook filled with writing, a few highlighters and pens, a pad of sticky notes, and an empty wine glass litter the surface. I zero in on the words in the notebook when Sam snatches the Maglite from my hands and turns it on my face.

"Quit snooping," she snaps, then brushes past me and heads to the door.

I chuckle and follow her down the stairs and to my truck. She climbs into my passenger side as I slide behind the wheel.

"You can take off your trash bag," I tell her, and she does without comment.

I'd put a towel or something down for her, but it's honestly pointless. We're both soaked completely through, and her robe has become almost like a second skin. It's so bad that I have to make sure to keep my eyes on her face and not on her body. The last thing I need right now is to see her curves encased in soaking wet silk.

"There are CDs in the glove compartment," I tell Sam, half expecting her to make fun of the fact that my truck is so old that it has a CD player.

She doesn't. She just opens the glove compartment and starts digging around in there. She ignores the CD case, though, and instead zeroes in on something else.

"What's this?" she asks, her fingers wrapping around the worn copy of *Walden* I keep in there. "Thoreau?" She opens it and flips through the pages, no doubt noticing the penciled notes, underlines, and highlights throughout. She smirks to herself. "I didn't know you could read."

I snort a laugh.

"Smartass." I take the book from her and put it back where it belongs, closing the glove compartment and putting my keys in the ignition. "It was my grandfather's copy, but yes, I do read it. Surprising, right?"

She hums, then rests her wet head on the seatback.

"I remember him," she says quietly after a moment.

My grandfather worked at the post office, so everyone knew and loved him. I was fifteen when he died of a stroke.

"Are the annotations his?"

I nod, but I don't look at her as I pull out of the lot and turn the truck toward my house.

"Some of them, yeah. Some of them are mine."

"Multifaceted," she says, and I smile but don't respond.

We stay quiet the rest of the ride to my house, me with my eyes glued to the terrible road conditions, and Sam with her eyes closed. Most of the town is pitch black, confirming what I'd already assumed. Almost everyone has lost power, so it will probably be afternoon at the earliest before everyone is restored.

When I pull into the driveway of my small house, though, the porch light is on, and I can hear the hum of my generator as soon as I turn off the truck. It came with the house, and it's come in handy on more than one occasion. I glance at Sam just in time to see her smile of relief.

"Let's get you cleaned up, princess."

I climb out of the truck before I can hear her scoff at the nickname.

She follows me inside and peels her dick slippers off at the door. I raise a brow at them, and Sam rolls her eyes.

"A gag gift from Lennon." She returns my smirk. "I got her rose gold anal beads."

I almost choke on my laugh. "Real gold?"

Sam's smile disappears. "Of course. Eighteen karats."

*Of course.* I shake my head, then gesture for her to follow me down the hall.

"Here's the bathroom." I open the door and point to the shower, then to the linen closet. "Towels and washcloths are in here." I turn to face her. "Just holler if you need anything."

She blinks at me.

"I do not *holler*," she says seriously, then steps into the bathroom and says thank you before shutting the door in my face.

## NINE

## Sam

I heave a sigh of relief as soon as the door closes.

The tension in my shoulders lessens once I turn the shower knob and hear the water start to run, but then I turn to face myself in the mirror and gasp at what I see.

A drowned rat.

That's what I look like. A drowned sewer rat.

There are still patches of mud mask stuck to my cheeks, and when I gingerly run my fingers through my hair, I find it feels just as greasy as it looks. Meanwhile, Chris is looking like something straight out of a Hollywood film set with his bulging, tattoo-covered biceps and glistening rain-slicked skin. Add in his playful smirk and boy-next-door charm, and he's a recipe for disaster.

Fuck this whole fucking day.

I shed my ruined silk robe onto the white tile floor, followed quickly by my bra and underwear, then pull back the shower curtain and step beneath the hot spray. The moment water hits my body, I have to fight back tears. Not because it hurts, but because for the first time in days, my muscles fully relax. I hadn't even realized it had gotten this bad. This week has put my emotions through a meat grinder, my composure resembling a precariously built house of cards, and this shower acts as a balm, soothing my invisible wounds.

I keep hearing the same three words in my head. I keep repeating them.

*Whatever it takes.*
*Whatever it takes.*
*Whatever it takes.*

No cost too high, no risk too great.

Whatever. It. Takes.

I just needed a moment to recharge. A few days to catch my breath before, once again, donning my snakeskin and diving into that pit of vipers in D.C. Instead, I got a terrifying thunderstorm and an even more terrifying blackout that frayed my nerves to ribbons.

Tilting my head up to the ceiling, I let the shower spray cascade over my body. I scrub my face clean of mud mask remnants and wash my hair three times. When I'm certain I no longer resemble a diseased rodent, I turn off the water and step out.

I towel dry my hair enough that it's no longer dripping down my back, then reach for the pajama set I grabbed from my sad excuse for an apartment. I button up the short-sleeved silk top and step into the silk pair of shorts. When I look in the mirror once more, I'm a different person. My face is fresh and clean, my skin flushed pink from the hot water and the scrubbing. It's free of mud mask, but it's also free of makeup, and that makes me uncomfortable.

My fingers itch to reach into my toiletry bag and apply a coat of red to my lips.

My suit of armor. My shield.

I don't. Blinking at my reflection, I scowl at how much younger I look, then wipe my expression clean of any vulnerability. Take a deep breath. Practice a smirk. Then I leave the bathroom and enter the kitchen.

"Hey, I—"

Chris glances up from his spot at the island but stops mid-sentence when he sees me. He closes his mouth and looks me over, something strange passing over his features as he does.

"What?" I ask, sounding more annoyed than I feel, and he shrugs.

"I just can't remember the last time I saw you so...I don't know...dressed down."

"Sorry to disappoint," I say sharply, "but I wasn't going to put on a full face of makeup for you."

"That's not what I meant." He chuckles. "I like it. That's all. It's different, but I like it."

I narrow my eyes at him, suspicious, and he laughs again. He must have changed while I was in the shower. He's wearing a pair of joggers and a long-sleeved Henley shirt, and he's got that damned camo ballcap sitting backward on his head. I open my mouth to comment on it, but then my eyes fall to the counter in front of him.

"Oh, you bastard." I grin.

I close the distance between us and pick up one of the two lowball glasses and inspect it. Judging from the bottles on the counter, it's a Boulevardier. Two ice cubes and two orange twists. I take a sip, and my eyes flutter shut. It's perfect.

"I thought it was a crime to make a cocktail with such fancy bourbon," Chris says, and I smile at him above my glass.

He barks a laugh and shakes his head.

"That's why you do it," he states, and I shrug, swirling the liquid in my glass as I speak.

"My father considers himself something of a whiskey sommelier. A bourbon snob. To him, mixing a fine bourbon like this into a cocktail is akin to sacrilege. For Senator Thom Harper and his highbrow friends, even more than one ice cube is a crime."

I take another sip, mentally cataloging the taste of the apéritif before swallowing, then set the glass on the counter. I make eye contact and hold it.

"I want to desecrate everything he loves."

Chris doesn't flinch. He doesn't laugh. He doesn't tell me I'm stupid or childish. He doesn't question me or insist that I don't understand the weight of my own words. He just holds my gaze without judgment, and something about it feels empowering. Thrilling.

I have a lot of faces I show the world, but this one—the one that's naked and honest—I keep hidden. Lennon's the only person who knows the true extent of my darkness, so to feel like I've revealed some of it—even if just a small, insignificant detail—with impunity?

Well. Let's just say I understand how villains are created.

When I start to smile, Chris's mouth curves with mine until a small laugh bubbles out of me.

"You're something else, princess," he says finally, his smile growing softer.

Soft enough that my arms prickle with goose bumps, and I have to look away.

"It sounds like the storm is calming," I say, changing the subject. "I should probably get back to my cave and try to sleep."

Silence blankets the kitchen until all I can hear is Chris breathing and the rain pattering on the windows. I take another sip of my perfect Boulevardier, and then my stomach growls. It's loud enough that my eyes widen, and my hand covers my abdomen on instinct.

"Did you eat dinner?" Chris asks, and I purse my lips.

"Yes."

He rolls his eyes and moves to the refrigerator as he speaks.

"What did you eat?"

"Food," I snap, and he chuckles.

I set my drink on the counter and watch as he pulls things out of the fridge. A hunk of something wrapped in aluminum foil. Shredded cheese. Jalapeño peppers. I get so distracted watching him that I don't even realize I start talking.

"I had some crackers and brie." Two limes. Sour cream. Some herbs. He shuts the fridge and opens a cabinet. "And I also had some blueberries and pepperoni." Tortilla chips. Olive oil. He grabs an avocado out of a basket on the counter. A bowl from a cabinet above the stove and a cutting board and cast-iron skillet from the cabinets next to the stove. "Some baby carrots and some pistachios."

He turns to face me with a grin.

"That's not dinner. That's a charcuterie board."

I arch a brow. "I had it at dinnertime, so it's dinner."

He grins wider. "Fine. It's dinner. Then how about you stay for a while longer, and I'll make prime rib nachos as a late-night snack?"

My stomach growls again and he laughs. He doesn't wait for me to answer. He just grabs a chef's knife and starts chopping the bunch of herbs, then tosses them into a metal bowl with some olive oil and garlic.

He chops the jalapeños next, leaving them in thin, perfect little rings. It's actually fascinating how smoothly he moves. How swiftly and expertly he wields the chef's knife. I find myself speechless, and every once in a while, he'll glance up at me with that lopsided, boy-next-door grin. It's all so overwhelmingly sexy that even the backward camo hat doesn't deter from it.

When he's finished with the jalapeños, he grabs the hunk of tinfoil and unwraps it. Even straight from the refrigerator, the divine scent of garlic and rosemary hits me, and it's enough to make my mouth water.

"Now, this is leftovers." He starts to slice the prime rib into strips, then cuts the strips into bite-sized pieces. It's a beautiful reddish pink. "It *was* a perfect medium rare, but I'm going to do a quick reheat in the cast iron so it will be more medium. I did a rosemary, thyme, and garlic rub on it, and I'll warm it up with a little more olive oil and herbs."

He puts a big plate on the counter and dumps tortilla chips on it. He mixes sour cream, lime juice, and lime zest in a small bowl, and he cuts open the avocado, slicing it into strips. Then he turns to the cast-iron skillet on the stove.

"I've never heard of prime rib on nachos," I say as I observe him work.

He laughs. "If we can drink fancy bourbon in a cocktail, we can have prime rib on nachos."

I can't help but smile at that.

When he drops the meat into the cast iron, it sizzles and the herbs waft toward me in the most delicious aroma. He only has it in the pan for a minute or two, just enough to warm it, and then he starts putting the reheated prime rib onto the tortilla chips, followed by the peppers and shredded cheese.

He opens a drawer in front of him and pulls out a kitchen torch, handing it to me silently. I take it slowly, and he tells me how to turn it on.

"Melt the cheese." He gestures to the platter of nachos, so I do.

I turn on the torch like he told me, point the flame at the cheese, and melt it until it's bubbly and gooey. I hand him back the torch, and he finishes off the nachos by decorating the top with slices of avocado and little dollops of the sour cream mixture.

It looks amazing.

Chris grabs a chip, making sure it has a little of everything on it, and then he holds it out to me.

"You first," he says, eyes intent on my face.

"Me first what?"

"Try it."

I hesitate, but then I figure fuck it. I'm actually really hungry, and these nachos smell and look phenomenal. When I reach for the chip, though, he pulls his hand back slightly. I flick my eyes to his and he arches a brow.

"Open." His voice is a little rougher than before, and I obey immediately.

I don't break eye contact until I close my lips around the chip, bite down, and the flavors hit my tongue.

"Oh my god," I mumble, my eyes falling shut briefly. I make eye contact with him and use my hand to cover my mouth as I chew. "This is amazing. This is, like, restaurant-level good."

His smile is full of pride as he pops the other half of my chip in his mouth and then nods.

"Yep. Pretty fucking good," he says, and I laugh.

"Another facet?" I ask around another mouthful, and he winks at me in response.

I follow him into the living room where he puts the platter of nachos and the bottle of bourbon on the coffee table. He takes a seat on the couch on one side of the table, and I sit on the love seat on the opposite side, so we're facing each other.

"How many tattoos do you have now?" I ask randomly, and he glances at the ceiling as he thinks it through. I can practically see him counting in his head.

"I don't know. A lot. They've all started to blend together at this point. Do you have any?"

I smile and nod.

"I have two." The surprise on his face makes me laugh out loud. "I have one on my shoulder that I got the day I turned eighteen, and I have this one."

I pull up the silky sleeve of my pajama top to reveal the small tattoo on the inside of my upper arm. He leans forward to get a better look, and when he sees it, an amused chuckle escapes him. I know what he's thinking. Why on earth would Samantha Harper have a linework tattoo of two tiny gnomes holding hands? I tell him the answer before he can ask the question.

"Lennon has the same one. We got them when she lived in Paris." I point to the gnome holding a daisy. "This one is Lennon. Daisy. Because she says I need to be reminded that it's okay to be soft."

He brings his eyes from the tattoo to my face.

"And the other one?" he asks playfully.

I point to the other gnome. The one holding a dagger.

"This is me, obviously. Dagger." I smirk. "Because Lennon needs to be reminded that it's okay to cut a bitch from time to time."

He breaks out into laughter, scrubbing a hand down his face and wiping at his eyes, and his laughter triggers my own. I'm giggling like crazy within seconds as I try to tell him the story of Lennon and me stumbling into the Parisian tattoo parlor on a random Wednesday afternoon. We'd had too much wine and not enough food, but the tattoo artist didn't turn us away. I think he found us amusing, and I know for a fact he overcharged us, but it's fine. I put it on my father's credit card.

"Okay, your turn," I say when I'm finished, my cheeks still aching from smiling so big. "Tell me about one of yours."

He cocks his head to the side as his eyes bounce between mine.

"A funny story or a sentimental one?"

"Sentimental."

He pauses as he thinks, and then he stands and leaves the room. He comes back within seconds and hands me what looks like a brass antique pocket watch on a chain. It's heavy and covered in intricately carved designs of vines and leaves. I turn it over in my hand gently as I inspect it.

"Open it," he says, so I do.

"A compass," I muse, turning it back and forth to watch the needle move and noting the numbers engraved on the inside of the brass cover.

"This is a two-fer," Chris says, and when I glance up, I see him pulling off his shirt.

I school my face into boredom, even though his tattooed, muscled torso is anything but boring. I hadn't realized he had so many. His arms and part of his torso are covered in ink, color and grayscale all throughout. I see flowers, a map, a sunrise, three dates, and some script before I tear my eyes away and lock them on his face.

"Real smooth," I say flatly, suggesting he picked this tattoo just to show off his sculpted chest, and his mouth tips up at the corner.

"Right here is the compass." He points to the inside of his left bicep.

It's an absolutely perfect rendition, right down to the numbers on the inside cover, but the needle is pointing east instead of north.

"This compass was my grandfather's. I used to carry it everywhere with me, but I cracked the glass once when I was working and scared the shit out of myself. Got it repaired, but now it stays safe in my bedroom."

"So you got the tattoo so it's still with you," I say, and he nods. "And the numbers? They're coordinates, right? Latitude and longitude?"

He turns slightly and points to a piece on his rib cage. A small log cabin sitting amongst pine trees with a lake in the distance.

"This was my grandfather's cabin. The coordinates lead to here."

It's beautiful. So serene and inviting. The longer I look at it, the more I find myself wanting to reach out and run my fingers over it. To close my eyes and imagine myself there. Away from everything and everyone.

"And the needle," I ask. "Why is it pointing east?"

"That's where my home is. My family. It's my true north."

His statement makes my eyes prickle with tears, and I have to look away.

*Home. Family.*

Fuck, what would it feel like to have that? To have those things and cherish them. To *be* cherished by them. The reality that I'll never know breaks my heart. It makes me angry that my heart could break so easily. I shouldn't care so much, but I do.

Do I even have a true north? What would it be? My hatred for my father? My soul-deep desire to ruin him? It wouldn't be a home or a family, that's for certain. Not for me.

Maybe it would be Lennon. Maybe. But she has Macon, and even she doesn't know it all recently. I'm even keeping secrets from her now.

I squeeze my eyes shut and breathe through my nose. My heart aches with loneliness and shame. My stomach swirls with the familiar sense of self-loathing. It's been getting stronger. It's been getting harder and harder to ignore.

I need to feel something else. I need a distraction.

"Favorite sexual position," I say quickly, and I can tell by the way Chris freezes in my periphery that I've shocked him.

I drag my eyes to his face and give him a taunting grin.

"Cat got your tongue, *Christopher*?"

## TEN

## *Chris*

I sit back on the couch across from Sam and take her in.

It's like a switch flipped. One breath, she seemed emotional, vulnerable, on the verge of tears. And the next? She's wearing that cold, unfeeling mask again. The one that says she'd chew me up and spit me out, and I'd love every second of it.

I can't help but feel like she's playing a game with me. She's the cat and I'm the mouse. But do I want to play along? Do I want to let her catch me?

When she raises a brow in challenge, I know my answer to both is *hell yes*.

"Missionary," I say after a minute, and she snorts out a mocking laugh. I knew she would. I shake my head slowly. "I guarantee it's not what you're thinking."

She leans back on the couch and crosses her legs, every bit that cold, regal royal who is deigning to interact with a peasant. She takes a dainty sip of her drink, and I want to shake her composure. I want that mask to slip again.

"Enlighten me." Her lips curve into a challenging smirk.

She's not wearing her signature blood-red lipstick, but she doesn't need it. She's just as cruel and sexy without it. I drag my eyes down her body for the first time since she climbed out of my shower. I've behaved. I've been a gentleman. It seems she's grown bored with that. I let my gaze linger on her exposed collarbone long enough to see her breath hitch, and then I look back at her plump pink lips.

"I like to be in control. If I'm on top, I can move you where I want you. Angle you how I want you. See and touch as much of you as I want. If I want your hands pinned above your head, I can do that. If I want your ankles on my shoulders, I can do that. I can suck on your nipples. I can play with your clit. I control the pace. I control the contact. Missionary means you're at my mercy."

Her next inhale and exhale are shaky, but she forces out a breathy laugh.

"*Me*?" she says incredulously, and I shake my head slowly.

"No. Not you. You wouldn't like it."

Her jaw drops and she blinks, and I have to bite back a laugh. She's stuck between shocked and offended, but she doesn't want me to know that.

I lean forward and prop my elbows on my knees. I lock my eyes with hers, and then I lower my voice like we're trading secrets. I speak low and slow, and I watch her pupils dilate with every word.

"See, princess, you wouldn't like it how I like it because I like my missionary *filthy*. I like fucking *sloppy* sex. Sweaty and sticky and gasping for breath. Hoarse voice and teary eyes. Bite me. Scratch up my back. Leave me bleeding. I like to fuck so hard that your muscles ache for days when I'm done with you. That you've been stretched in so many directions that your limbs feel like jelly afterward. I like my missionary fucking messy. And you? Well, I don't think you like messy very much."

Her chest rises and falls rapidly under her silk pajama top. Her cheeks and neck are sporting a deep pink flush. And just to be an asshole, I drag my eyes to her chest where her pebbled nipples are visible through the fabric.

"Or maybe I'm wrong." I sit back against the couch and spread my arms over the back of it.

Her eyes scan my naked chest. She chews the inside of her cheek and lets her eyes drop lower, resting first on my abs before dropping even lower and landing on the outline of my erection in my joggers.

"Do you ever think about it?" she asks finally. She uncrosses her legs and brings her eyes back to mine. "Do you ever wonder what it would have been like if we hadn't stopped?"

"Yes."

My answer is immediate and honest. Even when I was with Sable, I would sometimes find my mind drifting to that night with Sam in my truck. How fast things got hot between us. How she put a stop to them even faster.

And then she just fucking disappeared.

No call. No text. Not a single sighting for weeks after.

"Me too." She rises and steps around the coffee table until she's standing in front of me.

I widen my legs so she can step between them, but I don't reach for her. I made that mistake once before, and I won't do it again. I keep my arms planted on the back of the couch and watch with bated breath as she straddles my thighs and lowers her ass to my lap.

I hiss the moment she makes contact with my hard cock.

"I hate that hat," she says, eyes stuck on my camo ballcap.

"I know." I grin, then take it off my head and put it backward onto hers.

She rolls her eyes, but then she tentatively moves her hips, dragging her pussy over my cock. I groan and move my hands to her waist, halting her.

"What are you doing, princess?"

My voice is low, nearly a growl, and there's no mistaking the warning there. She smiles sweetly and moves her hips again.

"Finishing what we started," she says, and my restraint snaps.

My hand wraps around her neck and I pull her mouth to mine, finally tasting those plump lips again. They're so much softer this time without the lipstick, but they move just as commandingly as before.

She kisses me hungrily, whimpering as her body moves over mine, dry fucking my cock through our clothes. Her hands roam up and down my torso, squeezing my biceps and shoulders until I grab her arms and move them behind her back. I gather both of her wrists in one of my hands, locking them there, so her shoulders are pressed together, and her breasts are thrust toward my face. She struggles a little, but when I start to unbutton her top with my free hand, she goes pliant.

I press kisses to her jaw, neck, and chest while I undo her buttons, making sure my lips touch each inch of flesh as it becomes exposed. When her shirt falls open, I sit back and take her in. Arms pinned back, chest heaving, bare and begging to be worshiped, and my camo ballcap sitting backward on top of her head.

"Fuck, you're gorgeous."

I flick my tongue over one dusty pink nipple, and she moans. I suck it into my mouth and swirl my tongue around it before biting down lightly. She gasps and grinds her pussy over my cock, so I move to her other nipple and give it the same treatment. I can feel her growing wetter, her heat seeping through the thin silk fabric of her bottoms onto my pants, so I thrust up against her.

"Oh fuck." She gasps, and I chuckle.

Keeping her wrists captive in one hand, I take the other hand that's been gripping Sam's waist and move so it's splayed on her pelvis. I dip into her bottoms so I can rub on her clit with my thumb.

"Yes," she says, eyes stuck on my hand. "Like that."

She takes my mouth again in another possessive kiss, and I welcome it. She fucks my mouth with her tongue and dry fucks my cock with her hungry little pussy while I rub on her clit. She tugs against my grip on her wrists, but I tug back, making her arch her back more. She grinds down on my dick harder, her pelvis chasing the friction of my thumb on her clit.

"You're a greedy little thing, aren't you, princess?"

She whimpers and bites her lip, her eyes pleading with me so sweetly that I give in and give her what she wants. I rub her clit faster and pepper open-mouthed kisses to her neck and chest.

"I'm so close." She pushes harder onto my thumb. "I'm so close."

I sit back and watch her face as I tend to her. As she moves her body with her arms locked behind her. When she tilts her head to the ceiling and opens her mouth on a silent cry, it's got to be one of the sexiest things I've ever seen.

I give her a moment to catch her breath, and then I flip her quickly onto my couch so she's lying on her back and I'm kneeling above her.

"All that with just my thumb." I grin, giving my hard cock a squeeze through my joggers.

Sam huffs, but instead of giving me a snarky retort, she reaches for the band on my joggers. I grab her hand, halting her movements, and shake my head disapprovingly.

"Tsk-tsk. It's not polite to be so impatient."

She glowers at me, and fuck is it sexy.

"You're not in charge here," she snarls, her tone surprisingly authoritative considering she's lying half-naked and horny underneath me.

I don't argue with her. Instead, I hook my fingers into the waistband of her bottoms.

"Hips up, princess."

She obeys immediately. I slip her silky pajama shorts off her body and discard them on the floor, but I leave her white, lacy thong on. It's thin. I can see her bare pussy lips through the damp fabric, and I want to know how they taste through it, too.

I'm going to fuck her senseless in this white, lacy thong, and then I'm going to rip it off her and keep it as a fucking trophy.

"Jesus Christ." I marvel at her. I reach for the bottle of bourbon and uncap it. "You're a sight, you know that? Your body is fucking perfect."

She smiles, but it's sinister. It's all teeth. The warmth, the *humanity*, I'd seen in her just moments earlier is gone.

"Well, of course," Sam says, her tone biting. "I'm a

representative of the Harper family. *Every* aspect of my appearance matters."

I hold her scathing eye contact and debate my next move. I want to ask about that comment. I want to know more—I want to know *everything*—but her nostrils flare, and she raises an eyebrow.

"Are we fucking, or is it time for me to go?"

Without taking my eyes off hers, I lift the bottle of bourbon to my lips and pour some of it into my mouth. I set the bottle back on the table, brace one hand on the back of the couch, and lean over Sam's naked body. I allow myself one more visual perusal of her goose-bump-covered flesh and heaving chest, then I slowly spit the bourbon onto her.

She gasps as the liquid slides down her collarbone, breasts, and ribs. I move down her body, spitting more onto her stomach, into her belly button, onto her pelvis, and finally over her lace-covered pussy. The bright white fabric turns a rusty brown when the bourbon hits it, and she sucks in her stomach and moans. Her back arches, her breasts the perfect invitation, and I accept.

I lick and suck at her flesh, lapping up the taste of bourbon from her skin. Sucking on her nipples, biting them, and dragging my tongue over her sides and stomach. Her fingers thread into my hair as I run my tongue over her skin. I bite at her hips, I nip at her, and she whimpers sweetly the whole time.

When I close my mouth over her pussy, massaging her clit through the lace with my tongue, she groans.

"Oh fuck," she cries, tilting her pelvis so her pussy presses harder against my mouth. "Oh, fuck, yes."

I settle myself onto my knees on the floor and grab the bottle of bourbon once more. I run my knuckle over the thong, dragging from bottom to top and pressing lightly on her clit.

"I want you to go down on me," she pants.

I smirk.

"I don't do that."

Her face falls, disappointment and rage warring in her eyes. I drag my knuckles down over her thong again, then circle her clit as I speak.

"Going down is for the upper class. It's too formal. Too proper." I pour a little more bourbon between her legs, and she jerks, but I clamp my hand onto her thigh. "I eat pussy, princess, and I'm going to fucking devour yours."

I waste no time. I descend upon her, unleashing the fervor I've been restraining. I move her thong to the side and swipe my tongue up and down her pussy, dipping into her once before moving to her swollen clit and flicking. She bucks against me, and I chuckle.

"Greedy fucking girl," I say against her. "You taste so fucking good."

I slip a finger into her as I suck on her clit, and she moans. I slip in a second finger and her grip tightens in my hair as she tries to fuck my fingers. I let her. I let her thrust on me, dragging her bourbon-soaked pussy lips up and down my tongue as I pump my fingers into her.

I will never be able to drink bourbon again without thinking of this. Without tasting her pussy and hearing her sexy whimpers and moans.

She starts to flutter around my fingers at the same time her panting breaths become more ragged.

"Are you going to give me another orgasm, baby?"

"Yes. Yes."

Fuck yes, she is. I curve my fingers inside her and suck her clit at the same time. I stroke her inner walls as I thrust into her, and when she starts to chant *oh god, oh god*, I flick my tongue over her clit as fast as I can.

"I'm coming. I'm coming," she says, voice strangled as her body bows and her thighs clamp around my shoulders. "Oh, my *fuck*."

The moment her orgasm breaks free, I feel her arousal on my hand, pooling in my palm and dripping down my wrist. I don't stop stroking and thrusting, don't stop tonguing her clit until her body starts to jerk, and she pushes on my head, too sensitive for more.

I sit back on my heels and grin at her gasping, spent form.

"I didn't know you were a squirter, princess."

She shoots up on her elbows, and the look of horror on her face is enough to make me bark out a laugh.

"I did not! I do not!" she protests, sitting straight up and staring at my couch cushion, which is now dark and damp with bourbon and her.

I didn't realize until now that I never actually took her pajama top off, so it's just drenched in bourbon and sweat, hanging open and loose around her body.

"I am not a *squirter*," she hisses. "Porn stars are squirters."

I smirk.

"I mean, I've got a camera if you want to make that dream a reality. Because, baby, you're *definitely* a squirter, and it's fucking sexy."

Her lips twitch and her nose scrunches up as she fights her smile. I can tell she's embarrassed, but she's trying hard not to show it. Embarrassment is weak, and Samantha Harper would never show weakness.

She steels her spine and gets control of her expression, and it's like a curtain dropping. Her eyes turn seductive, her smile more predatory as she leans forward and slips her delicate fingers into the band of my joggers. My cock is so hard that it hurts, and it's pressing as far out as the fabric of my pants will allow.

"Well," Sam says, tugging me closer until I'm directly in front of her. She presses a kiss to my abdomen. "I think it's my turn, don't you?"

I breathe slowly through my nose and work to keep my excitement off my face. I run my knuckles over her cheek, then thread my fingers through her hair, gripping it at the back of her skull.

"If that's what the princess wants," I say smoothly, giving her hair a little tug.

She keeps her face tilted up and her eyes on me as she drags my joggers down my thighs until they pool at my feet. She licks her lips and smiles softly, then lowers her gaze to my exposed erection.

And then she freezes.

I laugh loudly, and she whips her eyes back up to mine, face full of shock. She giggles once, then again before she punches my thigh.

"You have your fucking *dick* pierced?"

## ELEVEN

*Sam*

"It's called a frenum," Chris says pointedly, and I blink up at him a few more times before bringing my attention back to his cock piercing.

Excuse me. His *frenum*.

I tilt my head to the side as I survey it from every angle.

"Why?" I ask finally, and his dick bobs as he shrugs.

"I played poker with a bunch of on-leave Marines and lost."

I chuckle. Makes sense. Sounds like something that buddies of Macon would do.

"Did it hurt?"

"Not as bad as I thought it would, actually."

"Huh." I glance up at him through my lashes. "Can I touch it?"

He laughs.

"By all means."

Gently, I run my fingers over the silver metal bar, and his abdominals flex. I press a little harder, feeling where the metal goes through the shaft of his cock, and he hisses. I snatch my hand back.

"Did I hurt you?" I ask quickly, and he grabs my hand while shaking his head.

"It doesn't hurt." He puts my hand around his dick and applies pressure, so I'm squeezing him. "Like that. Pulse it. It feels good."

I look up into his face as I do it, growing bolder with each flash of heat in his eyes. I run my hand up and down him, then rub my thumb on the underside of his head, making him groan.

Then I dip low and take him into my mouth.

When I run my tongue along the ridge of his head, his hand clamps into the hair at the back of my skull. When I do it again, he tugs harder, and I whimper around him.

"Don't do that, baby," he warns.

So I do it again, and he groans.

I drag my tongue down his shaft, paying special attention to his piercing. He murmurs encouragements. Whispers compliments that feel genuine despite the fact that I have his cock in my mouth.

I reach up and palm him, massaging his sack as I lick and suck his dick. I haven't taken him down my throat. Admittedly, I'm a little scared to with the piercing, but I want to make this good for him. I get high on the way he moans and tightens his grip on my hair. I get high on all of it.

When he tries to pull me off him, I resist.

"You keep working me like that, and I'll come in your mouth, princess."

I hum around his head, using one hand to pulse the base of his shaft and the other to massage beneath. I want him to come. I want to taste him. I want to know I did it to him.

"If you don't want me to come down your throat, you need to stop," he forces out, his voice almost pained.

In response, I grow more enthusiastic, and when I hum around him again, he mumbles a warning just before he shoots his release into me with a groan.

I take it all and swallow it, and I fucking preen under his appreciative gaze.

"Fuck me." He drops to his knees and takes my mouth. "Fuck, you're so sexy. Such a sexy, filthy fucking princess."

I smile, and then I stifle a yawn, suddenly exhausted. Chris presses a kiss to my forehead, then tugs me to standing and leads me by the hand to his bedroom. I clean myself off in the bathroom, we take turns brushing our teeth, then I crawl into his bed, curl up like a sated kitten, and fall fast asleep.

---

When I wake, the bed is empty and the clock on Chris's nightstand says 9:30 a.m.

I never sleep this late, but we were up until three, so I guess I needed the rest. I'm not sure when Chris left, but I remember him saying he needed to go to The Outpost first thing. I stretch in his soft bedsheets and smile to myself that he let me sleep instead of kicking me out.

When I sit up and reach for my phone, I find a torn piece of notebook paper on top of it. There's ink-scribbled script on it, and as I read it, my smile grows.

*Hellfire or Holy Water*

I dig through his drawers and find a pair of joggers and a T-shirt, then steal a pair of slides from the closet since my pajama top is bourbon-soaked and my slippers are ruined. I smile the entire time I get dressed, and right before I leave, I put on a fresh coat of lipstick and press a red kiss to the word *hellfire*. I leave the note on his pillowcase and skip out the front door to make my walk of shame across town back to my cave.

The whole way, I replay the night over and over. Every memory making me flush with heat and smile to myself. In all of the nights I spent wondering what it would have been like, I never considered this.

I get to my apartment and check my email. Three from Ashton, all with degrading tasks. I close out of all of them without responding.

It's the weekend, so fuck him.

I read the latest news articles that mention my father, all of which work to sour my mood. Then I take out my second cell and power it on for my morning check-in, expecting to see nothing, like usual. Instead, there's a meeting request for later today.

I groan and tip my head back.

I had plans to catch up on work today. I have two separate deadlines, and I'm dangerously close to falling behind. Instead, now, I have to drive three hours south, pretend to be interested in a rare handbag from a small boutique, then sit for an hour in a fucking coffee shop until my guest decides to show up and pretend she doesn't know me.

I don't want to. I don't want to do any of it, but I remind myself how good it's going to feel when I can finally light a match and drop it on all this gasoline I've spilled.

I've got a few hours before I have to head out, so I text Lennon and ask if she wants to move our brunch date up to now and meet in the next town over since half of Franklin is still out of power.

Thirty-five minutes later, I'm sitting at an outdoor table with my best friend, and for an hour or so, I can pretend that this is my life. This is *all* of my life, the entirety of it, and nothing else exists.

"Can I get a glass of orange juice in a flute with a dash of seltzer, please? And if you can drop a few raspberries in there, that would be great," Lennon says to the server.

"Of course." He writes it on his pad before looking at me. "And for you?"

"I'll have the same, please. And a coffee."

The server scribbles my drink and disappears, and Lennon turns to me.

"You can have a real mimosa, Sam. It doesn't bother me at all."

She reaches for her water glass at the same time I do, and I shrug.

"I don't mind. I got a little tipsy last night, so I should take it easy anyway." I go to take a sip of my water, then stop. "Did you know Casper has his dick pierced?"

Lennon starts coughing, choking on her sip of water and laughing at the same time with a look of shock on her face.

"Shit, sorry." I lean over to rub circles on her back. "Maybe I should have given some warning."

She waves me off and shakes her head.

"*How* do you know?" she forces out, and I bite back a grin and speak casually.

"I saw it, of course. I mean, it was kind of hard to miss at eye level."

"*WHAT?*" Lennon shrieks, then slaps a hand over her mouth and looks around apologetically at the other tables before zeroing back in on me. She lowers her voice to a conspiratorial whisper and leans across the table. "I'm sorry, but what *exactly* are you implying? *Why* would his dick be exposed at your eye level?"

I laugh.

"Lennon, I know you know. Or do we have to have *the talk* again? Have things with Macon gone stagnate, and you've forgotten what sex is?"

Her jaw drops.

"You shut up." When my smile grows, so does hers, and her eyes grow as wide as the mouth of her water glass. "You shut up right now, Sam. You had sex with him?"

I purse my lips.

"Well, technically, no, since it was only oral. But it was oral *sex*, so I guess also technically, yes."

"Oral." She gasps. "But you don't do oral. You're strictly in and out. Literally."

I smirk and shrug.

"I made an exception."

A laugh bubbles out of Lennon, and then one follows from me, until we both start to laugh until the server brings our mock mimosas and my coffee, and we have to calm down enough to place our food orders.

"Okay, I want to know everything," Lennon says as soon as the server leaves. "Every dirty little detail." When my lips curve into a smile, she gasps. "Oh my god, it was really good, wasn't it?"

I take a cooling sip of my mock mimosa and a few calming breaths, but when I speak, I still feel a blush creep up my neck. It's unsettling, and I am never unsettled.

"It was *surprising*," I say slowly, filtering through my memory to find the right words to explain it. "Different."

"Okay..."

Lennon raises her brows in question, and I open and close my mouth twice more before finally continuing.

"I like sex, right? I have a decent amount of it. But it's always with a certain kind of guy..."

"The kind of guy you hate," Lennon says, and I shrug in confirmation.

"It's enjoyable, don't get me wrong. But it's..."

"Clinical? Detached? Emotionless?" she supplies, and I snort a laugh.

"Yes. And formulaic. Predictable. I don't know. Sterile, I guess."

Lennon laughs.

"And Casper was dirty?" she asks, and I nod.

"Fucking filthy," I whisper.

I cover my face with my hand because I can feel myself blushing again.

"Lennon, he said things, and he did this thing with his fingers, and the sounds—"

"The sounds?!"

"The sounds were all squishy and wet and *debauched*, but insanely sexy. Oh, and there was bourbon involved. Expensive bourbon."

"You *drank* bourbon...?" she asks, voice giddy.

"Yes... And he also kind of drank it off of me..."

I gesture to my lap and Lennon lets out another laugh.

"Chris Casper." She shakes her head in disbelief. "A filthy fuck with a pierced cock. I never would have guessed it."

Now it's my turn to laugh, and I ball up my napkin and toss it at her grinning face.

"Anyway...then I fell asleep and didn't wake back up until I texted you." I avert my eyes because I know the weight of my statement.

The way Lennon grows quiet tells me she knows, too.

I haven't been sleeping well since the campaign kicked off. I never sleep well, but it's been worse than usual. Working with my father is more stressful this time than it's ever been, and being relegated to Ashton Cartwright's subservient assistant has only added to my shitty disposition.

At least once a week, I have to call Lennon.

At least once a week, she has to read to me like I'm a child just to get my mind to calm down. We've gone through all of Jane Austen's catalog and are now working our way through the Brontë sisters.

I hate feeling like this, hate depending on someone else, but Lennon and I are well-versed in being each other's lifeline when shit gets difficult. And shit has gotten *really* difficult for me.

Lennon reaches over the table and takes my hand in hers.

"You know you can talk to me, right? You can tell me what's going on. It might help if you just let it all out."

Tears prickle my eyes, and I clamp them shut. I shake my head.

"I can't, Lennon," I whisper. "God, I fucking want to, but I can't."

I drop my forehead into my palms and breathe through my nose, willing the tears to retreat. I detest crying. It hurts. I don't need anything else to hurt.

"Sam... when you come back from D.C. these days..." Lennon hesitates and squeezes my hand. "When you come back, you're angrier. You're more agitated. You laugh less. You have these shadows under your eyes that just won't clear. It's like that place is sucking your soul from your body."

I laugh sardonically because she couldn't be more right.

It is. It *is* sucking my soul from my body. It's taking every shred of decency I've managed to cultivate in my twenty-six years of life, and it's poisoning all of it. I keep telling myself to stick to it. To stay focused. To stay the course. But what if I fucking ruin myself in the process? What if my lies catch up to me, and I become just as black as the rest of them?

Or worse. What if it all blows up in my face?

If Lennon knew the extent of it, she'd ask if it was worth it, and the sickest part of it all is that I truly believe it is.

Flaying strips from my soul is a small price to pay if it all works out.

*If.*

I clear my throat and force a smile, sitting up straight. I let go of Lennon's hand so I can reach into my handbag. I pull out a compact mirror and my lipstick, and she watches silently as I fix my eyeliner and apply a fresh coat of red.

"The offer stands," Lennon says firmly, a hint of defeat in her voice. "It doesn't matter what it is. You can tell me, and I will be here. I will always be here."

I nod.

I know, and that's exactly why I don't tell her. If I tell her everything, that puts her at risk. If I tell her everything and fail...

I don't want to think about the consequences and how they could affect her. I've got enough pressure on me right now. I cannot have Lennon on my conscience, too.

"How's Evie doing?" I ask, changing the subject, and like the fucking saint that she is, Lennon plays along.

## TWELVE

*Chris*

The note with Sam's perfect lip print sits in my wallet, burning a hole through my jeans as I try to work.

I knew she would be gone when I got back. It didn't surprise me.

What does surprise me is the sting that comes after more than a week without a word from her. It brings me back to that night in my truck. The way she disappeared after. It brings me back to Sable's words. It doesn't matter how glad I am that my ex didn't say yes when I proposed, her reasoning still fucks with my head.

*Not good enough. Too blue collar. Too small town.*

Knowing Samantha Harper, she's probably thinking the same thing, and I shouldn't fucking care so much, but I do.

I replay my night with her over and over, pulling me away from work. From conversations. From everything. What was supposed to be a single night to finish what we started last year has instead turned into some distraction under my skin.

That night with Sam in my truck, I thought I glimpsed something in her. Something uninhibited and wild. Some fire that she keeps tamed for everyone else. Different than the rebellious girl I knew in high school and completely opposite from the conceited royal I barely know these days. I *felt* it, but she doused it quickly, and then she ghosted me.

After a while, I just assumed it didn't exist. I'd imagined it thanks to cheap wine and lust.

But in my house the other weekend?

I know that wasn't my imagination. I watched the ice thaw around the princess. I saw someone else entirely come out from behind her perfect mask. It's as unsettling as it is exciting.

She's usually untouchable, unfeeling, but for one night, she was malleable and eager, responsive and soft under my lips and palms. The way she sounded when she came. The rapture on her face. The perfect princess was made mortal, and it was addictive to watch. I want more of it. I want to see if I can do it again.

Does she have everyone fooled? Which Sam is the real Sam?

Perfectly polished and cold as ice, or wild, free, and hot as hellfire?

It's hard to believe both women can reside in the same body, and I can't help but obsesses over it. I've always loved puzzles. I'm a fixer by nature, a solver, and she's the most fascinating equation I've encountered.

I finish up my shift at the garage, drive home and shower, then head to the bar. The whole time, I think about Sam, and then I scold myself for thinking about Sam. But I continue to think about her.

Five minutes after I pull the chain on the open sign, Macon comes strolling through the front door and slides onto one of the many empty barstools. I fix him a Dr. Pepper with lime and set it on the bar top in front of him.

"Where's Len?" I ask, glancing at the door before bringing my eyes back to my best friend.

"She's with Harper. They'll be here soon." He takes a sip of his soda and then glances at me with a smirk. "I thought you were kitchen tonight? Figured you'd cook me dinner."

I halt my movements briefly, just enough to let it sink in what he's said—Sam is on her way—and then I busy myself by wiping down my already clean bar top.

"I am kitchen. I'm just waiting for Paul to get here. He's got to drop his kid off at his mom's on Thursdays."

Macon nods, then slides a bar menu in front of himself and looks it over. I watch him scan the items, knowing full well he already knows everything that's on it. He helped me come up with it after I bought into the bar before Alan left. Lennon and Sam must have kicked him out of the apartment for girl talk, and it makes my lips curl up into a reluctant smile.

"Hey, you given any more thought to quitting the garage now?" he asks, and I shrug.

"Yeah," I say honestly. "But I don't think I will just yet. I don't know. I like the people. Keeps me busy."

Macon nods. He knows the only reason I started working at the garage a few years ago was to help out Tiffany and Michael, but they no longer need my help financially, and I'm still working two jobs.

I'm not complaining, though. I really enjoy my job at Franklin Auto Body, but I'm down to part-time now. While owning half the bar wasn't originally my plan, when Alan offered to sell me half at a fucking steal, I jumped at it. It's the closest I'll probably ever get to running my own restaurant. Moving into Alan's old house made it possible for me to move out of The Outhouse Penthouse and rent it out, too, so it's all worked out for the best so far. I don't see a reason to change anything at the moment, despite Sable's comments about me being *stunted and unwilling to improve my status*. I like my life. I like my jobs. I like my home. I don't need anything else.

Macon sets the menu down. Then takes another drink from his soda. Then pulls his hat off so he can push his hands through his hair and put the hat back on. He's fidgeting. I raise a brow.

"What's goin' on? You and Lennon get into a fight or something?"

He chuckles and flares his eyes.

"Not exactly." He drums his fingers on the bar top.

Flicks his gaze to me and then away again. I watch as he fights a smile as he tries to harness all of his nervous energy.

"Macon, what the fuck?" I laugh. "What's going on?"

He drags a hand down his face with a sigh, then finally looks at me. His giant smile has me smiling, and I don't even know what we're smiling about yet.

"Lennon's pregnant," he says, and my jaw drops. "Doc confirmed it this morning. Ten weeks."

I'm immediately filled with happiness for them. I've never met two people more perfect for each other, so the idea of Macon and Lennon starting their own little family makes me ecstatic.

"No shit? Congrats, man. How long have you known?"

He grins.

"'Bout four hours. Neither of us had any idea. She just went in because she's been more tired than usual, and she thought she was vitamin deficient or something. Turns out she is, but only because she's growin' a kid."

I bark out a laugh, my smile so big that my cheeks hurt, and I reach over and pat him on the shoulder.

"Congratulations, Macon. I'm really happy for you. You're going to be a great dad."

"Thank you." His voice cracks a little. "I wasn't expecting it, but I'm fucking thrilled. So Lennon called Sam and she showed up, and then I came here to tell you. We haven't told our parents yet. I think we might wait until she's officially out of the first trimester, but we wanted you and Sam to know."

My smile softens.

"Thank you. I'm honored that I'm one of the first to know."

"Well, also, there is something else," Macon says, smirk still affixed to his face. "I don't know if there's, like, a protocol for this, and I know we're not religious or anything, but Lennon and I want to know if you will be the baby's godfather."

Well, shit. Now I want to cry. I can't even make a *The Godfather* joke because I'm so fucking touched. I just nod and smile.

"Yeah, man," I finally say. "I'd be honored."

The door opens, and we both turn to find Lennon and Sam walking in. I round the bar and scoop Lennon into my arms, giving her a twirl while she giggles.

"Congratulations," I say before finally setting her on her feet and kissing her head. "I'm so happy for you, Len."

She's beaming at me with shimmering emotional eyes.

"Thank you. Did Macon ask you yet?" she asks, and I nod.

"It's my honor, Lennon. Truly. I am honored."

She throws her arms around my neck with another soft laugh, and I let my eyes flick to Sam. She's quiet, but her smile for her friend is genuine. Nothing but total happiness and love. Lennon releases me, and Macon snags her, pulling her onto his lap at the bar.

"So we're going to be godparents," Sam says wryly, and when I look at her, she's smirking. I open my mouth to make a snarky comment, but she holds up her hand. "Do not."

I snap my mouth shut and narrow my eyes playfully, then I look her over. From the way she's dressed—designer dress slacks, button-down, and jacket, shiny high heels, and a sleek bun in her hair—I'd guess she came straight from work to be with Lennon.

It's a nearly four-hour drive from D.C., so she must have left as soon as Lennon called her. I smile. Sam is as prickly as they come, but when she cares about someone, she cares with everything she has. Another sign that she does have a heart underneath all that icy bravado.

"I have every intention of being the favorite," I say to Sam, and she rolls her eyes.

"Dream on."

She brushes past me to go stand by Lennon, so I go around the bar just as Paul comes in from the back. He takes over the bar and I move into the kitchen. Five minutes later, he comes into the kitchen with a green server ticket, chuckling to himself.

"What?" I ask, and he arches a brow before sliding the server ticket to me. I glance down and read it, and then I laugh. "I'll take care of it."

I drop a basket of fries and fix Lennon's and Macon's orders as they requested, but I make Sam a simple bacon cheeseburger, taking a moment to draw a crown in ketchup on the inside of the top bun.

I place the top bun front and center, and then I bring the orders to their table.

The moment I slide the burger in front of Sam, she hits me with a glare.

"This isn't what I ordered," she says, tone bored.

"If you're looking for seared sea scallops on a bed of baby spinach, you're in the wrong town, Harper. But I did put some lettuce on the burger for you."

Macon and Lennon laugh, but I don't take my eyes off Sam. I'm smirking, and from the way her lips are twitching, she's trying hard not to.

"And this?" she asks, waving her hand over the decorated top bun.

I shrug.

"Personalization. A crown for the princess. I thought you rich folk enjoyed custom things."

She sighs, loud and unamused, despite the smile she's fighting.

"Fine. If this is all you're capable of, I suppose it will do..."

My grin widens, and I wink.

"My goal is to satisfy you, princess," I say slowly, dropping my eyes to her lips before scanning her face once more. "I've got a perfect track record so far, so maybe you should trust me on this one."

I walk away without letting her respond, Lennon and Macon's laughter trailing me into the kitchen.

Once again, my smile doesn't fade, and the night goes by in a blur of burgers and fry baskets. When a flash of blond hair catches my eye through the kitchen door, I grab my other line cook and have him take over my grill. We're slowing down, anyway. It's the last few orders before we switch to just appetizers.

I step up to the bar in front of her and she arches a brow before sliding her eyes to my backward camo ballcap.

"Done in the kitchen, then?" she asks, and I grin.

"How was the burger?"

She shrugs.

"Fine."

I place my forearms on the bar and lean into her space. She doesn't back away, and I don't miss the hint of excitement that flashes over her features.

"Did you finish?" I ask, my voice lower than before.

Suggestive, despite the topic. Her lips twitch, but she doesn't answer.

"Were you satisfied?" I try again, tilting my head to the side as I scan her face. "Do I still have a perfect track record? Do I know how to please the princess?"

She huffs, failing to hide her smirk, and rolls her eyes.

"You're an idiot." She folds her arms over her chest. "I hate your hat."

I laugh.

"I know." I nod. "But I can't stop picturing you wearing it. You on my lap. You with y—"

"Shut up," she snips, eyes flashing back and forth to the customers flanking her.

My grin grows. If it weren't for the wild excitement she's trying to hide, the blush coloring her cheeks and neck would probably offend me. She might be embarrassed, but she's thinking about it now, and it's got her heart racing. That's what I focus on.

I drop my voice to a whisper and lean closer so only she can hear me.

"What's wrong, Harper? Don't want people to know you were caught in a *compromising position* with me? Worried how that might make you look?"

"Please." Sam laughs. "What these people think doesn't even register on the list of things I care about. I just don't want my...*personal* business...advertised to every drunken fool in this town."

I drop my eyes to her lips, then to her neck. Her delicate skin flutters over her rapidly thrumming pulse. I curl my fingers into a fist against the desire to reach for her.

"You want to keep it just between us, then? The fact that my mouth has been on you, my tongue has been inside you. You want it to be our little secret?"

Sam's lips curve into a flirty smirk.

"Secret is such a juvenile term. I just prefer to act with discretion." She reaches up and pulls my baseball cap off my head, then brings her hands behind her back before meeting my eyes once more. "Can you be discreet, Christopher?"

Sam takes two steps backward without breaking eye contact, and then she turns and heads toward the exit. I tell Paul I'll be right back, but I don't take my eyes off the spot where Sam disappeared. Then, like I'm being pulled, I follow.

Through the crowded bar, out the door, and into the cool night air of the parking lot.

I expected to see her climbing the stairs to the penthouse, but instead, I find her sauntering toward the back of the lot where my truck is parked. I pick up my pace, then scoop Sam up into my arms. She yelps, and I smack her ass playfully.

"Shush, princess. Can't you be discreet?"

I hear her laugh just as I get to my truck. I open the door closest—driver's side—and sit her onto the seat. I take my camo hat from her hands and put it backward on her head, and then I plant my arms on either side of her body and step between her spread thighs.

She's panting, her eyes sparkling with humor and the thrill of whatever it is we're doing, and her full, crimson lips are curled into an addictive smile. Fuck, she's gorgeous. I can barely tear my eyes away from her. I don't even want to blink. This smile? The one she's giving me right now? It's not something just anyone gets to see. This smile is unbidden. It's not for show. This one is real.

"Now that you got me out here," I say slowly, eyes dropping to her parted red lips, "what are you going to do with me?"

She threads her arms around my neck and leans in close, so her lips brush mine.

"You're a clever boy," she whispers. "I think you can figure it out."

I kiss her.

I wrap my arms around her body and pull her to me, the hot place between her legs lining up perfectly with my already hard cock, and I take her lips in a deep kiss. The moment she opens her mouth, I groan, licking my tongue over hers in a frenzied, tangled massage. I drag my hands up her back and arms, reaching between us to cup one of her breasts as she wraps her legs around my waist.

There's nothing elegant about the way we collide—all greedy hands and lips and tongues. Fueled by need and desire. When she digs her heels into my back, pulling me closer, my hips buck into her and she whimpers. She shoves her hands under my shirt and scrapes her fingernails down my chest before palming my dick through my jeans.

My phone rings in my back pocket, but I ignore it, and she drags her lips from my mouth to my neck.

"Fuck, princess," I grind out as she massages me, pressing kisses to my neck and collarbone. "Your mouth on me, your hands. It's fucking torture."

I feel her smile.

"Why torture?" she asks, pulling back enough to look me in the eyes.

She blinks innocently, and I have to clench my teeth and breathe through my nose to control myself. Her hand never leaves my cock. She never stops massaging me.

"I'm trying to be a gentleman here," I say slowly, "but you're making it difficult."

She cocks her head to the side coyly and pops the button on my jeans, then slides the zipper down. She sinks her teeth into her lower lip.

"Difficult how?" she asks, slipping her delicate fingers into my boxers and wrapping them around my cock, pulsing on my piercing the way I like.

I drop my own hand and cup her pussy, feeling her heat through her dress pants. She gasps, her eyelids fluttering as I apply light pressure.

"Because all I really want to do is flip you around on this bench seat and sink into that hot little cunt from behind. I want to feel you clench around my cock the way you did on my fingers."

She whimpers, then kisses me again, jacking my bare dick while I rub her pussy through her pants. If she keeps this up, I'm going to come in her hand, and I'm not even ashamed of it.

Gracelessly, she scoots farther back into the truck cab, urging me to follow with her hand wrapped around my erection, but when I do, my shoulders hit the steering wheel, and the horn honks. We both freeze, lips still pressed together, and wait a few seconds.

"Whoops," I say, and she laughs against me.

I open my mouth to suggest we go to her apartment, then my name is called from the bar.

"Casper!" Paul shouts. "Casper, yo! You good?"

I sigh, and we break apart.

"Yeah, I'll be right there," I call and turn back to find Sam checking herself in the visor mirror.

I tuck my painfully hard cock back into my pants and do up my zipper, then offer Sam a hand to help her down out of my truck.

"Sorry." I give her a rueful grin.

She shrugs, then rubs her thumb over the corner of my mouth.

"Lipstick." She takes my hat off her head and pushes it into my chest with a smirk. "You've got some on your neck, too. Might want to get that. It's not very *discreet*."

She brushes past me and walks back toward the bar, and for a few breaths, I just watch. Her hips sway with her confident stride, hands swinging loosely by her sides. She looks completely unaffected, and I'm still sporting a raging fucking boner.

"You're torturing me, princess," I call out.

"You'll live," she says, and I can hear the grin in her tone as she disappears back around the front of the bar.

I give myself five more minutes to get my dick under control, and then I head inside through the back entrance. I stop in the bathroom and check myself in the mirror. Sure enough, there's a lipstick smudge on the place where my neck meets my shoulder. It's not a perfect kiss print, but it still makes me think of the paper I have tucked in my wallet, and instead of washing it off, I leave it. My collar mostly hides it, anyway, and no one says anything about it the rest of the night.

A little before midnight, one of my servers pops her head into the kitchen and tells me my friends are leaving, so I wash my hands and head out to say goodbye.

I hug Lennon. I shake Macon's hand. I glance around for Sam, but she's nowhere to be seen.

"She's outside," Lennon says with her eyebrow raised. "Since you're looking."

I RAISE MY EYEBROW RIGHT BACK AT HER. "I WASN'T, BUT YOU MIND your business."

Lennon runs her eyes over my face and shrugs.

"Her car is at our place," Lennon says, and I shrug back.

"Goodbye, Lennon."

Lennon smiles sleepily and then walks out the door. I turn to Macon.

"You and Sam?" he asks, and I eye him warily.

He doesn't sound angry or jealous, not that I think he would be, but he's curious. There's a hint of humor in his voice that I can't read. I don't bother answering.

"Would that be weird?" I ask, and he shakes his head.

"Nah." His voice trails a bit before he lifts a single shoulder in a shrug. "I think she could use someone like you in her life."

I arch a brow.

"That mean I've got your blessing, *Dad*?" I say jokingly, and Macon barks out a laugh.

"Fuck, you better be more concerned about getting *her* blessing over mine. Even if she likes you, it's going to be hell getting her to admit it."

I nod. I've figured as much. Knew it the moment she ghosted me. Sam Harper abhors feelings. Intimacy? Don't even try it. Winning her over would be a challenge.

"I hope she does, though," Macon says suddenly, glancing away from me before speaking again. "You know I was a shit to her in high school. You watched it happen. She needed someone, and I failed her. I fucking failed everyone, myself included. But I feel more guilty that I've taken Lennon from her."

I shake my head. There's a lot I could say to that, but I can only come up with one thing.

"I don't think it's that serious, man. Me and Sam..." I shake my head and glance around the bar. "It's just not that serious."

I'm surprised at the slight disappointment I hear in my voice, but I don't acknowledge it. It is what it is. I might be fascinated by her, a little fucking thrilled at the idea of a challenge—at the idea of cracking her open and seeing what's really inside—but I'm not an idiot.

Me and Samantha Harper? We couldn't be on more opposite planes.

Polar fucking opposite.

Macon moves out of my peripheral, folding his arms across his chest with a shrug.

"Sure," he says. "I'm just sayin' that if it ever is, I don't think it would be a bad thing."

I don't say anything. I just nod and pat him on the shoulder. I tell him congratulations again, then watch him walk out the door to meet the girls. The rest of the night in the kitchen, I find myself on high alert. Waiting. I don't even know what for until I pull the chain on the open sign and head out into the parking lot. Sam's car isn't there. The lights in the penthouse are off. She didn't stay in town, and the realization fills me with a disappointment I don't want to acknowledge.

*Nothing serious*, I repeat to myself.

I tell myself this, but I still leave her lipstick on my neck. I don't scrub at it, I don't wash it away in the shower, and when it inevitably disappears, I pretend like it doesn't bother me.

Because me and Sam? It's nothing serious.

It's nothing at all.

## THIRTEEN

*Sam*

"Your dry cleaning."

I lay the garment bags on Ashton's kitchen counter and smile at him. I wonder if he can tell I want to use the hangers to gouge his eyes out. Weeks of being the perfect little assistant have my patience wearing thin. If I don't get out of this city soon, I might actually commit a violent crime and Ashton will be my victim of choice.

"Thank you, Samantha," he says smoothly, buttoning up the cuffs of his white shirt. "You've been such a help lately."

I act like the praise pleases me. It doesn't.

"I also scanned these into the computer like you asked," I say casually, pulling a stack of papers from my oversized tote and setting them on top of the garment bags. I pretend the papers are nothing special, despite the fact that they contain a long list of names and donation pledges. "I've noticed that Belinda has been...*preoccupied*...lately, so if you'd like me to check over her spreadsheets, I don't mind."

He furrows his brow.

"Belinda?"

"The campaign finance manager?" I blink innocently. "She's been spending a lot of time with Daddy lately. I would hate for it to affect her job performance. Having pristine records is very important for this campaign."

"Denise," he corrects, but I don't acknowledge it. I don't care what her name is. "I'm sure she's fine, Samantha, but thank you for the offer." He smiles tightly. "I don't mind helping her out where she needs it."

"If that's what you want." I sigh. "I'll see you at the office."

I turn to leave, but he reaches out and grabs my hand, stopping me. It takes every ounce of strength not to snatch my hand out of his. When he rubs his thumb over my wrist, I have to hide a shudder.

"Samantha, I suppose your father spoke to you about the dinner tomorrow night?"

"He did," I say curtly.

Though *spoke to me* is an interesting way to put it. More like ordered me via text message at four in the morning. I keep my spine straight and my shoulders back, and I don't cower even though I want to.

"I'd like to pick you up at your condo," he says. His thumb never stops rubbing over my wrist. "It only makes sense since you're going as my date."

I clear my throat and gently pull my hand from his.

"That's unnecessary. I have a driver."

He grabs my hand again, but this time, his touch isn't gentle. I bite the inside of my cheek.

"I insist." His grip tightens to painful before he drops my hand. "I'll be there at seven fifteen tomorrow evening to drive you to the dinner."

He reaches into his suit jacket pocket and pulls out a long black velvet box. He opens it and turns it toward me, displaying a diamond necklace. My stomach clenches.

*Gifts.* The last thing I want from this man are gifts. Especially not expensive ones. They always come with strings attached.

"I have something for you." He takes the necklace from the box and closes the distance between us. "Turn around."

I open my mouth to protest, but then I hear *her* voice in my head.

*Whatever it takes.*

I turn around, and to be even more *agreeable*, I move my hair from the back of my neck.

He hums his approval, then reaches around me and drapes the string of platinum and diamonds on my collarbone, making sure to drag his knuckles over every centimeter of my skin along the way. Goose bumps flare up on my body, but not the good kind. His hands rest on my shoulder blades as he does the clasp, and I'm grateful for the high collar and fabric on the back of my button-down shirt. I can feel the heat of his hands, the pressure, but it's not skin on skin anymore.

When the necklace is clasped, he takes a step back and I turn around.

I smile.

"Thank you."

"It looks beautiful on you." He surveys the necklace, then allows his eyes to drop down my body in a disrespectful and shameful display of his interest.

Like a butcher assessing a piece of meat.

"A woman like you, with a body like yours, should be draped in fine jewels so everyone knows your worth."

Ugh. I want to throw up on his shoes, but I don't let my smile slip. I nod gently in thanks, but I can't bring myself to say the words.

"Wear it tomorrow night," he says.

Ashton brushes past me and leaves me standing in his kitchen, but he stops before disappearing into the hallway. He doesn't even turn to face me. He just speaks his patronizing command into the air.

"Do try to be on time, Samantha. This is a very important event for your father."

Then he's gone, and my jaw aches from how hard I'm clenching my teeth. The muscles in my legs tremble from how tightly I had them locked, fighting the urge to knee him in the groin.

He's just like my father. He's just like his father. He's just like all of them.

These men? They're all the fucking same.

I turn and calmly let myself out of his brownstone, then take the steps to the street and unlock my car. I climb inside, pull out of my parallel parking spot, and drive to the coffee shop. The whole time, the gaudy diamond necklace sits cold and unnatural on my skin, but I don't dare take it off. I'm to pick up a large coffee order and an assortment of muffins and deliver them to the campaign office—a small thank you from Ashton to the team—then I'm to curate his calendar for the week, confirm his lunch reservations, and filter through his emails.

And I need to do it all without delay or complaint.

Gaining Ashton's trust and staying on my father's good side is imperative, and the way it pummels my pride and sense of self-worth doesn't matter. It's not that I think I'm above assistant tasks. It's that assisting evil makes me an accomplice, and it's getting harder to identify the rapidly blurring lines.

*I can do it,* I tell myself. I can.

Whatever it takes.

---

AT SEVEN FIFTEEN, NOT A SECOND EARLIER, I WALK OUT OF THE lobby and climb into the waiting car.

The driver shuts the door behind me, and I smile at Ashton.

"You look beautiful." His eyes drop to my neck and settle on the necklace there.

He reaches up and fingers the necklace, and there's no hiding the flare of pride in his expression. The hunger. I'm a pretty pet, a symbol of status, and he thinks he's going to use me for all I have to offer.

He hands me a glass of champagne. I take the flute and hold it, but I don't drink it. Despite my mother's proclivities, I know that alcohol and Valium don't mix well, and I don't trust Ashton as far as I can spit.

"Thank you." I cross my legs slowly. "You look nice as well."

We sit in silence for the short trip to the restaurant. Ashton scrolls on his phone, occasionally chuckling to himself, and I wouldn't be surprised to find him looking at nudes or watching cheap porn. For a moment, I feel bad for his future wife because I'm probably sitting exactly where she will sit as he does exactly what he will do.

I take a deep breath and find solace in the fact that his future wife will not be me.

The driver pulls up to the flashy restaurant and opens the door. Ashton slides out first and offers me his hand. I take it and follow. As we enter the restaurant, he places his hand on my lower back, just above my ass, and escorts me to our reserved private room in the back.

I hear my father as we approach. His campaign finance manager is sitting to his left, but to my surprise, I find my mother sitting on his right. From the looks of her, she did not turn down the champagne with the Valium. She smiles when she sees me, and I force a smile in return.

I scan the tables and take note of the faces I see. I recognize all of them, and I wish I didn't. All big names in politics and money, some of whom donated to my father's senator campaign in the past, and the others he's courting now. Thankfully, one face is mercifully absent, and I let myself relax a little. That's one mask I don't have to worry about tonight.

"Excuse me," I say to Ashton and turn to leave.

He grabs my wrist tightly, and I stop, glancing at him over my shoulder.

"Where are you going?"

I swallow back a smartass retort and give him a mild smile, instead.

"To the lady's room."

He drops my wrist, and though he doesn't say it, I read the command in his eyes loud and clear.

*Hurry back, pet.*

Inside the restroom, I remove my second cell phone from my handbag and power it on. I set it to silent, then set it to record, and place it back into my handbag in a pocket containing an assortment of tampons and panty liners. I doubt anything of importance will happen tonight—my father is pompous and overconfident, but he's not stupid—but I am always prepared.

I check myself in the mirror.

My lipstick is perfect. My eyeliner is perfect. My blond hair is pulled into a perfect low bun with just a few loose strands artfully framing my face. My dress is the perfect blend of classy and suggestive. Form-fitting enough that not much of my shape is left to the imagination, but the neckline is high, the hem is long, and the sleeves come just past my elbows. The gaudy silver necklace is the only thing that's ostentatiously over the top, but I ignore it.

I smooth my hands over the black fabric, then turn and check my back.

Even the zipper is hidden.

When I exit the bathroom, I run smack into a hard chest and am hit with the strong scent of alcohol. I glance up into the face of my big brother and scowl.

"You smell like you bathed in tequila," I say to him. "I thought you were getting sober."

He grins and reaches into his suit jacket, pulling out a flask. He offers it to me, and I shake my head, swatting it away.

"How's that for a hello." He laughs. "Are *you* sober?"

I roll my eyes.

"I'm a responsible prescription drug user, Chase, something I know you can't grasp."

He chuckles.

"Don't be a bitch, sis. I was trying to be nice. I want to share with you so you can get through the evening with dulled senses."

"I don't need your help."

I brush past him without saying anything else. No *hello*. No *goodbye*. No *how have you been?* I don't even check after his health.

I don't fucking care.

If Chase is smart, which he is not, he'll make the required bullshit appearance, and then he'll get the fuck out of here. It's sure to be a disgusting night full of blustering and bragging. It's likely no money will change hands and no secrets will be shared, but I still have to be present. Chase, on the other hand, does not. If I were him, I'd run as far and as fast as I can.

The moment I step foot in the private room, Ashton is at my side. His hand never leaves the spot on my lower back except to occasionally lead me by the elbow from one cluster of men to another. I am the perfect arm candy. I smile, nod, and laugh politely when expected. I literally bite my tongue. I taste blood, and the metallic flavor does little to calm my rage.

But I am nothing if not a stellar actress.

I play the pretty puppet, the submissive pet, and they all fucking buy it because in their minds, that's where I belong. Several times, I rethink the champagne, but I need to be alert in this den of snakes. I just pretend I'm my mother, and I can almost forget that I hate everyone in this room.

Myself included.

Right before dinner is served and we move to our assigned tables, I notice my brother is no longer here. I saw him a few times throughout the cocktail hour, but there is no empty chair for him. It seems he might be cleverer than I gave him credit for.

My father rises and gives a pre-dinner speech, thanking everyone for attending. He thanks my mother for her continued support, and he thanks Ashton for agreeing to take the night off from his important role as my father's campaign manager. Then my father makes a sly remark about how I'm Ashton's date tonight, and all I can do is smile and avoid eye contact with everyone staring at me. Ashton, on the other hand, uses the opportunity to put his hand on my thigh, and he doesn't remove it until the first course is served. I release a small sigh of relief the moment the contact is severed, but it's short-lived.

At the end of the night, when I slide into Ashton's car, he replaces his hand on my thigh. This time, though, he uses his thumb to massage my leg through my dress. I'm grateful the fabric is thick.

He leans into me, and I can smell alcohol on his breath.

"Thank you for behaving tonight, Samantha," he murmurs into my ear, using the hand not laying claim to my thigh to fondle the strands of hair that are framing my face. He twirls it tightly around his finger, so it tugs at my temple. "You seemed to be enjoying yourself."

I have to swallow back a scoff and force my body not to grow rigid. I inhale and exhale slowly before speaking, and though I want to, I don't lean away from him.

"It was a nice evening."

He hums, and his nose grazes the shell of my ear, his heavy breathing fanning my neck. When he presses a kiss to my jaw, I remain still despite every instinct in my body screaming at me to shove him away.

"We should do it again." He presses another wet kiss to my neck.

I fist my hand on the seat beside me and keep my eyes wide open and fixed on the rearview mirror. The driver makes eye contact with me twice but says nothing.

"Wouldn't you like that?" Ashton whispers, moving his hand to grip my waist and his lips to just below my ear. Another kiss. More hot, moist breath. Another repulsed shudder I have to shove down. "I think you would."

He plants another kiss on my jaw, then moves to my mouth. I turn a fraction of a second before he makes contact, so the kiss lands on the corner of my mouth instead of flush on the lips. I'm relieved for half a second, but then he grips my face, turns it to his, and forces his mouth on mine.

I don't move. I don't kiss him back. He moves a hand to my breast and squeezes hard before pushing me further into the seat. When he forces his tongue into my mouth, I let him, and I think of

Jane Austen. I think of the scene where Mr. Darcy confesses that he still loves Elizabeth Bennet and pretend it's being read to me in Lennon's voice.

I will not cry.

"Ms. Harper, we're here," the driver says, and Ashton reluctantly climbs off me.

Ashton pulls his face from mine so I can finally breathe, but he doesn't remove his hands. We're still almost a minute from my building. The driver announced us early, and suddenly I want to shower him with gratitude. I wonder how many other women he's had to do that for.

"You're like kissing a corpse," Ashton says, his tone bored. "We'll have to work on that."

I say nothing.

When we pull to the curb outside of my building, the driver wastes no time getting to my door and reaching for my hand. Just as I place mine into his, Ashton's voice stops me.

"Let me come up."

It's not said as a request. It's not a suggestion. It's an order.

I flash pleading eyes to the driver, a silent request to intervene should he need to, then turn softer ones to Ashton. The words I speak taste like dirt.

"Rain check."

I allow the driver to help me from the car and close the door behind me.

"Thank you," I whisper to him, and he nods but doesn't look me in the eyes.

"Be safe, miss."

I walk calmly into the lobby. I say hello to the security guard. I wait for my private elevator, then ride it in silence to my condo. Once inside, I set the alarm and head to my kitchen. I pull a wine glass from the cabinet and a bottle of white from the beverage fridge.

I get the full glass all the way to my lips before I remember the Valium, and then I let out a scream and hurl it at the floor.

The glass shatters and wine splatters everywhere.

It's not enough. I still feel his hands on me. I still smell his breath.

I pick up the wine bottle and slam it hard against the stone countertop with another scream. I have to hit it twice before the bottle breaks, then I hurl that at the floor too. I pull more wine glasses from the cabinet and throw them, one by one, at the spot on my kitchen floor now littered with broken glass and a large puddle of expensive white wine.

The crystal decanter I got in Italy goes next.

Then I go for a drinkware set made of imported crystal. I can't remember where I bought it, but it was paid for with my father's credit card. Another pointless, luxurious purchase. Another way to waste my father's stolen, inherited blood money.

I throw each piece against the tile with a scream, mentally calculating the cost of the damage. Martini glasses, champagne flutes, rocks glasses. They all crash satisfyingly on the ground until they're nothing but sharp shards of crystal. No longer rare and valuable. No longer coveted.

Now they're nothing but treacherous garbage.

I stand for several minutes and catch my breath, surprised at how disheveled I've become. My hair is falling out of my bun. I'm sure my eyeliner is once again smudged. My father's voice filters into my head, followed by Ashton's.

*Stop being so dramatic, Samantha.*
*Thank you for behaving, Samantha.*
*You kiss like a corpse.*
*We'll have to work on that.*

I choke back another scream while I unzip my dress and let it fall to my feet. I kick it into the mess of glass shards and wine. Then, slowly, I walk through the mess in just my lingerie and my heels. When I reach the edge of my kitchen tile, I step out of my heels and leave them behind me. In my bedroom, I take off the horrible necklace, stashing it in my dresser drawer, then take my real phone out of my handbag and dial the building maintenance team. I make my voice sharp and cold, just like the glass and wine now covering my floor.

"I require a clean-up in my kitchen. There's been an accident involving glass."

"Of course, Ms. Harper. We'll send someone right up."

"Tell them to get rid of the dress and shoes as well. They've been damaged."

"Of course, Ms. Harper."

I hang up without saying thank you and pull up my email app. I send a single email to my father and Ashton, excusing myself for the rest of the week. I tell them I have the flu and will be unreachable. Then I power my phone off and pack a bag.

I don't get to Franklin until three in the morning. When I walk through the door of my dark cave above the now quiet bar, I allow myself to take one of my prescription sleeping pills, and then I pass out into a deep, dreamless sleep.

## FOURTEEN

*Chris*

"They're six, Chris. They aren't going to appreciate your culinary degree."

Michael's laughing voice sounds from behind me, and I smile, but I don't look toward him. I don't bother reminding him that *no one* really appreciates the degree because I haven't done shit with it. I don't even know where the piece of paper is.

"Maybe not, but turning six is a big deal and I'm not half-assing this."

I don't look at him as I pipe little flowers out of icing onto half of the assortment of cupcakes. I already piped footballs onto the other half. I prefer cooking to baking, but I can make a mean fucking cupcake when the situation calls for it.

I can hear my dad laughing in the other room with my sister, and Luke and Lucy keep running in and out of the kitchen in their little matching birthday T-shirts, asking Michael how much longer until their party starts. There's a bounce house in the yard, streamers strung from the ceiling, and balloons fucking everywhere. In thirty minutes, this house will be overrun with six-year-olds, and the twins are ready.

I finish piping icing on the last cupcake when my phone buzzes in my pocket. I take it out and open a text from Macon.

**MACON**
Be there in five.

Heads-up. Len is bringing Harper.

My stomach jumps with excitement just before it falls to my feet. It's been a few weeks since I've seen Sam, and the idea of seeing her today thrills me. But the reality of seeing her here, with my sister and father, sets my nerves churning.

"Fuck, I'm sorry in advance," I mumble to Michael, and then I shout toward the living room. "Tiff. Dad. Can y'all come here a minute?"

My dad ambles into the kitchen, followed by my sister, and they join me at the counter.

"Oh, those look great, Chris," my sister says. "Lucy is going to love those little footballs."

"I know." I grin. "And I did the daisies for Luke because he's our little Ferdinand."

My sister laughs and swipes a finger full of icing from the bowl. When she *mmmms*, I waggle my brows.

"The cake is even better," I tell her, swatting her hand away when she reaches for a cupcake. "They're for the children."

"I am carrying a child," she argues, gesturing to her pregnant stomach.

I shake my head *no* anyway, and she rolls her eyes.

"Right, so, anyway, I have some news," I say quickly, looking from my sister to my dad and then back. "And I need you guys to be on your best behavior and to remember that this is a birthday party, and that we, *of all people*, should understand that a child should not be punished for the crimes of their parents."

"What would we punish the twins for?" Michael asks, obviously confused.

"Not them," I say slowly, then I look at my sister and my dad. "Sam Harper is coming to the birthday party."

My sister's face goes from shocked to enraged at the drop of a hat.

"The hell she is," Tiffany says. "I'm not letting anyone from that family into this house. Who the fuck even invited her?"

"You said fuck," Lucy shouts from the stairwell, and Tiffany flinches.

"She's coming with Lennon and Macon." I keep my voice hushed so no more little ears overhear. "I don't know why, but I just found out. They're probably pulling into the driveaway any second now."

"No." My sister shakes her head rapidly. "Absolutely not. No."

She turns to head toward the door, but my father puts his hand on her shoulder and stops her.

"Don't make a scene," my father says. "We don't want that to be something the twins remember about their sixth birthday."

Tiffany opens her mouth to protest, but I speak up, cutting her off.

"Sam's not her dad, Tiff. She's not her brother. Just...just cut her some slack, okay? I know I'm asking a lot, but...please."

Her nostrils flare as she flicks her eyes from me to Michael.

"I'm fine, babe. It's fine."

"It's not fine," she hisses. "You expect me to let someone from that family into our home? Around our kids? You expec—"

Tiff's voice stops at the sound of the doorbell, followed by the sound of the twins shouting "DOOR" and running down the stairs. I know it's Macon and Lennon because as soon as the door opens, Lucy squeals Evie's name, and Macon and Lennon's voices chime in with happy birthday wishes.

I give my sister a tight smile and raise my eyebrows in question. She frowns at me and looks away. Awesome. I glance at my dad and Michael and am relieved to find that they both look significantly less pissed.

"Good?" I whisper, and they both give me half-hearted nods. Good.

I school my face into something that looks less like a grimace, then head toward the living room.

"Hey, hey." I slap Macon's hand, then pull Lennon in for a hug.

"Glad you guys could make it. I see you've already lost your gremlin."

"They stole her as soon as we walked in." Lennon laughs.

I can hear Evie giggling with Lucy and Luke upstairs. It's already chaos and there are only three kids here. I don't know how the house is going to withstand the seven more coming.

"Harper." I finally let my eyes settle on her. She looks paler than usual, and there are faint purple shadows under her eyes. She looks miserable and lifeless, and I have to resist the urge to reach for her. "Welcome."

"Casper." She nods, and I note the strange hoarseness in her voice. "Thanks for letting me crash your niece and nephew's birthday party."

Macon and Lennon head into the kitchen, but I don't follow. Instead, I stand in my sister's living room and find myself scanning my eyes over Sam. Her signature red lipstick washes her out in a way it normally doesn't. Her hair, usually glossy and straight, is pulled up into a messy ponytail, and she's wearing a plain T-shirt and cutoff jean shorts.

I've never seen Sam in anything so casual, and it catches me completely off guard. Even in high school, she dressed like something out of a fashion magazine. The last time I saw her, we were making out like teenagers in the parking lot of The Outpost. Now, she's standing in my sister's living room wearing jean cutoffs and flip-flops and looking like something out of a psychological thriller.

Something happened. Something not good.

"How you been?" I ask softly, and she snorts.

"Is this what we're doing now?"

I raise a brow at her tone. Cold. Unfeeling. Dead.

"Is *what* what we're doing?"

"*How you been,*" she repeats, voice low and mocking. "Don't make things weird, Casper. It was just sex and some fooling around. We can be adults about it."

I force a grin and take a step toward her, closing the distance so there's little more than a foot of space between us, then lower my voice to a whisper.

"It wasn't *just sex*. It was a little oral play. We haven't even gotten to the sex yet."

"Yet?" She tilts her chin up and narrows her eyes. "Who says there will be a next time?"

I run my eyes over her face. Take note of the way her pupils flare and her chest rises and falls more quickly. The way she shifts on her feet and her pulse thrums in her neck. A flush of color returns to her pallid cheeks, and I reach up and drag my knuckles over her jaw. Her breath hitches, and I press my thumb to her pulse point. I lean down and put my lips to her ear.

"You do, princess. Your whole body says there will be a next time."

She pulls back just enough that our cheeks brush, and I consider kissing her right here, but then my niece shouts "*WATCH OUT*" and all thoughts of a kiss vanish.

Sam and I jump apart just in time to see a pink remote-control car come zooming through the living room. The car runs into Sam's foot, then backs up into my foot before looping around us and zooming back out again.

"Sorry, Uncle Chris," Cheyenne shouts from somewhere in the house.

Then Luke, Lucy, and Evie go bolting past us after the remote-control car.

"Sorry, Uncle Chris!"

"Sorry, Uncle Chris!"

"Sorry, Uncle Casper!"

I chuckle. Uncle Casper is new. Evie usually just calls me Casper, but I'm not mad about it. I turn my smile toward Sam, but she's still staring in the direction of the car.

"Was there a rodent in that car?" she says finally, and I bark out a laugh.

"Probably."

She blinks at me.

"Probably?"

I shrug.

"Chy has a hamster named Puma. He's pretty chill. He was probably in the car."

She gives me a surprised smile, scrunching her nose up in disbelief. Fuck me, she's beautiful.

"Really?" She laughs.

I nod.

"Yep. Really. Now, c'mon before they think we skipped out on the party."

I put my hand on her shoulder and steer her into the kitchen. I introduce her to my dad and Michael, but my sister is noticeably absent. When the rest of the kids arrive for the party, it's not as obvious that Tiff is avoiding Sam, but I can tell, and I'm pretty sure Sam can tell, too.

I watch her cautiously and the way she interacts with everyone.

Her posture is easy and natural with Lennon, but with everyone else—even Macon—there's a rigidity to her. Michael engages her in conversation for a while, and I overhear him telling her about his prosthetics and his plans for the Boston Marathon. She laughs. She asks questions. When he mentions that a car accident took his legs, she expresses sympathy. She tells him how amazing it is that he's accomplished so much since then. She's rightfully in awe of my brother-in-law, but there's still a level of discomfort in her that I can't ignore.

It's made worse when she has a stilted conversation with my father, and exacerbated further when she attempts to talk to my sister, only to be blown off entirely. Sam stands awkwardly in the yard next to the food table and watches as my sister walks back into the house.

"Here." I hand Sam a plate. She takes it but doesn't speak. "This barbeque is supposedly some of the best in the county. Masterfully rubbed, smoked to perfection, and the sauce is a secret recipe."

I put a hamburger bun on her plate, then use the serving tongs to put a large portion of barbeque pork on top of it. When I reach for the coleslaw, she throws a hand over her plate and shakes her head.

"Are you allergic?" I ask.

"No," she says.

"Have you tried it before?"

"No," she repeats, and I laugh.

"Then trust me." I grab her hand and gently move it so I can put a scoop of coleslaw on top of the barbeque.

She doesn't stop me, but she sneers at it with disdain. I put some chips on her plate, then a hunk of watermelon before finally steering her toward a picnic table where Macon and Lennon are sitting.

"Moment of truth," I say as she eyes the sandwich. "Don't be a wuss, Sam. Go on."

She looks at Lennon. "Did you eat this?"

"I did." Lennon grins. "It's very good."

She scowls at it, and Macon laughs.

"C'mon on, Harper," he says jokingly. "Take a polite bite."

Sam flips him off on instinct, then quickly puts her hand in her lap and looks around to make sure no kids saw her. I shake my head at her, and she rolls her eyes.

"Fine." She picks up the sandwich and carefully takes a bite.

The moment her eyes flare with surprise, I let out a whoop of victory.

"Told ya," I say smugly. "Smoked it ten hours."

"You did this?" she asks while chewing, and I nod.

She smiles and raises her sandwich in my direction before taking another bite, so I pretend to take a bow at her applause, then I stand and gather Lennon's and Macon's empty plates.

"Be right back," I tell them and head into the house.

When I walk through the sliding doors, I hear hushed arguing coming from the laundry room off the kitchen. It's my sister's and Michael's voices, so I turn to head back outside and give them privacy until I hear Sam's name. Then mine. I sigh at the ceiling and head toward the laundry room.

I knock once and the arguing halts, so I open the door and bounce my eyes between Tiff and Michael.

"This isn't subtle." I lean on the doorframe and fold my arms across my chest. "I could hear you in the kitchen."

"This is ridiculous, Chris. Having her here? My blood pressure is through the freaking roof," Tiffany hisses, and Michael rubs his hand over her back.

"You're overreacting," I say, and Michael glares at me.

I realize my mistake just as Tiffany punches my shoulder.

"You do not *ever* tell a pregnant woman she's overreacting," Tiffany snaps.

I wince.

"I know. I'm sorry. But, Tiff, I really think you're making this bigger than it needs to be," I say cautiously, though the way she scowls tells me she doesn't appreciate my not-so-clever rewording.

"She's not hurting anyone or anything by being here," I say, and when Tiff opens her mouth, I shut her down. "Dad is fine. Michael is fine."

I look at Michael.

"Are you fine?"

He nods at my sister.

"I'm really fine, babe."

"Sam is not her father, Tiffany. She's not. You can't hold the sins of her family against her. She's not guilty of them."

Tiff shakes her head and wipes away a few stray tears.

"I don't believe that, Chris. After everything that family has done? You want to sit here and expect me to believe that that woman is innocent? That she hasn't had some hand or influence or knowledge of all of his corruption? I don't buy it. Harpers are not good people, Chris, and you're too naïve to see that it applies to her too. She is a Harper, and Harpers are poison."

"You're wrong, Tiff," I say, and she scoffs.

"I'm not. You just can't see past her pretty face. It's going to be Sable all over again."

I rear back like she's slapped me. In a way, I guess she did.

"Low blow." I shake my head. "You're angry. You've held a grudge. I get it. You have every right to be angry. Hell, we all do, but you're taking it out on the wrong person. That ax you're grindin' isn't meant for Sam. Remember that."

In the quiet, my sister and I look at one another. She's stopped crying her angry tears, but she's still mad. She won't back down. Before I open my mouth to say something else, I hear the faint sound of the sliding glass door in the kitchen. My eyes go wide, and I whip around just in time to see Sam's retreating back to the yard. She's halfway to the picnic table now, but her empty plate is sitting on the kitchen table, which means she probably heard us arguing.

"Fuck," I mumble, tipping my head to the ceiling.

Sam already looks like a beaten-down version of herself right now. I don't want to consider what this will do.

"The party is almost over," I say to Tiffany. "Just fucking be civil, okay? And then I'll get her out of here."

I head back out the door. When I sit down next to Sam, she's alone, and I see Macon and Lennon in the bounce house with Evie and a bunch of kids. I consider what to say, how to bring it up, but in the end, Sam does it for me.

"I'm fine. I've heard worse," she says coldly. "And anyway, your sister isn't wrong. Harpers are poison, and I am very much a Harper."

"You're not poison, Sam."

"Aren't I, though? I'm not ignorant of the shit my father has done. I know he's a terrible person. Yet, I've actively worked alongside him and others to help elect him to a government office. What does that say about me? Purposely putting power in the hands of someone like him. My father is pure evil, but I'm an accomplice. I've got blood on my hands, too."

I shake my head and take in her profile. She still hasn't looked at me, but there's no emotion on her face. Her eyes are cold. Her mouth is flat. I want to shake her.

"You're not accountable for anything your father has done," I say, but she lets out a derisive laugh and turns her ice-blue eyes on me.

"You don't know me, Casper. You think just because I let you between my legs that means you know anything about me? It doesn't, it *never* does, so quit making assumptions. I don't need you standing up for me. I don't need you fighting some invisible battle with your family—with *anyone*—for my honor. I don't need it, and I don't want it."

My eyes narrow on her. A sharp tongue spitting sharper words, but it's all fucking bullshit.

"You think I don't know what you're doing," I say quietly. "I do. I know it pisses you off, but I'm not falling for the act, princess. You can't hide from me."

She shakes her head with a mocking smile, her teeth seeming too white against the blood red of her lips.

"You are delusional," she says cruelly. "Is this how you are? You get off one time and suddenly you think we have a connection? You think that gives you the right to have opinions about me and my life? You *know* nothing. You *are* nothing."

She chuckles and arches a brow, dropping her eyes down my body as if seeing me in a whole new way.

"No wonder Sarah turned down your proposal," she taunts. "You probably dreamed up the whole relationship in your head."

I clench my jaw, my nostrils flaring at the insult, but I don't argue with her. Instead, I reach my hand up and slide it to the back of her neck. She doesn't flinch or push me away, but her blue eyes stay frigid. Her mask never slips.

I run my thumb over her jaw and press my fingers into the soft flesh of her neck. It's becoming one of my favorite things to do, hold her like this. I can feel her pulse thrumming, reminding me that she's human. She's real, with warm blood and a breakable heart, just like the rest of us.

"You're not fooling anyone." I can tell by the way the muscle in her cheek jumps that it's the worst possible thing to say.

"What you think doesn't matter," she says.

She wraps her hand around my wrist and pulls it away, dropping it back into my lap. Then she stands and leaves.

Minutes later, Lennon and Macon return to the table.

"Where's Sam?" Lennon's smile falls from her face.

"She left."

"She what?" Lennon glances around the yard. "She came with us. Do you know why?"

I shrug. "Guess she had enough of mingling with the unwashed."

Lennon doesn't acknowledge my barb as she pulls out her phone, then she sighs and tips her head to the sky.

"She doesn't have her phone with her." She looks at Macon. "Can I have the keys? I'm going to pick her up and drive her home."

Macon fishes into his pocket and drops the car keys into her hand, and she kisses him quickly before bolting from the yard.

"What happened?" Macon asks.

"I'm not sure yet," I say honestly, and he nods in my periphery.

"Sam's complicated."

I look at him finally. He's standing with his arms crossed, staring toward the sliding glass doors.

"I've gathered that," I say, and then he smirks.

"Her bite fucking hurts." He laughs, then makes eye contact with me. "But her bark is worse. And usually the nastier she is, the closer you are to something she's trying to protect."

I don't ask him to elaborate. I just nod, then look back toward the doors until Lucy comes running over with a football under her arm.

"Uncle Chris! Macon! Wanna play?"

"Heck yes, I want to play," I say to Lucy, and Macon scoops her up and throws her over his shoulder.

"Let's go kick some Uncle Chris butt, little lady."

# FIFTEEN

## *Chris*

I USE MY PROPERTY KEY TO UNLOCK THE DOOR TO SAM'S APARTMENT at 6 a.m.

I expected her to be sleeping, so I'm surprised to find her awake on the couch with a cup of coffee in her hand and a laptop in front of her. She blinks up at me with surprise, her blue eyes magnified slightly by the glasses she's got on. I take her in quickly and notice she's wearing a very familiar pair of sweatpants and T-shirt, but because I realize I'm walking a thin line right now, I don't point them out.

"What are you doing awake?" I ask, making my way to her kitchen and putting the reusable grocery bag I brought on the counter.

She studies me warily and takes a sip of her coffee before answering.

"I don't sleep well," she says finally, sliding her glasses to the top of her head. "Why are you letting yourself into my cave at six in the morning? Pretty sure this is illegal under tenant's rights."

"Cave?" I chuckle. "Macon calls it the penthouse."

Sam arches an unamused brow.

"Please. My place in D.C. is a penthouse. This place? This is a cave."

I shake my head, but I don't argue. I'm sure her place in D.C. is way nicer than this place. It just makes me more curious as to why she's here and not there.

"Figured I'd make us breakfast before we got on the road." I rummage through cabinets to find a frying pan and a rubber spatula.

As I suspected, her kitchen is lacking. Luckily, I pre-chopped the vegetables and pre-shredded the cheese before I came. I even brought my own spices.

"I'm having breakfast," Sam says, and I look up just in time to see her raise her coffee mug. "And what do you mean *get on the road*?"

I ignore the question and address the statement.

"That's not breakfast," I tell her. "That's a beverage."

She takes a slow sip, then sighs contentedly and gives me a sarcastic smile.

"I'm having it at breakfast time, so it's breakfast."

I don't respond. I just get to work cracking eggs and whipping them with a fork since I can't find a whisk.

"What do you mean get on the road?" she repeats. "I have work to do. I'm not leaving this couch for the next four days."

I glance at the makeshift office she's made on the couch. Laptop, notebooks, pens.

"Bring it with." I go back to my task without looking at her.

She stands and puts her hands on her hips in my periphery.

"I'm not going anywhere with you, Christopher. Are you forgetting what I said yesterday?"

*Christopher*.

Not *Casper*.

I bite back my grin and take it as a good sign. I shake my head once as I pour the egg mixture into the pan on her stove.

"Heard you loud and clear yesterday, princess."

"Good. Then hear me now. I am not getting *on the road* with you, and I already had breakfast."

I don't respond. I just focus on the eggs, adding the chopped bell peppers, shredded cheese, and seasoning. Pretty soon, I feel Sam's presence and look up to find that she's moved to the counter and is silently watching me cook. It makes me nervous but in a thrilling way.

"Are you making omelets?" she asks after a moment, and I flash her a grin.

"I like my eggs the way I like my women..." I trail off, and she raises an eyebrow. I can't help but laugh a little when I finish. "Folded, with their insides scrambled."

"Oh my god." Her lips twitch in an attempt to fight a smile. "That is terrible. That is so dumb."

She's right. It's a horrible joke, but that little smile I just earned? I feel like I struck fucking gold.

I plate her omelet and set it in front of her, sprinkling some parsley and chives on top of the perfectly melted cheese, then I top off her coffee. I lean my hip on the counter and watch, arms folded, as she studies the plate.

"I'm not hungry." She flicks her eyes from me to the omelet and back.

I hold a fork out to her and wait. She looks at the fork, then at me.

"If I take that, I'm going to stab you with it."

I sigh, then step up to the counter. I use the fork to cut into her omelet, then raise the bite to her mouth.

"Open wide." I smirk.

She doesn't. She just glares.

"Don't be so stubborn. One bite, and if you don't like it, we can trash it."

She doesn't budge, so I try a different approach.

"This is a smoked bourbon gouda. Don't make me throw it away before you at least taste it."

She huffs, then opens her mouth, so I feed her the bite of omelet and watch intently as she chews.

"Wasn't so hard, was it?"

She glowers, but then her eyes flutter shut, and she hums in appreciation. When she swallows, she opens her eyes and hits me with a look of pure annoyance.

"How are you so good at this? This is amazing. Prime rib. Barbeque. Cupcakes. Now omelets? I can make *one thing* well: shrimp alfredo. That's it."

I hand her the fork so she can eat some more, then cut into my own omelet and take a bite, chewing and swallowing before answering.

"I went to culinary school for a while," I confess. "Even had a job working in the kitchen at Rosa Mare. You know that fancy restaurant in Arlington?"

Her eyebrows shoot up to her hairline.

"Yeah, I know it. It's almost impossible to get on their reservation list. There was a write-up about them in the *Post* "Food and Culture" section a few years ago and they blew up."

I laugh.

"Yeah, I remember that write-up. The braised purple carrots they raved about? Those were mine."

"You lie," she says, and I shake my head.

"Nope. They credited everything to Chef Oliver, but that was my recipe. I did the steak the food critic ate that night, too."

She blinks at me with her mouth agape, then shakes her head.

"What happened?"

"What do you mean?"

"I mean, what happened? Why aren't you working in some five-star kitchen somewhere demanding everyone call you Chef? Why are you *here*?"

I furrow my brow, wincing a bit at her words.

*Why are you here?*

Meaning, why aren't you doing something better, something more? I laugh it off, but it stings.

"I used to want to run my own kitchen, own my own restaurant or something like that, but my home is here. My family is here. I didn't want to live in D.C. or New York because then I'm not here if they need me, and there's really not much opportunity to further your culinary career in Franklin, so I let it go."

Her eyes widen some more, and she lets out a shocked little laugh.

"You gave up your dream of being a chef and owning your own restaurant because you didn't want to live far away from your family? You gave up working at a Michelin-star restaurant in Arlington to come back to *Franklin*, of all places?"

The confusion that laces her every word is so thick that it's comical.

She doesn't get it. She doesn't know my family's history, sure, but even if she did, I doubt she'd understand. How could she? I've seen her family. I know who she grew up with. If our situations were flipped, I'd probably be confused, too.

"When I was working in Arlington, my brother-in-law was in an accident. He had left the house to go on a run—he was training for a marathon at the time—and when he didn't return when he was supposed to, my sister called the county sheriff's department. They found him unconscious on Old Courthouse Highway. He'd been a victim of a hit and run and needed surgery, and they had to amputate both of his legs. Michael couldn't work, obviously, and Tiffany was home with three small children, so I dropped everything and moved back. I took on two jobs to make sure they didn't lose the house and that the kids had food on the table, and I don't regret it. They needed me, so I came, and we got through it together. That's how it should be, and it made me realize that I never want to be that far away from them again."

I take a deep breath, then let it out slowly. I don't look at her. I can't. I don't want to know what I'll find on her face if I do.

"They're my true north, Sam," I say, and then I end the conversation.

I wash my plate in the sink, then wash hers. I make sure everything is clean and put back where I found it, then I turn back to her.

"Ready to head out?" I check my watch. "It's almost a four-hour drive, so I'd like to get on the road. Macon and Lennon are going to meet us there."

She tilts her head to the side and studies me, her expression giving nothing away.

"Lennon will be there?"

I nod.

"Head to where?" she asks, but I make a show of checking my watch again.

"Go on. I'll wait while you pack."

She steps closer, puts her hands on her hips, and studies me, something almost sad flickering over her features.

"I can't be what you want me to be."

I can't help the way my lips curl up on the side. It should feel like a brush off. Like a rejection. But somehow, it doesn't.

"Presumptuous of you to think I want you to be anything other than what you are," I say honestly, holding her eye contact. "Now, are we ready to head out?"

She sighs and rolls her eyes.

"Head to *where*, Christopher?"

I give her a small smile, then reach up and run a strand of her soft hair through my fingers. She doesn't bat me away.

"Want to see heaven, princess?"

---

IT'S ALMOST NOON WHEN WE PULL UP TO MY GRANDFATHER'S CABIN.

It's a perfect day. The early summer weather is not too hot, and the breeze off the lake is gentle and refreshing. The forest is a vibrant green, and the birds are singing in the trees. I can tell from the way Sam's taking it all in that she's going to love it here.

I saw the way she'd looked at my tattoo, the way she acted when I mentioned the cabin that night in my living room. Something's been eating away at her, and I've always found that the best medicine comes in the form of lake water and mountain views. I took a gamble, but we've only been here three minutes and I'm already sure it will pay off.

We stopped on the way to get groceries, so I grab those bags out of my truck and tell her I'll come back out for her LV suitcase and my duffle.

"I'll give you a tour," I say, then she follows me up the stairs and into the house.

I drop the groceries in the kitchen, taking a minute to put away the things that need to be refrigerated, then I lead Sam through the cabin and point out all the important things. She walks slowly, surveying everything. She runs her fingers over the spines of the books on the living room bookshelf, then reads the names on the boxes of board games. I watch her eyes widen when she sees the clawfoot tub in the bathroom. I show her the office and tell her she's free to use it to get her work done, and she comments on how nice the natural light is in the room. Her eyes bounce between the final two doors in the hallway, and I grin.

"This will be where Macon and Lennon will stay when they get here." I push the first door open to show the small guest bedroom. Then I move to the door across the hall and open it. "And this will be where you will stay."

It's not much larger than the guest bedroom, but we've always treated it as the primary bedroom. Sam raises an eyebrow.

"And you?"

"The couch is a sleeper sofa." I wink, and she gives me a curt nod. "C'mon. There's more."

The moment we step out the back door, she gasps at the view. It's beautiful. The cabin is at a higher elevation than the lake, so you can see it clearly from the back, and the mountains make for an absolutely breathtaking backdrop.

"Nice, right? This area used to be all trees and pine straw—no real yard, just two rocking chairs on the back porch. But when I renovated it, I wanted to make this more of a gathering space."

Sam laughs to herself, shaking her head lightly as she takes in the stone pavers, firepit, and patio furniture.

"You renovated this place, too?"

"Me and my dad, yeah. Didn't do much except update it a little. Make it a little more energy efficient and modern."

It's an understatement. We did a complete kitchen remodel and knocked the wall down that used to separate the kitchen and living room. We replaced all the windows, light fixtures, and plumbing, and restored the original hardwoods. This whole place used to be outfitted with a hideous brown shag carpet. I don't brag, though. I just let the appearance speak for itself.

"Dock's this way."

Sam follows me quietly down the trail to the lake, and we stop next to the small, private boat shed and dock. There are already boats and jet skis on the lake, but since it's a Thursday, it's not as busy as usual. On Saturday, the place will be a party.

"Wow," she says. "This is beautiful. How big is this lake?"

"About thirty-two square miles. The place is really popular now —I'll take you out in the boat tomorrow and show you some of the giant houses around here—but this land has been in our family since the sixties. My grandfather built the cabin himself."

She grows quiet and takes a deep inhale and exhale before closing her eyes and tilting her face to the sky. It's probably my imagination, but I think I can already see the color returning to her cheeks.

"It's so peaceful out here," she says after a moment. "I feel like I can actually think clearly. No distractions. No unrealistic expectations. Just the lake and the trees and me."

I smile. That's exactly what I was hoping.

"It's my favorite place in the world," I tell her, and she smiles to herself.

"I can see why," she says before turning back to me. "If you could have one wish, one wish for anything at all, what would it be?"

I blink at her. She's caught me off guard, and I don't know how to answer the question right away.

I walk to the water and search the stones, picking up a few smooth ones as I think it over. What would I wish for? Anything at all? So many things come through my mind—financial stability for my sister's family, Michael's medical bills paid, my dad to stop aging, an update on my mom.

I consider all of it before settling on one.

"I think I just want to enjoy life without doing too much damage."

I hand Sam one of the stones, then turn and skip one of mine on the surface of the lake. It skips three times before sinking.

"That's it?" Sam asks. "You wouldn't want to own a restaurant or run your own kitchen or something?"

When I look at her, she's frowning at her rock.

"Owning a restaurant would be great—it used to be my dream—but it's not the most

important thing anymore. If I could have that and never have to leave my family, sure. I'd love it. I'd want it. But I'm not losing sleep over it."

I skip another rock. Five.

"I don't need to own a restaurant to be happy," I say to the lake. "All I really need are my

family and friends. To make some good memories with them. If I could do it all without hurting anyone, then I'd die happy."

I shrug and turn back to her, slipping my hands into the pockets of my jeans, and find her

staring at me. I'd find her attention flattering if she didn't look so confused.

"What?" I ask with a laugh. "What's wrong?"

"I just can't figure out your angle," she says finally, and I arch a brow.

"What if I don't have one?"

She shakes her head.

"Everyone's got an angle, Chris. Everyone."

"What's yours?"

She narrows her eyes, then looks out at the water. She's quiet for so long that I think she won't answer me, but then she drops her rock into the lake and speaks to the ripples.

"I think it's probably the opposite of yours."

We fall back into silence. I don't ask her to elaborate, and she doesn't offer to. I just stand next to her and watch her as she looks out at the lake with her eyebrows scrunched in thought.

I wait. I let her take it all in.

She's battling with something inside herself, and my instincts say not to interrupt. I let her work it out, and when she does, when she finally looks back at me, we head to the house.

"Is that a shower?" she says randomly, just before we step inside the cabin.

I turn and find her staring at the side of the house, and I chuckle.

"Yeah, it is." I walk to the outdoor shower and push it open, showing her the inside. "Nothing fancy. Just here to shower after fishing or swimming. It's nice, though."

She glances up at the sky and furrows her brow.

"There's no roof."

"Very astute."

She rolls her eyes.

"You should try it out tonight. You can shower under the stars."

She gives me a look that suggests she thinks I've lost my damn mind, and I laugh out loud.

"Never mind." I walk past her and back toward the house. "It's probably not fit for a princess, anyway."

She scoffs just before the door shuts behind me, and I don't see her again for over two hours. When Sam finally comes back inside, I'm in the process of prepping pizza dough for dinner.

"When will Lennon be here?" she asks, leaning on the doorframe and watching me work. "I left my phone in D.C., so I can't text her."

I flick my eyes toward her, then look away.

"They'll be here Saturday."

"What? Saturday?" Her voice rises with her temper. "You said they were meeting us."

I glance at her again and have to swallow my laugh. She's so irritated that her face and neck are flushed with pink and her blue eyes are wild.

"They are," I say calmly. "They're meeting us Saturday."

"Today is Thursday," she shouts. "Why didn't you say they wouldn't be here until Saturday? What the hell am I supposed to do until Saturday?"

I drop the pizza dough into a large bowl, then wash my hands in the kitchen sink as I speak.

"Honestly, I didn't mention it because I figured it would be harder to get you here."

Her jaw drops.

"So you tricked me?"

I nod, feeling a little ashamed now that she's said it out loud.

"Yeah. But I think you're going to be glad I did. Now, go wash your hands. I need your help with dinner."

"I'm not hungry," she says, then storms off into her bedroom and shuts the door loudly behind her.

Fuck.

I wanted to bring her here to help her feel better, but I might have just made it worse. I knew getting her here under false pretenses was a shitty thing to do, but I did it anyway. Sometimes I think I've got her figured out, think I know her, and other times I feel like I'm clawing in the dark for any sort of clue. I just can't figure out *why* I care so damn much, because I fucking do.

I knock on the door to her bedroom a few hours later.

"Come in," Sam says, so I open the door and enter plate first with my other hand up.

She's sitting on the bed with her laptop in her lap, and she slides her glasses to the top of her head when she sees me.

"Pizza," I say. "Peace offering."

I set the plate on top of the dresser, then turn to face her completely.

"I'm sorry. I should have been up-front with you. I withheld the whole truth, led you to believe a lie, and I never should have done that. If you want, I can bring you back to Franklin tonight."

The shock on Sam's face is unmistakable, but then it's wiped away just as quickly as it came. She purses her lips, frown lines appearing briefly between her eyebrows while she thinks over what I said, and finally she sighs.

"Thank you for apologizing. You're right. It was shitty."

"It was." I nod.

"But I don't want to leave," she adds, and a small spark of hope ignites in my chest. "I'm glad I'm here. It beats sitting in my cave all alone, and I figure I can get work done until Lennon gets here."

"Okay." I ignore the disappointment flooding me.

She's just going to hole up in here until Lennon arrives, and that upsets me more than it should.

"Thank you for the pizza," she says softly, and I give her a smile.

"Just holler if you need anything," I tease, and she smirks.

"I do not *holler*."

Memories of the night in my house flash through my mind, but I tamp them down.

"Good night, princess."

"Good night."

## SIXTEEN

*Sam*

I MANAGE TO GET A DECENT AMOUNT OF WORK DONE IN THIS TINY bedroom.

I finish and submit one article, then begin another. I email some clients. I accept a project. I enjoy this job much more than working for my father. In a perfect world, this side hustle would be my only hustle. The promise of that world is what keeps me going.

I can hear Chris moving around in the cabin the whole time, but he's not distracting. I noticed there's no television in the place. I wonder if he's reading. If he were anyone else, I'd guess he was scrolling on his phone, but something tells me he doesn't do that. He's too present. Too grounded.

I smile to myself just as soon as I frown, his words from earlier playing over in my head.

*I want to enjoy life without doing too much damage.*

The statement was like a slap to the face, made worse by the fact that I'm pretty sure he actually means it. He's not lying. He's not trying to make himself look better. He's *actually* that good, that kind.

Chris and I? We couldn't be more different.

Sometimes when I'm around him, I almost forget what kind of person I am. I can almost believe I'm like him. Like I'm good and kind and unwilling to hurt anyone.

But then I remember.

I remember the cruel things I said to him yesterday just because I was hurting. I remember wanting to lash out and hurt him more.

I remember my name. I remember my past. I remember my goals.

I remember everything, and then I feel like a naïve fool for ever trying to wish for something else.

*She is a Harper, and Harpers are poison.*

A sad laugh escapes me, then I fall back on the pillows.

Chris's sister was right; he just doesn't see it. He looks at me like I'm something to be worshiped, not something to be feared. He looks at me like I have nothing in the world to be ashamed of, like I have good inside me. Like I could *be* good if I wanted to be.

But Chris is wrong.

---

I sit up with a jolt, and it takes a moment to get my bearings.

The unfamiliar room is dark, lit only by the moon shining through the windows, but I can tell I'm on a bed surrounded by my work supplies. My laptop sits open, but asleep, on the pillow beside me, and my notebooks lie atop the bedspread.

I must have fallen asleep, and a dream woke me up.

I scrub a hand down my face, then throw my hair up using the elastic on my wrist. I lie back on the bed and close my eyes again, but I can't get comfortable. My mind won't quiet.

I reach for my phone to call Lennon seconds before I remember I don't have it with me. I brought only my second phone, and I don't use that for personal contacts. I don't have my sleeping pills either.

I tap the trackpad on my laptop to wake it up and check the time. It's a little after midnight. I won't be falling back asleep for a while, or possibly at all, so I make up my mind to not even try.

Quietly, I climb out of bed and tiptoe into the kitchen. I rummage through the fridge, find the leftover pizza, and pull out a slice, then I open all the cabinets until I find a glass to fill with water.

Then, as quietly as possible, I walk down the hall and out the back door.

Grateful for the full moon and starry sky, I make my way down to the boat dock. I keep my eyes on the gravel path, careful not to trip over a stray stick or rock. When I can hear the soft sounds of the lake, I glance up and find that the dock is occupied.

"Are you coming to keep me company?" Chris says as I step onto the wooden slats.

"Do you want company?" I ask, and he shrugs with a smile.

"From you? Always." He scoots over and pats the spot on the dock next to him. "Couldn't sleep?"

I slip off my sandals and leave them next to his, then I hand him my plate and water and lower myself awkwardly beside him so my legs are hanging off the edge. I take my slice of pizza off the plate, take a bite, and chew slowly to delay answering.

"Figured I'd come out here so I didn't wake you," I say after I swallow, then I turn and look him over. "What are you doing out here, anyway?"

He picks up a paperback book and waves it at me before setting it behind him.

"Reading."

"But it's dark."

He grins.

"It wasn't always dark."

"Hm."

I look back out over the lake. I don't ask him what he's been doing since the sun set. I suppose he doesn't want me to know. I take another bite of my pizza and chew.

I wonder what it was like to grow up coming here for the summer. I bet it was fun. I bet he laughed a lot. I hope he has pictures of it. Of him and his sister and his dad and—

"Hey, where's your mom?" I ask, and I feel him stiffen beside me. "Sorry," I say quickly. "That's none of my business."

"No, it's fine. Last I heard, she was in New Mexico."

I don't know what to say to that. He doesn't sound sad. Just resolved to the reality of it. I bite my lip and focus my eyes on my pizza. I'm seconds from going back to my tiny room when he starts talking.

"She had an affair when I was in fifth grade. My dad found out and filed for divorce, but when my mom's lover wouldn't leave his own wife, she skipped town. I guess the idea of living in Franklin forever just wasn't enough for her."

I turn toward him and run my eyes over his face. I had no idea. I remember seeing his mom a few times at school when we were kids, and then nothing. I didn't know there was a divorce or that she left. I didn't know any of it.

"I'm sorry," I say honestly, and he bumps my shoulder with his.

"She'd have left either way."

The statement gives me pause. Not so much the meaning, but the way it's said. There's no anger. He's not harboring a grudge. In fact, I think the news pisses me off more than it does him. I'm livid on his behalf. I'm ready to track his mother down and give her a tongue-lashing for abandoning her ten-year-old son. To scream at her lover for breaking up a family. But for Chris? It's just something that happened to him once. Lake water under his grandfather's dock.

"What were you working on?" he asks, and I'm grateful for the subject change. "Don't lie and tell me it was campaign stuff."

I narrow my eyes at him and bite back a laugh.

"What makes you think it would be a lie?"

He holds my stare and arches a brow, and my laugh bubbles out of me despite my fighting it.

I don't know why I tell him the truth. Maybe part of me—a small, hidden part that's been getting louder the closer I get to the end—wants him to know that I'm not *all* Harper. I'm not just some old money, nepotism baby leeching off her trust fund. I'm not just an accomplice to evil deeds. I'm not just what everyone thinks I am.

I want to be so much more than that.

I want *him* to know that I'm more than that.

I want to be what he believes I am.

It gets lonely in the dark, and recently, I've been worried that if I hide too well, I won't be able to find my way back out.

"I do freelance writing," I confess finally, feeling like a brick has been removed from my chest. "Articles for journals and stuff, usually. Political commentary and op-eds. Some creative nonfiction. Sometimes I'll do contract work. Right now, I've got a project where I'm writing blog content for a business marketing firm. I enjoy it."

His white teeth sparkle in the moonlight as he smiles at me. I've shocked him in a good way, and I like this feeling. I want to do it more.

"Wow, Sam. That's really awesome. Have I read anything you've written?"

"Probably." I flit my eyes away and shrug. "I'm in the *Post* 'Politics' section almost weekly."

His jaw drops, and I watch as he pulls his phone out of his pocket and searches my name.

"You're not going to find anything searching Samantha Harper." I laugh. "You think I could get away with criticizing my father's politics while publishing under my real name?"

His eyes widen with surprise, his smile stretching over his whole face.

"You criticize your father's politics?"

I shrug it off, but it's a bigger deal than I let on. If my father knew, if the media knew, it would be chaos. My cover would be blown, and my plans would be ruined.

But I can't just sit by and stay quiet.

My silence would fester inside of me, and I would hate myself even more than I already do.

"Wouldn't you?" I ask flatly, and Chris holds my eyes.

He looks at me like he's searching for something—like I'm a puzzle he's trying to piece together—and as thrilling as I find it, it also scares me.

I look away.

"You have an alias?"

I nod.

"Sam Harper has an alter ego," he says playfully. "You're basically Batman."

The laugh that escapes me bounces off the lake and surrounding trees, echoing into the distance, and I slap my hand over my mouth and widen my eyes with surprise.

"It's fine." He chuckles. "We've got neighbors, but they're not that close."

I look around again. I can see houses and lights on the other side of the lake, but when I look from side to side, it's nothing but trees. His dock's on a little inlet, jutting off from the larger spans of water, and I feel...*safe*. Secure. Like it's just him and me right now, and nothing else matters. No one is watching my every move. No one is scrutinizing me. No one is expecting anything from me.

"Did you ever swim out here? When you were little, I mean."

"Yeah. All the time."

I smile to myself, then set my pizza and water on the dock beside me.

"Close your eyes," I say as I stand.

Instead of doing what I told him to do, he glances up at me with his lips pursed, fighting a smile.

"What are you doing, princess?"

I shrug and strip off my T-shirt. I feel his eyes on my chest and my nipples harden under my simple white lace bra.

"Going for a swim. Now turn around, Christopher."

I make a twirling motion with my finger, and slowly, he turns his back to me. I push off my shorts and underwear, nudging them next to my shirt with my foot, then I unclasp my bra.

"It's going to be cold," Chris says.

"I can handle the cold."

"It's deeper than it looks," he adds. "'Bout six to eight feet in the center."

I smirk to myself as I drop my bra onto my pile of clothes.

"I can handle six to eight."

His back shakes with a laugh, and then I jump.

The water envelops me, and he's right. It's cold. Colder than I was expecting, but it feels good too. I stay under the water for a moment, willing my body to adjust, and then I swim up. When I break the surface, I run a hand over my face, wiping away the lake water, and take a huge breath of the night air. When I open my eyes, Chris is standing at the edge of the dock with his arms folded across his chest. It's too dark to make out his features, but I can see his white teeth.

"Cold?" he asks, and I laugh.

"Yes. Very."

I dip back under for a moment, then float on my back so I can see the starry sky. I drift farther from the dock. Farther into the center of the inlet. My nipples are peaks, but every light breeze adds to the thrill, adds to the excitement and arousal. I've never skinny-dipped before. I should have done it sooner.

I feel Chris's eyes on me, so I tilt my head back to the dock. He's taken off his shirt and has his thumbs hooked into his shorts.

"Are you going to come in?" I call out, and he shrugs.

"I'm considering it," he says slowly. "I just don't know if I want to risk waking the alligator."

"What?" I shoot my knees to my chest, making my body smaller, and dart my eyes around. It's so dark. I can't see anything clearly. "Are you joking? You're joking."

"Haven't seen him in a while, but the neighbors have. He could be sleeping."

Oh, Jesus Christ. I am going to fucking kill him. If I don't get eaten by a goddamn alligator, I am going to murder Chris Casper.

I start to swim quickly back to the dock, my breaststroke rusty as hell, and I curse myself for not going to the pool more. I hear a crash of water behind me and swim faster. I feel the wake rushing over my body from the crash, and then I'm grabbed around the calves and jerked back. I scream and try to kick, try to throw an elbow, but my naked body is wrapped up, my arms pinned to my sides with a hard, warm chest pressed to my back. I freeze.

"There are no alligators in the Blue Ridge, princess. I thought you were smart? You think Georgetown will give you a refund?"

His chin rests on my shoulder, his soft lips brushing against my ear as he speaks, and despite my irritation, I shiver and sink into his hold. My heightened emotions, my racing heart, and the contrast of the heat from his body and the cold lake water sends my senses into a tailspin. Goose bumps cover every inch of my skin and my pussy aches.

"You're an asshole," I force out, still trying to catch my breath. "I should kick you in the balls for that."

His chest rumbles against my back as he laughs, but he doesn't let go of me, and I don't want him to.

"You're right," he says. "I should give you one free shot."

I hum and wiggle a little so he loosens his hold. I'm not angry anymore. Instead of swimming away from him, I turn in his arms, then wrap my legs around his waist so he's supporting us. Our bodies submerge a little more, only our necks and heads cresting the surface. His cock, thick and hard beneath me, rubs gently as he kicks his feet to keep us afloat.

"I don't think I want to kick you anymore," I say quietly, running my eyes over his face as his do the same to mine.

Lake water clings to his long eyelashes, glistening in the moonlight. My pale skin is stark next to his sun-kissed tan, cold meets warmth, light meets dark. We almost look like different beings. Polar opposites both inside and out.

I shouldn't want him this badly.

He's too good. Too kind. Too naïve.

"What do you want to do with me, then?"

Chris drops his eyes to my lips and keeps them there, as if he can hear my thoughts. Then his sister's voice flits in, and I almost flinch at the invasion.

*Harpers are not good people. You're too naïve to see that it applies to her.*
*You can't see past her pretty face. It will be Sable all over again.*

I fight the urge to push away from him. To drown myself in the truth of his sister's statements. But I'm stubborn. I won't let her ruin this moment with blunt honesty, so I shove her voice out of my head and fuse my mouth to his.

Our lips glide together flawlessly, aided by the lake water, and the warmth of his tongue caressing mine sends a tremor through me. I tighten my legs around him and he groans, deepening the kiss.

I slide my fingers to his hair, and we dip lower into the water. He breaks the kiss and presses his forehead to mine.

"How would you feel about moving this to the cabin?"

There's no mistaking the hint of hope in his voice, laced in every syllable of his deep rasp. It emboldens me. It makes me want him more. I nod, and he slowly starts to swim us to the dock. He stops at a ladder and takes one hand off me to grab it. Our bodies steady, so I know he can touch the bottom, but I don't untangle my legs from his waist.

"Close your eyes." I smirk, and he does.

I wait a few breaths, and he peeks one eye open. I arch a brow.

"No peeking."

His lopsided grin sends a spark of lust straight to my clit, then he closes his eyes again. I wait another few seconds to see if he'll peek, but when he doesn't, I let go of him and make my way up the ladder. When my feet are on the dock, I slip on his T-shirt and my sandals, then gather my clothes and his book in my arms.

"Okay," I tell him.

He opens his eyes and smiles when he sees what I'm wearing. He says nothing, though. Just makes a little twirling motion with his finger, so I turn around and give him my back. I hear the water sluicing off his naked body. I can imagine it. I bet he looks beautiful, all colorful tattoos and starlight. His clothing rustles. The waistband of his athletic shorts snaps. His sandals tap on the wood as he closes the distance between us.

Then gently, he gathers my hair away from my neck, his knuckles dragging over my still-wet skin, and his warm lips land on the sensitive spot where my neck and shoulder meet. It's soft and sexy, and it makes my core throb with need.

I sigh and lean my head back against him, and he takes my hand in his. Without speaking, I let him lead me to the cabin. When we get to the patio, he takes the book and clothes bundled in my arms and sets them on a lounge chair.

"Use the shower," he says roughly. "I'll get you a towel."

He kisses me again, this time on my lips, then he disappears into the cabin. I wait, and within seconds, he reappears with two fluffy towels.

"Do you want me to show you how to turn it on?" he asks, and slowly, I shake my head no.

Then, without taking my eyes off him, I grip the hem of his T-shirt and raise it over my body, exposing myself to him inch by inch until I'm dropping the shirt onto the lounge chair and standing naked before him. His eyes rove over me, every glance a sensual touch. My heart is threatening to burst out of my rib cage as I take a few steps toward him and slip my hands into the band of his shorts.

I smile shyly, suddenly more nervous than I have ever been, and push his shorts over his ass and down his thighs. When he's naked, I trail my fingers down his chest and abs. I revel in the way his body quakes under my touch, the way his eyes fill with heat. I trace the deep V of his pelvis, then wrap my hand around his hard cock and pulse the way I know he likes.

His answering groan makes my thighs sticky with arousal, and I moan when he leans down and takes my lips in a possessive kiss.

I want him.

I want him more than I have ever wanted anything in my entire life. Nothing before this moment exists, nothing after it matters. All I know is him, here and now.

For right now, in this minute, standing naked under the stars wrapped up in this man—this is my true north.

## SEVENTEEN

*Chris*

Slowly, I walk her backward toward the shower.

I don't break our kiss. I don't stop touching her, and she doesn't release me. She pulses her hand around my cock, squeezing my piercing, and I grow impossibly harder. I fist her wet blond hair in my hand and kiss her relentlessly until we're stumbling into the outdoor shower and I'm fumbling with the knob.

When the shower turns on and the water rushes over us, we both gasp. It's cold, but it warms quickly, and she presses her naked body closer until every inch of her front is covering mine. I use my hands to push her hair back off her face, kissing her lips and cheeks and neck.

I reach for the bottle of bodywash I brought and squeeze a little on my hand, and then I run my palms over her. I lather her up, taking care to soap every inch of her body. I caress her breasts and tease her nipples, then run my hand between her ass cheeks. I cover her in bubbles, then she reaches for the bodywash to do the same to me.

"Should I get you clean, filthy boy?" she teases as she soaps up my abs, moving to my ass cheeks before finally taking my dick in her hands again.

I grin and thrust into her grip, groaning at the way my piercing feels against her palms.

"Only if you'll let me dirty us up again after."

I spin us and move her back under the showerhead, and she giggles with surprise. It's the sweetest fucking sound. I slide my hands down her back and give her ass a squeeze before lowering myself to my knees in front of her. The cement bites into my skin, but I barely feel it. My awareness is focused solely on Sam's hands in my hair and the soft, needy whimpers I'm drawing from her. I kiss her pelvis, bite the soft flesh at her hips, then use my hands to push her thighs farther apart.

When I look up into her face, what I see captivates me. She's backlit by the moon and stars above as water cascades down around us, her blond hair almost shining in the darkness with an aura of starlit steam around her head. Like an angel's halo. Like a queen's crown. It makes my breath catch in my throat.

"You're gorgeous, princess," I whisper over her skin. "You are the most beautiful thing I have ever seen."

She brushes her fingers through my hair and smiles, but it's sad. Wistful in a way that breaks my heart.

"No." Her voice cracks. "You are."

She trails her fingers to my face and rubs her thumb over my cheek. Softer than I've ever seen her. A tenderness I'd never expect. I could stay here forever, on my knees, supplicating at her feet.

I press another kiss to her body, just above her pussy, and her eyes flutter shut. Gently, I kiss her clit before licking her thoroughly, tasting the arousal pooling between her thighs. I lap at her, tonguing her pussy before moving up to suck on her clit again.

"Oh fuck," she whispers to the sky, tightening her grip on my hair. "Oh, Chris. Please."

I lift one of her legs and drape it over my shoulder, baring her more to me.

"Fuck, you're perfect," I say, then blow lightly on her clit.

Sam sucks in a breath and tightens her hold on my hair. I press my knuckle onto her clit, then drag it through her pussy lips until I get to her entrance. Slowly, I slip my finger into her, and she hums before pushing against my hand for more.

"There's my greedy girl." I chuckle, blowing lightly on her clit again as I thrust into her with my finger. "You've got such a greedy little pussy, princess. This perfect, greedy little cunt."

I put a second finger into her pussy, and she moans, bucking against me.

"Patience, baby." I give her swollen clit a kiss. "Be patient, and I'll give you anything you want."

"I want your mouth on me," she rasps, so I lick her, making her whimper. "Yes, like that. God, I love your mouth."

I smile as I lick her again, thrusting my two fingers in and out of her as she writhes on me. I suck her clit into my mouth and hum around her.

"Oh, god, do that again," she says. "Do it again, please."

"Do I have the princess begging?" I tease. "A royal begging a peasant." I graze her clit with my teeth, and she sucks in another harsh breath. "I'm the one on my knees, but you're the one begging. I think I like that."

She opens her mouth to sass me, but I don't give her the chance. I thrust my fingers into her harder and take her into my mouth again. I flick my tongue faster, then swirl and suck in a torturous rhythm until she's quaking around me.

"You taste so good, baby. Your pussy is my new favorite thing to eat. I want you for every fucking meal."

I thrust my fingers into her, curving them to stroke her, and her body starts to bow.

"I'm going to come," she gasps out, and then she does, throwing her head back and arching against me until her legs start to shake.

Slowly, I remove her leg from my shoulder and set her foot on the ground, then I stand up and kiss her pouty lips. Her hands stay on me, twining up my shoulders and around my neck, and she kisses me back feverishly. Hungrily.

"I need you inside me," she says between kisses, "but I don't know if my legs will work yet."

I chuckle against her mouth, then grip her ass and lift her.

She wraps her legs around me on instinct, and the feel of her hot, wet pussy rubbing on my hard dick is enough to make me see stars. I turn off the water and we both gasp at the rush of cold air. I walk us out of the shower and Sam rests her head on my shoulder, kissing my neck and cheek softly. I wrap the towel around her back, then carry her into the cabin, stopping to grab the condoms I'd stashed in my duffle before taking her back to her room.

"Down," I whisper, and she releases me so I can set her back on her feet.

I toss the condoms on the bed, then take the towel from around her shoulders and dry her off, and she smirks at me as I work the water out of her hair.

"I could get used to this kind of treatment," she teases.

I hold her gaze as I reply, "You could."

The smile falls from her face and her brow furrows, but I don't say anything else. I just hold her eyes and continue to towel her off, and we don't speak again until we're both dry enough that we won't soak the sheets on her bed. I drop the towel on the floor and take a step back before nodding at the bed.

"Lie down, baby."

She does, sitting first on the mattress, then scooting back until she can lay her head on the pillows. God, she's fucking beautiful. My cock aches with the need to be inside her. To feel her come again around me.

"Bring your knees up and open your legs for me," I say as I stroke myself. "Nice and wide, princess. Give me a good view of that greedy little cunt."

She does what I tell her to, and fuck me, she's swollen and glistening. Perfectly pink and waiting prettily for me.

"Do you like what you see?" Sam asks, and I flick my eyes to her face in time to see her smirk at me. "Do you like knowing that I'm wet for you?"

God, her mouth. I nod, and then my eyes widen as she snakes

her hand down her body and cups herself, rubbing slowly on her clit before dipping her fingertips into her pussy.

"Greedy, greedy girl."

I stalk toward the bed and kneel between her spread legs, wrapping my hand around her wrist and bringing her fingers to my lips. I suck her index and middle fingers into my mouth, swirling my tongue around them, tasting her arousal, and licking her clean. I set her hand gently on the bed and lower my face to her pussy. I lick her once more, then grab a condom, tear open the foil, and roll it down my aching dick.

When I glance back at Sam, she's propped up on her elbows with her pupils blown wide, and her need for me is unmistakable. Without taking my eyes off her face, I grab my dick and slap her clit with it. She gasps, so I do it again, slapping the head of my cock against her clit before moving down to pulse at her entrance. As soon as my cock makes contact, her hips thrust, trying to force me in. I chuckle. I fucking love how eager—how unapologetically needy—this woman is for my cock.

In one smooth, steady motion, I push into her until I'm fully seated, and we both let out low moans of pleasure. She feels perfect. She sounds perfect. She *is* perfect.

"Holy fuck," she says, her pussy fluttering around my cock. "Is that your piercing?" She moves her hips in a circular motion, then groans. "Oh my god. It feels amazing."

I stay still as she moves on me, pulsing her hips and swirling them while she explores my dick. I want to tell her it feels even better without a condom, but I keep my mouth shut. I let her move until I can't handle it anymore, and then I take over.

"My turn."

I pull out slowly, then slide back in a few times before picking up pace, her breasts swaying with every thrust, and she bites her lip to stifle her moans. When I lower my body to cover hers, bracing myself on my forearms and grinding my pelvis against hers, she opens her mouth with a gasp, and I swallow it, taking her lips once more. Our tongues tangle, breaths mingling as we pant, and I start to move faster. Harder. I want to draw every ounce of pleasure from her body until she's spent. Every sound she makes—every whimper and gasp and moan—I want to hear, and I want to know she's making them because of me. *For* me.

When her nails bite into the flesh on my back, I groan against her.

"Mark me, princess." I press my face into her neck as I move inside her. "Scratch me up. I want to feel it. I want to see it for days just to remember this moment. The moment I made you scream with pleasure."

"You feel so good, Chris," she says. "I can't handle it, it's so good."

I bite her earlobe, then rise back up on my knees so I can hook her legs on my left side. When I bend her knees to her chest, her moan is guttural, and it's like a fucking trophy. Like a medal of honor I can wear around my neck. The way her eyebrows scrunch, the way her full lips part in ecstasy. I want those images burned into my brain. I want to see her face when I sleep. I want to hear her voice in my dreams. I twist my body, hitting her at a new angle, and she whimpers, clenching around me so tightly that I have to work to steady my breathing.

"Oh my god," she cries, arching her back and thrusting her hips in time with mine.

I feel myself approaching the edge of climax, but I don't want this to end. After this weekend, I don't know how long it will be until I see her again. Will it be days or weeks? Months? I'm not ready for it to be over, so I pull out and spread her legs, pushing her knees to her chest so I can feast on her pussy again.

"Chris. Fuck, Chris." She gasps, fisting her hands in my hair, pulling tighter as she comes again on my lips.

When I push my aching cock back into her, I kiss her so she can taste herself on me.

"I'm going to come soon," I tell her, pushing in as deep as I can and pulsing slowly.

Our sweaty, sticky bodies meld together, and she meets my

thrusts. I brush her hair back, cradle her face in my hands, and gaze at her. Fuck, she's beautiful like this. She's beautiful always, but especially like this. Raw and stripped down. No walls. No masks. Bare for me and only me.

When I come, it's with her mouth fused to mine, her legs and arms wrapped around me, and her name in my mind like a prayer.

---

I WAKE WITH SAM NAKED AND PLASTERED TO MY SIDE, AND FOR A moment, all I can do is stare at her.

She is the most beautiful thing I have ever seen. How long do I have her like this? How long do I get to keep her this time? I twirl the ends of her hair around my fingers, then softly trace her jaw and lips. She whimpers and tightens her hold on me, and I have to swallow back my laugh.

Slowly, I slide out from under her until she's snuggling with the pillow, and then I slip beneath the sheet. I maneuver her leg so it's bent up, giving me perfect access to her pussy, and then I kiss my way up her inner thigh until I am able to lick her freely.

The moment my tongue hits her, she groans and pushes back onto my face. I can tell the moment she wakes because she widens her legs farther and tilts her pelvis to give me better access. I press a kiss to her ass cheek and slip a finger into her pussy.

"Good morning," I say against her skin, and then I hook my hands around her waist and tug her up on her knees so I can eat her fully from behind.

"Holy shit," Sam says, and her fingers fist into the mattress.

When I move my mouth to the soft, sensitive flesh between her pussy and asshole, she yelps and jerks forward, falling face first into her pillow.

"Too filthy for you, princess?" I laugh, rubbing my fingers back through her pussy lips.

"You were *not* just going to eat my ass," she breathes out, staring at me over her shoulder with wide, shocked eyes.

I laugh some more. I feel like we're two kids in a poorly made blanket fort beneath this bedsheet, and it makes me feel fucking giddy. I press another kiss to her ass cheek and flash her a smirk.

"I was most *definitely* going to eat your ass." I start rubbing fast circles on her clit, and her eyes flutter shut. "But if you're not ready for that, I can make you come this way instead."

She nods and whimpers into her pillow.

"Yes. Please," she says, and in under a minute, she's coming on my hand.

"I can't walk," she whines, and I roll my eyes as I slip out from under the bedsheets and lie on the pillow next to her. "I'm never leaving this bed."

I don't say anything. I just run my gaze over her face until she gives me a sweet smile.

"I can feel you looking at me," she says, and I shrug.

"Stop being so pretty, and I'll stop looking."

She opens her eyes just so she can roll them at me, and then she sits up, letting the sheet fall to her waist, giving me a perfect view of the tattoo on her back. I realize of all the times we've been together, I've never seen her naked back. Even last night in the lake, I didn't get a good view. The artwork is breathtaking.

"Wow, Sam." I reach my fingers up to graze them over the image of Medusa inked onto her skin. Goose bumps trail her skin in the wake of my fingertips, but she doesn't flinch away. Instead, she leans into my touch. "How long did this take you?"

She'd said she had a tattoo on her shoulder, but this is much bigger than I expected. It covers half of her back, and the detail is impeccable, even down to the face on every single snake. I move her hair off her back and drape it over her shoulder so I can study the tattoo better.

"A couple of sessions," Sam says. "Maybe twelve hours total."

The tattoo is mostly grayscale, but the snakes are shadowed with various shades of green and gold, and Medusa is sporting dark red lips and ice blue eyes.

I blink and study the tattoo again, and then it hits me.

The tattoo of Medusa has Sam's face.

My throat tightens.

"Why Medusa?" I ask, and she glances at me over her shoulder.

"Strength. Protection. What better way to take down dangerous men than with the very monster they created?"

She stares at me for a moment more, then turns away. When she speaks again, I can hear the vengeance in her voice, and I bet her eyes are burning with rage.

"If I could turn them all to stone, I would."

We're quiet for a moment, and I trail my fingers over the tattoo once more.

"You're the picture of deception, you know that?" I say finally. "Polished, classy, refined. But underneath the gold jewelry and designer labels and high society manners, you're all fire and retribution. Like Nemesis. Like an avenging angel."

She shakes her head with a sigh.

"I'm hardly an angel, Chris."

I move on the bed so I'm facing her, taking in every one of her features as I speak.

"I don't know, princess. I'm not religious, but I think you're divinely made." I trail my knuckles down her cheek, then give her a teasing grin. "A face that could launch a thousand ships, anyway."

She rolls her eyes with a laugh.

"So I'm Helen of Troy now?"

I shrug.

"I would go to war for you."

The statement is said lightheartedly, almost jokingly, but something about it makes her wince, and the playfulness that was there before vanishes in a breath.

"I fight my own battles." She stands, gathers some clothes from her suitcase, and disappears out the door.

A minute later, the shower in the bathroom kicks on.

I lie back on the pillow and stare at the ceiling, not wanting to believe what my mind has put together, but the more I think it over, the more certain I am.

Sam didn't just tattoo Medusa from Greek Mythology onto her back. She tattooed a portrait of herself as Medusa, and I've read enough of Greek Mythology to know the story of Medusa.

Medusa was a mortal woman who was violated by a god and then punished for her pain. A victim who was made into a monster.

*The very monster they created,* Sam had said.

*What better way to take down dangerous men...*

I breathe slowly and deeply to calm the rising anger in my chest. The protective feeling swirling in my stomach.

That tattoo is more than just a tattoo. It's a symbol. It's a purpose.

And all I can think is, who hurt my princess and what is she planning to do to them?

## EIGHTEEN

*Sam*

As soon as the shower kicks on, I sink to the ground and drop my head into my hands.

*I would go to war for you.*

His statement echoes in my head, bouncing off the sides of my skull until it aches. I squeeze my eyes shut and press my fingers into my temples, trying to block out his words. Trying to erase the memory of them on his tongue. Trying to forget he ever said them at all.

I need to scream.

I need to knock some sense into myself.

I need to not feel *anything* for this man.

How? How did he get through my defenses? How does he always know what to say to unsettle my carefully crafted façade? How does he know which buttons to push? The most effective ways to seduce me?

How did I get here with him?

If it were anyone else, any other man, I would swear it was a game. A trick. An angle he's playing to get on my good side, or to get close to my father, or to gain access to the money attached to my family name.

But with Chris? I'm starting to believe he doesn't care about any of that, and that's the most terrifying thing of all.

I think of the way he touches me. Like I'm something precious.

The way he treats me. Like I'm something worth protecting.

And god, I want it to be true so badly.

*I would go to war for you.*

Every man I have ever trusted has let me down in some egregious way. In a way that has left permanent scars. Every single one. No man has *ever* fought for me. No man has *ever* seen me as something worth fighting for.

And now? Now, when I might have found someone who does, I don't deserve him.

When I feel tears leaking down my cheeks, I tell myself it's just the water from the shower. When I feel my heart breaking in my chest, I ignore it. I force away the truth—that I'm fucking falling for Chris Casper, and it hurts more than anything ever has.

He says he'd fight for me, but my fight is already promised for another, and I don't have the energy left for anything else. And when he finds out? He'll realize the person he sees in me is just a figment of his imagination. A side effect of his hopeless romantic state of mind. The woman he sees when he looks at me doesn't exist.

He wants to see the good in people, but there's no good to be found in me.

I stay in the shower for a few more minutes. Enough to stop my emotions from spiraling, but not enough to warrant concern.

It's just a shower, after all. Not an emotional breakdown.

I towel off and get dressed. I avoid looking in the mirror. I don't know if I could handle what I'd see. I don't particularly want to look at myself right now.

When I step into the hallway, I run right into Chris as he leaves the living room.

"Good, you're ready." He smiles, then shoves a folded blanket into my arms. "C'mon. We're going fishing."

My eyebrows scrunch together in confusion.

"I don't fish," I say, and he shrugs, his lopsided boy-next-door grin on full display.

"Grab a book from the shelf, then. But I told you I'd take you out on the boat, so we're going out on the boat."

He brushes past me without another word and leaves me staring at his back with the blanket in my arms. When the screen door shuts behind him, banging on the wooden frame, it jerks me out of my fog, and I hurry into my room to hunt down my sandals.

He's already at the boat dock by the time I catch up to him, and he has the wooden shed open and a little aluminum fishing boat in the water. It's little more than a bucket with a motor.

"That's your boat? It looks like it will sink if we both get in there."

He grins.

"It will hold up just fine. I've got a speed boat at the marina, but this one will work for now."

He pulls down two fishing rods from some hooks in the shed, then picks up a tackle box before setting it all in the tiny boat.

"I don't fish," I repeat, but he ignores me.

He steps into the boat, never losing his balance despite the way the whole thing wobbles back and forth, and then he holds out a hand.

"Give the blanket first, and then I'll help you in."

"What do we need a blanket for?" I ask as I hand it to him. "It's warm out."

He drops the blanket on one of the two little seats, then puts his hand out for mine.

"It's warm, but the breeze once we're on the water can get chilly. Give me your hand. I'll help you in."

I bite back the instinct to tell him that I don't need his help, and instead, I let him take my hand as I step off the dock and into the metal bucket. I mean boat.

"Get comfortable," he tells me, so I lower myself onto the tiny seat across from him and fold my hands in my lap while he starts up the engine with a loud rumble. "Ready?"

I nod, and he pushes us away from the dock and steers us out into the lake.

We don't go out far. We stick close to the shoreline, and Chris points out different houses. He was right. Some of these places are massive, and it surprises me that my father never wanted to buy a house here just for the status of it. From the looks of it, some of these places are multimillion-dollar homes. Then again, when I really consider it, I'm glad he hasn't. My father would ruin the peace. He'd suck the joy out of it.

Chris steers us into another inlet similar to the one near his cabin, but this one is nothing but trees and rocks and a sharp cliff. When he turns off the engine, I sit up straighter and look around.

"This is where we'll fish." He gets to work fixing up one of the fishing rods.

Mercifully, he doesn't urge me to grab the other one. And then my shoulders droop in disappointment.

"I forgot to grab a book."

He smiles, but he doesn't take his eyes off the fishing line he's messing with.

"Check the tackle box," he says.

I lean forward and turn the tackle box so I can see inside, and there, on top of extra fishing line and some little red-and-white bobbers, is his copy of *Walden*.

I don't speak. I just open the text and thumb through the pages, noting the flashes of yellow highlighter and pen and pencil margin notes. There are so many annotations. Plus, the spine of the paperback is broken and multiple pages look like they at one time were dogeared.

This is an example of a well-loved book, and it makes me eager to read it. To soak up a bit of whatever magic Chris and his grandfather have found within the pages. I spread the blanket over my legs because Chris was right and the breeze is a bit chilly, and then I sink back into the tiny seat, stretch my legs along the floor of the boat, and start the first essay.

It's a struggle.

While I'm no stranger to reading books with nineteenth-century rhetoric, I have difficulty with Thoreau's. The sentences are long and drawn out. The passages feel clunky. And as hard as I try not to, I can't help but read the tone of the text as if being spoken down to by a patronizing man.

This is why I prefer to read books by woman authors.

Am I prejudiced? Yes, I am. Do I care? No, I do not.

The only parts I find interesting are the highlights and margin notes that Chris and his grandfather made, but I don't give up. I'm plodding my way through the second essay when Chris laughs, and his foot bumps against my thigh. I look up to find him grinning at me from the other tiny boat seat.

"What?" I ask, and he laughs again.

"You look like you hate it," he says, and immediately I blush.

I feel bad. He loves this book. His grandfather loved this book. And I might be a bitch, but I'm not going to insult something he loves.

"No," I say quickly. "No, I don't hate it."

He shakes his head. He obviously doesn't believe me, but that lopsided, good-natured smile stays on his face.

"It's okay. It's very dense and parts of it really drag." He holds the fishing pole out to me and gestures for me to give him the book. "Trade me."

I stare at the fishing rod with distrust.

"I don't fish," I say, and he rolls his eyes.

"You won't be fishing. You'll just be holding the rod so I can read you some of my favorite parts."

My jaw drops, and my eyes sting. I blink quickly, grateful I'm wearing sunglasses, then clear my throat. Fuck, my heart aches.

"You want to read to me." I try for humor. I try to make a joke of it. But instead, I just sound...*young*.

Chris's smile falters, and his eyes scan my face before he nods slowly.

"Yeah, princess. I'd like to read to you."

I can't speak. I can't say anything for fear of crying, and when I hold the book out to him, I can't hide the way my fingers tremble. He either doesn't notice or doesn't want to embarrass me by bringing attention to it, and I'm certain it's the latter.

He hands me the rod, tells me how to hold it, and then lifts the end of the blanket and throws it over his own legs before settling back in his seat.

I turn my head toward the side of the boat so it looks like I'm watching the fishing line, but I keep my eyes on Chris.

When he starts to read, it's like a soothing balm has been applied to my muscles. With every passage, every sentence, my body relaxes, and I find a new appreciation for the text. Every so often, he'll even stop reading to tell me about his or his grandfather's thoughts on the passage, or to recite the annotations from the margins.

"This line here, *the sun is but a morning-star*, is why I got this tattoo." He sets the book down and lifts his shirt to show me the script and a sunrise on the side of his rib cage.

I smile.

"This book is that important to you," I say, and he nods.

"Some parts of it more than others, but yeah. I like the idea of wanting and needing less. Of enjoying time as it passes instead of dreading it. Of finding happiness in the simplest of things."

I pull my sunglasses off my face and hold his gaze for a moment. I take in his big brown eyes and thick lashes. The sincerity and kindness behind his soft smile. He's talented and humble and caring. He's the best kind of person, and it makes my chest tighten when I realize how much more beautiful he's become to me. Every minute I spend with him makes him more beautiful in my eyes, and I hate it. It scares me. If it continues, it will ruin me.

"I'm sorry for what I said about Sable," I say finally. "It was cruel, and I didn't mean it. I don't believe that."

His mouth tips up on one side.

"So you *do* know her name," he teases, and I roll my eyes and flip him off on instinct, making him laugh.

He grabs my ankles and props my feet onto his lap, then turns his attention back to the book.

"I told you I heard you loud and clear at my sister's, princess, but maybe you didn't hear me. You don't fool me. You can't hide from me. I see right through it."

He doesn't wait for me to respond before he starts reading again, and I'm grateful for that. I can't make sense of everything going on in my head. I feel like my heart's been riding on a rollercoaster, or like someone made me a passenger on a broken, ever-spinning tilt-a-whirl.

I want things I know I shouldn't want.

I long for the impossible, yet I find myself thinking maybe, just maybe, I can have it.

I want to laugh and cry at the same time. I feel joyful and frightened. I feel everything, and I can't understand any of it. It's been so long since I've felt even a whisper of attraction to someone. Even longer since I've been interested in spending time with a man. I feel all of that and more with Chris. I need to breathe slowly through the ache in my chest.

When we decide to quit for the morning—thankfully without a single fish sighting—Chris steers us to a local marina where we get sandwiches and listen to live music while watching people on jet skis in the middle of the lake. The whole time, I find myself stuck on two particular lines from *Walden*. Both from the book's conclusion. Both important enough to Chris that he'd highlighted them.

They war in my brain. They dominate my thoughts. I think too much, struggling to decode the omen within them.

*"Things do not change; we change,"* and, *"Rather than love, than money, than fame, give me truth."*

Can I change enough to give Chris the truth he desires?

I don't know.

But if things don't change, then how can I?

I turn to him on the boat ride back to the cabin and ask him a question that's been plaguing me since that night in his house during the thunderstorm.

"What if I don't have a true north?"

He tilts his head and looks me over as he considers my question.

"What do you mean?"

"Yours is your home. Your family," I say, fiddling with the hem of the blanket. "But what if I don't have one?"

Or worse, what if mine is cruel? What if it's something I'm ashamed of?

He grows quiet for a while, and I wonder if he's even going to answer, but then he speaks, and his tone is so encouraging, so full of hope, that it makes me want to cry.

"You have one, princess. You just have to let yourself find it."

---

I WAKE LEISURELY, NAKED AND TANGLED IN BEDSHEETS.

I stretch, noting the sun shining through the windows and the smell of bacon wafting into the room from the kitchen. I smile to myself. I'm alone now, but I wasn't. I haven't been all weekend, and from the warmth in the bed beside me, I'd say Chris only just woke up.

When I sit up, I find a piece of paper lying on the bed beside me next to a single white wildflower. My smile is so big, my cheeks hurt, and I pick up both the paper and the flower carefully. I bring the flower to my nose and inhale as I flip the paper over and read the familiar messy handwriting.

*for the princess*

Under the single scrawled line of script is a crude drawing of an alligator that makes me giggle like a fool, then I immediately blush when I remember our nighttime swim in the lake. I drop my face into the pillow and squeal, then I sit up and take a deep breath.

I need to calm down. I'm acting like a preteen with a crush.

I give my head a shake, then stand and pull on Chris's discarded T-shirt before tucking the note safely into my suitcase and threading the flower through my ponytail.

"Good morning," Chris says when I stroll into the kitchen. "Perfect timing."

He slides me a plate full of French toast and bacon, and my mouth waters.

"Good morning to you, too, and thank you."

I cut a piece and put it in my mouth, and I immediately sigh with happiness. I don't know how he's so good at this. So far everything he's made has been absolutely perfect.

"I have a surprise for you," he says, and I pop my eyes open to find him leaning on the counter with his arms crossed and a smile on his face.

"I get breakfast and a surprise?" I take another bite and don't even bother trying to tame my giddiness.

"Lennon should be here in"—he checks his watch—"fifteen minutes."

"Really!" I dart to my feet, excited to see my best friend. "Okay, I'm going to go put on some clothes." I hurriedly shove another bite of French toast in my mouth, then rush to the bedroom. "I'll be right back," I call behind me, and he chuckles to himself as I shut the door.

I slip on some shorts and a tank top. I dig through my toiletry bag for some lip balm but come up short, so I move to my handbag. As soon as I stick my hand in there, though, I freeze.

Fuck. My second phone.

I pull it out quickly and power it on. I'm supposed to check it twice daily—once in the morning and once in the evening—but I haven't looked at it since Wednesday night. I tell myself it's probably fine, usually the messages are empty anyway, but then my heart falls to my feet.

I have five messages, all with varying degrees of urgency, and the final is demanding that I make a phone call as soon as possible.

Quietly, I sneak down the hall and out the back door, and I press call on the only number saved. It only rings once. When Agent Sexton answers, I can hear the fury in her voice.

"Ms. Harper, where the hell have you been?" she seethes, and I bristle at her tone.

"I've been busy," I say. "It's only been two days."

"You are to tell us when you leave town. You are to check in every morning and every evening. These were the t—"

"I don't owe you every aspect of my life," I snap, cutting her off. "Jesus, Agent, it was two fucking days."

She takes a deep, irritated breath before she responds, and when she speaks, each word is like a lashing. I wince, and my shoulders cave inward as tears threaten to fill my eyes.

"Are you forgetting that *you* came to *us*, Ms. Harper? *You* sought *me* out. You requested my assistance because you aren't capable of achieving the desired results on your own, and in doing so, you agreed to do this my way. You said this was the most important thing. The *only* important thing. Has something happened? Has that changed in the last two days?"

I swallow hard and shake my head, blinking away the tears, willing them to disappear. She's ruthless. Unwavering and unforgiving. She'll stop at nothing to succeed, and that's exactly why I chose her.

"No. Nothing has changed," I force out, hating every syllable.

"Okay." Agent Sexton sighs. "Because there's been a development."

## NINETEEN
### Chris

I glance up from the sink full of soapy water just as Sam hurries to the door, dragging her brown-and-gold designer suitcase behind her.

"Whoa." I drop the plate back into the sink and dry my hands on my shorts as I rush out after her. "Whoa, hold up. What's going on?"

I grab her wrist and she stops walking, but she snatches her hand away from me, and my heart falls to my stomach.

"What's going on, Sam?" I ask again warily. "Where are you going?"

She's wearing her sunglasses, but I can tell she won't look at me.

"I'm having Lennon take me back to Franklin," she says quickly, glancing everywhere but in my direction. "I need to go."

"I don't understand."

"I've been here too long, Casper," she snaps. "I need to get back to civilization. I need good internet and a facial, and I have things to do. I can't hole up out here in the woods with you and ignore my real life any longer. I don't belong here."

I flinch, but I don't say anything right away. I blink slowly. I breathe deeply. Then I choose my words very carefully.

"What happened in the last ten minutes, princess? Is everything okay?"

"Stop fucking calling me that," she says, her voice cruel. "I have a name. It's Samantha. Use my fucking name."

My head is spinning. I can't get my bearings. I don't understand what's happening. I feel like everything is slipping through my fingers, like the bubble that had been keeping us safe all weekend has popped and I'm plummeting to the ground.

"You didn't mind me calling you princess before…"

It's the only thing I can think to say. I'm grasping for clues.

"That was before it started to sound like a term of endearment."

Her voice cracks on the words, showing me the first fissure in her façade, and I shake my head. I take a step closer. I slide my hand to her neck and rest my fingers on her pulse point, then press my forehead to hers. Her muscles are so tense, her inhales and exhales shaky. She's coiled so tightly I'm worried she'll snap.

"Okay," I whisper. "Take a deep breath. Whatever happened, we can work through it together."

She's quiet for a moment, and for a fraction of a second, she leans into me. A brief moment of tenderness, of surrender before she steps back, widening the distance between us, and my hand that was holding her drops empty to my side.

Sam clenches her teeth and sniffs. Every ounce of real emotion that I felt flowing from her a breath earlier disappears. And then she laughs. I can tell she's going for cruel, but I hear the sadness there, and then I remember Macon's words from just days earlier.

*Her bite fucking hurts, but her bark is worse. And usually the nastier she is, the closer you are to something she's trying to protect.*

"The only thing that happened is that I've grown tired of this," she says pointedly. Regally. "I'm bored. I need Pilates. I need brunch that isn't swimming in grease. I need air conditioning, a professional massage, and conversation that doesn't put me to sleep. I need to go back to D.C. where I belong, and you may remain here."

Her thinly veiled insults almost land how she intended—right to my chest—and each one threatens a blow to my confidence. My last conversation with Sable tries to gain attention, followed by my sister's words at the birthday party, and I have to grit my teeth against the force of it all.

*Can't see past her pretty face.*
*Sable all over again.*
*You're too naïve.*

Sam has me in a cyclone and I can barely keep my feet on the ground. A big part of me knows for certain that something is wrong, and this is just her tried and true method of self-defense. But another part is still trying to recover from her expertly crafted blow.

The sound of tires on gravel brings me out of my spiral, and I glance up to see Sam hurrying toward Macon's car. Macon strides toward me as Lennon and Sam exchange words. The concern on Lennon's face and the slight droop of Sam's shoulders are what set my feet in motion.

I go straight to my truck and open the driver's side door, then dig through the center console for the small, black velvet bag. I look up to see Lennon climb into the driver's seat of Macon's car and Sam in the passenger seat. When Lennon cranks the engine, I bolt to the car and bang on Sam's window.

She jumps but won't look at me.

"Roll down the fucking window, Sam."

Lennon whispers something to Sam, then flicks her eyes to me. I can't read them, but I release a sigh of relief when Lennon reaches to the window button on the door. Sam's window rolls down, but she still doesn't acknowledge me. She says nothing. She doesn't even look at me. Her designer sunglasses stay pointed at the windshield.

It's fine. She can listen.

"You can be as vicious as you like, princess, but I told you I'm not falling for it. I've got a thicker skin than you're used to. Your bite may bruise, but it doesn't cut. I don't know what happened, but I know whatever this is has nothing to do with you and me. When you finally admit it to yourself, I'll be waiting."

"There is no you and me," she whispers.

I don't say anything. I don't argue. I just reach into the window and drop the velvet bag into her lap.

"A gift. For your true north." I look at Lennon. "Drive safe, Len."

I walk back to where Macon is standing with a stick of licorice hanging from his mouth. I can hear Lennon put the car in drive and disappear down the gravel lane.

"So," Macon says around his licorice. "You want to stay, or you want to head back?"

I look back toward the cabin and my heart clenches in my chest. I can't go back in there right now. I can't sleep in that bed.

"Let's head back," I say, and Macon nods.

He helps me pack the contents of the fridge into the cooler and clean up, then I turn off all the lights and lock the doors. On the drive back to Franklin, Macon and I don't speak. He plays music from his phone, and when we get back to town, I go straight to his apartment above the community rec center.

I park my truck, and we head inside to the rec center gymnasium. Macon tosses me a pair of boxing gloves and then flashes a grin.

"Loser buys dinner."

---

IT'S BEEN A WHILE SINCE I'VE LAST HEARD FROM SABLE.

Not a whisper since she "accidentally" tagged me in her social media post almost two months ago.

In the weeks after she turned down my proposal, I would find myself wondering how I would react if I ran into her. Would it hurt? Would I be angry? Would I want her back? Would *she* want *me* back? I could never decide. I was never sure just how much damage she'd done.

When I see her car pull up to the garage on the morning of my shift, though, I get my answer: *Annoyed*.

All I feel when I see her is *annoyed*.

"Chris," she calls as she steps out of her car. "Hi! Hi, Chris!"

"Hi, Chris, hi!" one of my coworkers whisper-mocks, and I flip him off as I walk to where Sable is now standing at the garage door.

"All service appointments need to be booked at the service desk, Sable."

I grab a towel off a nearby tool cart and wipe some grease off my hands. I don't bother washing them for her, though. I don't care what she thinks.

"If you head inside those doors, someone will be right with you."

She smiles and slides her sunglasses to the top of her head.

"I was actually hoping to talk to you," she says.

I note the way she's made her voice kind of low and raspy. Like she's trying to be sexy. Trying but failing. Did this use to work on me?

What the fuck does she want?

"I'm at work," I clip. "So if you aren't here for an oil change or a new set of tires, it is going to have to wait."

I turn to walk away, but she clamps her hand down on my bicep, halting me in my tracks.

"Baby," she coos, "just give me a minute, okay? I just want to talk."

I face her, and she beams. It does nothing for me.

"How are you? How have you been? How are Luke and Lucy? I saw Tiffany posted pictures of their birthday party. I'm sad I missed it."

"They had a good time," I say slowly.

"That's good. I wish I could have been there."

We fall back into awkward silence. She continues to smile and blink at me as if she's waiting for me to say something, and it's just...weird. It's fucking weird, and I don't have the patience for it.

"Sable, I don't have time for small talk, okay? We got cars scheduled all the way up to closing, so if you're here for something, just say it so I can get back to work."

Her smile grows strained, and she lets out an irritated little laugh.

"I saw Samantha Harper is coming back around," she says.

I arch a brow, but I don't say anything. She blinks again.

"In Tiffany's pictures online? Samantha Harper was there at the birthday party with you."

"Okay...?"

"So you guys are all close again? Like, Lennon and her are friends, right?"

I furrow my brow and nod. I can't figure out where she's going with this.

"Yes, Sam and Lennon are friends, but we all went to school together. I've known Sam since kindergarten."

I state the information even though I know Sable already knows. We had multiple conversations about Sam when Sable and I first started dating. She was jealous of Sam, and even after Sam stopped coming around entirely, she was still a point of tension in our relationship.

I'll admit that Sable was right to be jealous at first. Hell, my initial attraction to her was that she looked and acted a bit like Sam. Her hair wasn't as blond. Her lips weren't as red. She wasn't as, I don't know, queen-like. She wasn't Sam, but she was similar, and she soothed the ache of Sam's rejection.

I let it go too far. I know that now. But after a while, I thought I was in love.

I was wrong.

Looking at Sable today, though, I can't seem to find a single similarity between her and Sam. Sam has something that Sable doesn't. My heart.

"So are any of you going to the gala, then?" Sable asks, trying to sound casual and failing.

I know it's a trap, but I walk into it anyway.

"What gala?"

Her lips turn up at the sides, her pink gloss popping in the sunlight, and as she speaks, she looks predatory and fake. She looks nothing like the girl I fooled myself into thinking I loved.

"The fundraising gala that her father, Senator Thom Harper, is hosting next month? It's supposed to be huge. Five thousand a chair. Anyone who's anyone is going to be there."

Ah. There it is. Now it makes sense.

"Well, Sable, I guess none of us are anyone because we are not going."

Not to mention, no one I know would be caught dead willingly attending anything in support of Senator Harper. That includes Sam, with emphasis on *willingly*. I turn to leave, and she grabs my wrist again.

"That's a shame, but it's not really your scene, is it? I was thinking, though, since you're friends with her again—you know, now that we broke up and it's fine—that maybe you could talk to her about getting a ticket or two? I'd love to attend that gala. We could even go together if you want? I'm a very big fan of her father's, you know. And of the Cartwright family—"

"The who?"

"The Cartwrights, Chris." She lets out a condescending laugh. "Judge Cartwright and his son Ashton?"

When the confusion doesn't leave my expression, Sable sighs.

"I swear, it wouldn't kill you to socialize outside of your...*circle*," she mumbles. "Ashton Cartwright is Senator Harper's campaign manager. Judge Cartwright is a family friend of the Harpers. They will be in attendance at the gala."

The fact that she came to my work in the middle of my shift and interrupted my day to ask for a favor but *still* has the audacity to act like she's irritated with me is what kicks the little patience I'd had left right over a cliff. I close my eyes and release a slow breath.

"Sable. I will not be getting you a ticket to Senator Harper's gala. Even if I could, I wouldn't, so I'm sorry that you wasted my time. Now leave before I have Bobby spray you with the water hose."

She lets out a loud, offended gasp as I walk away, but I don't look at her. I don't turn around at all. Not even when her car door slams and her tires squeal out of the parking lot.

"Dude, I'm so glad you're not dating her anymore," my coworker Andre says.

"For real. She was a total bitch," Bobby agrees with a nod. "I was really hopin' I'd get to hose her."

I bark out a laugh, and he winks.

"I was gonna use the gun," he adds, holding up the high-pressure hose attachment that we usually use for cleaning tires.

Everyone in the garage hoots and hollers at that, and my cheeks hurt from smiling.

I shake my head.

"Keep it on hand just in case she circles back," I tell him, then head back to my work.

I didn't lie when I said we had cars scheduled all day. It keeps me busy even through lunch. But later that night, after one too many shots of expensive fucking bourbon, I do an internet search on Ashton Cartwright.

Prep school student. Princeton graduate. Rich as fuck.

When I find a picture of him with Chase Harper at some exclusive restaurant in D.C., I hate him on principle. But then I find a picture of Ashton with Sam at the same event. According to a caption, it was some sort of dinner party for her father. It's dated the week of my niece and nephew's birthday, right before I took Sam to the lake, and Ashton looks to be practically glued to Sam's side.

They are both smiling, and he has his hand wrapped around her waist. But while Ashton's smarmy smile is directed at Sam, Sam's smile is forced. Her eyes are tired and angry, with no joy to be seen.

I look her over.

She's wearing a formfitting long-sleeved black dress and tall, black heels. Her hair is in a low bun, and on her neck is a thick string of diamonds. Then I realize that's what Ashton Cartwright must be smiling at. Not at Sam, but at the necklace around her neck.

I know immediately he gave it to her. I know it in my fucking gut that Ashton Cartwright gave Sam that flashy-ass necklace of diamonds, and I can't help but laugh a little at myself.

The necklace I gave her can't even compare.

Sam's got fuckers like Ashton Cartwright spending hundreds of thousands of dollars on a piece of jewelry for her, and what do I have to give? A beat-up truck and a worn, hand-me-down copy of *Walden*. A cheap, tarnished necklace my grandmother got from a department store sixteen years ago. A small house, two jobs, and a heart that's too fucking soft.

I click my phone off and set it beside me, then drop my head to the couch.

She wasn't smiling with him, though. That's what I tell myself. It wasn't her real smile. It wasn't the smile I can draw from her. That matters more than the cost of the jewels on her neck. It matters more than the money he has in the bank or the power attached to his last name.

Sam would never be happy with someone like Ashton Cartwright.

But she would be happy with me.

## TWENTY

*Chris*

The apartment above the bar stays dark. My phone never rings.

I suppose that shouldn't surprise me. Sam and I have never texted or talked on the phone. She's always just breezed in whenever she wanted and left when it was convenient for her. I heard from Macon that Sam came down for Lennon's birthday, but I never saw her.

As the weeks stretch on, it feels like last time, but worse.

The last time she disappeared without a word, it was right after she put a stop to our heated encounter in my truck, and I didn't harbor any hope for a redo. My pride was hurt, and I was fucking horny, but I wasn't heartbroken.

This time, though. This time is different. I'm not being naïve. I'm not being fooled by rose-colored glasses. This heartache is real. This longing, bone-deep and ever-present, is real. And this time, it's painfully fucking obvious.

I am in love with Samantha Harper.

My cold queen. My avenging angel.

That's why, when I see her car in the bar parking lot a month later, I don't hesitate to text Paul and ask him to cover my shift. The moment he shows up and takes over the bar, I leave through the back exit and head up the stairs.

She opens her door after the third knock, and her unfeeling eyes drag down my body as I lean on her doorframe with my arms crossed.

"I didn't order a maintenance check," she says, voice bored.

I smirk even though it hurts, then I step past her and into her living room. As I expected, she has her little writer's nest set up on the couch.

Laptop, notebooks, water bottle, snacks.

I study the plate full of cheese, crackers, and some unwrapped dark chocolate squares.

"Let me guess." I reach down and snag a chocolate square. "Dinner?"

I pop the chocolate in my mouth and chew as she glares at me from her spot at the door. She doesn't have to say it. I can hear it in my head. *I'm eating it at dinner, so it's dinner.* I smile, and she narrows her eyes.

"Why are you here?" she asks with an annoyed sigh.

I shrug and choose to go with honesty.

"We said goodbye on bad terms at the lake. I wanted to make sure you were okay."

She waves her hand dismissively, then gestures to the door.

"I'm great. You may leave now."

I cock my head to the side and do a once-over. She looks like she just got out of the shower, with her hair wet and twisted into a clip. She's wearing another pajama set and her face is free of makeup. She's sickly pale. Her lips are chapped. She appears thinner. The circles under her eyes are a dusty purple. There's no sparkle in her blue irises. When I zero in on her nails, they are perfectly polished, but her cuticles look red and swollen, like she's been picking at them.

She's a ghost of who she was at the lake.

She looks how she did at my sister's, but five times worse.

"You're a good liar, princess," I say slowly, closing the distance between us. "But I told you before. I'm not fooled."

"Get out of my house, Casper," she says through her teeth.

"Have you been sleeping? Have you been eating?"

She doesn't answer. She won't make eye contact. A muscle in her jaw pops as she grinds her teeth.

"What the fuck are they doing to you up there?" My voice shakes from the restrained anger and worry. "You're wasting away. Is it drugs? Are you—"

"I'm not on fucking drugs," she snaps, finally looking at me. "Christ, just leave me alone. I am not your concern!"

"You are my concern."

"I'm not!"

"You *are*, Sam. You are my concern because I've made you my concern."

"Why?" she shouts, eyes welling with tears. "Why, Chris? I don't need you. I don't need you worrying about me. Stop. Just stop."

"I can't," I shout back. "I can't. I *care* too much to just stop. I care about you, Sam. You're going to have to fucking accept it because I'm not going anywhere, and I know you care about me, too."

She closes her eyes and shakes her head quickly. I know she's fighting like hell to keep the tears from falling.

"I don't," she says shakily. "I don't care about you. I don't."

"Another lie," I murmur, then reach up and hook my finger in the collar of her pajama top, tugging it open just enough to reveal what I hoped I would find.

She's wearing the necklace I gave her before she left me at the lake.

The chain is cheap and thin, and the small brass compass is tarnished, but it shines like gold against her skin. It looks like she's polished it or had it cleaned since I dropped the velvet bag in her lap and she drove off without me.

My grandmother gave this necklace to me when I was a kid because I loved my grandfather's compass so much. I wore it every day for years until the clasp broke, and once I got it fixed, I kept it safe in that little velvet bag. It's been in my truck with me since I was sixteen, and seeing it around Sam's neck fills me with more emotions than I can identify.

I put my index finger under her chin and tilt her head up so I can look into her face. Her eyes stay clamped shut with silent tears sliding down her cheeks.

"Look at me," I say, and she shakes her head. "Look at me, princess. Please."

When she finally does, hitting me with red-rimmed eyes glistening with tears, it's like a knife to the stomach. She looks lost. She looks scared. She's hurting, and all I want to do is fix it.

"Stop lying to me. Talk to me. Let me help."

Her face crumples, then, and she starts to sob outright. I pull her body against mine and hold her. I walk us backward until I can sit on the couch and pull Sam into my lap and cradle her against my chest. I rub my hand in soothing circles on her back and press soft kisses into her hair. She smells like floral shampoo and bodywash, and I want to breathe her in.

"Talk to me, baby, please. Please, just talk to me."

She buries her face in my shirt and shakes her head.

"I can't," she whispers. "I can't. I want to, but I can't."

It's not what I want to hear, but it's something. It's an admission. It's a crack in her armor. She's letting me in.

"But something *is* going on, though?"

She hesitates briefly, and then she nods.

"Are you in danger? Are you being hurt?" I ask quickly, and her body tenses right before she shakes her head. "That's a lie, Sam."

She presses her face against my neck and inhales and exhales deeply before speaking.

"There *is* something going on, but I can't talk about it. It's...*precarious*...and I can't take risks. I'm not in any real danger, but I'm drained. I'm not sleeping well because I'm stressed, and I'm trying so fucking hard to just make it to the end, but I'm exhausted. I just...God, I just need a respite. A moment of peace. I need a breather. I need to recharge before I have to dive back in headfirst."

My heart fucking breaks at the pain in her voice and the way she's trying to push through it. My strong, courageous, warrior princess. She's so accustomed to fighting alone.

I smooth her hair back and cup my hand around her neck. I kiss her forehead, willing my pulse to sync with the one thrumming against my fingers, then lean back just enough to catch her gaze and hold it.

"I know you want to fight your own battles. Fine. Then let me be your peace. Let me be your place to rest."

Her bottom lip trembles and I rub my thumb over it as more tears fall. Even broken, she's beautiful.

"You don't have to do everything alone," I whisper, then take her mouth with mine in a soft kiss. "Let me be your peace."

When her lips glide over mine, I taste the salt from her tears. She doesn't agree, but more of her wall has come down. I've earned the removal of another mask, and that's good enough for now. When she opens her mouth for me, tangling her tongue with mine, she whimpers and pulls me closer. I try to go slowly, to be gentle, but she deepens the kiss and moves to straddle my waist.

"We don't have to do that." I put my hands on her hips and halt her movements. "I just want to be here for you."

"I know," she whispers, pressing another kiss to my lips before climbing off my lap and rising to her feet in front of me. "Then be here."

Slowly, she unbuttons her top, then slides it down her arms and drops it on the floor. She's not wearing a bra underneath, so she's standing before me in just a tiny pair of silk shorts, and my dick aches with need for her. I reach down and palm my cock through my pants, pulsing at the piercing.

Sam swirls her fingers around her nipples and smiles softly. Then she walks toward her bedroom, and like I'm tethered to her, I follow.

When we're feet from her bed, I scoop her up into my arms and lay her out flat on the mattress, then I strip her shorts off so she's on full display for me.

"Take off your clothes." She moves her fingers to her nipples once more. "I want to see you."

I take my shirt off and drop it onto the floor, followed quickly by my jeans and boxer briefs. Sam's eyes zero in on my cock, and I wrap my hand around it and stroke once. She whimpers, and I do it again.

"You like that?"

She nods, then snakes her hand down her stomach and teases her clit. I squeeze and stroke myself some more, and her fingers dip lower.

"Show me my greedy little cunt, baby. Spread your legs wide for me."

She does, and fuck me, she's already wet. Her eager little clit is swollen and ready for me. I stroke myself again, and Sam moans. The sound is torturously sexy.

"Where are your toys, princess?"

Her eyes widen at me, and I smirk.

"I want to play."

"Top dresser drawer," she says almost shyly. "In the black box."

I stalk to her dresser and open the top drawer, then take out the black box. I carry it to her bed, set it on the comforter beside her, then open it to find two vibrators, a dildo, and some lube.

I flick my eyes to hers.

"What's your favorite?" I ask, and her lips twitch into a smile as a pink blush colors her cheeks and chest.

"The purple one," she says, so I reach in the box and pull out the tiny purple vibrator.

I click it on, and it buzzes to life. I lower the vibrator and tease one of Sam's nipples, then the other, and she starts to wiggle her hips in anticipation. I drag the toy to her belly button, then up and down her inner thigh.

"Do you want to show me how you do it, or do you want me to just explore?" I ask, reveling in the way her breaths have quickened, and her face has flushed.

I drop my eyes to her pussy and find it glistening. I have to take my cock in my hand again and squeeze, pulsing on my piercing then stroking a few times to relieve the ache.

"You do it," Sam says, and I flash her a grin before bringing the toy to her clit. "Oh, god," she moans, gripping at her breasts and teasing her own nipples as her body arches.

I lower myself to the bed and lick her once before shoving my tongue into her pussy while the vibrator teases her clit. She moans and jerks, and I lick her again, removing the toy so I can suck her clit into my mouth.

"Oh *fuck*, Chris," she cries out.

"I love hearing you moan my name." I bring the vibrator back to her clit, then spit on her pussy before slipping two fingers inside her. "Fuck, princess, you're choking my fingers. You like when I play with your clit like this? When I fuck you with one of your toys?"

"Yes, yes."

She jerks again, moving her pelvis so she can fuck herself on my hand, and my dick is throbbing so badly that I have to press my own pelvis into the mattress for relief. I scissor my fingers inside her cunt, feeling her clench around me, and then I click the button on the vibrator, raising the settings.

Her groan is low, almost pained, and she moves faster on my hand.

"That's right, princess, fuck my hand like that. Fuck my fingers until you come."

She does. She moves on me while I finger-fuck her and hold the vibrator mercilessly onto her clit, until she shatters with a scream. The moment she catches her breath, I put the vibrator in her hand.

"You hold this on your clit. Don't take it off until I tell you to."

Then I flip her onto her stomach and pull her up to her knees, so her ass and pussy are gloriously on display for me. I slap her ass once and she whimpers. I chuckle. How did I know the princess would like to be spanked?

"Put your toy on your greedy little clit, princess."

When she does, she hums in pleasure and her whole body shudders. For a moment, I just have to stroke my cock and stare. She's positioned almost like she's trussed up, with her ass in the air and her hand holding the vibrator between her legs. My bright red handprint mars the pale skin of her ass, and her pussy is swollen and dripping wet for me.

I lower myself to the bed and eat her pussy from behind. I knead her ass cheeks with my hands as I tongue her cunt, and she moans into the mattress. When I ease my tongue higher, she flinches, but she doesn't stop me like she did at the cabin. I massage my tongue over the sensitive flesh between her pussy and asshole until she starts to whimper, then I move higher and swirl my tongue around her tight ring of muscle. She groans, low and guttural, and pushes herself into my face, eager for more. I lick her up and down, then I thrust two fingers back into her pussy.

"Oh my fucking god," she cries out, and her pussy pulses around my fingers.

"My filthy princess likes when I eat her ass, doesn't she? Look at what a mess I've made of you." I start to thrust my fingers faster. "Turn the toy up one more, baby."

She hesitates and I smack her ass again.

"Turn up the vibrator and come on my face, princess."

When she does, I devour her. I lick and suck and thrust my fingers, moving from her ass to her pussy hole until she starts to quake. When she comes, it's with a full-body spasm and an animalistic cry that almost coaxes my own orgasm.

She drops the vibrator onto the bed, and I grab her hips with my hands and shove my cock into her pussy from behind. We moan together, and my vision whites out before I realize exactly why it feels so fucking good.

I pull out immediately and step back.

"I forgot a condom. Do you have any?"

Sam pushes up onto her forearms and looks over her shoulder at me. Her face is red and sweaty, and her blond hair is sticking to her skin, and it just makes me want her more.

"No," she pants out. "I don't have any. But I'm on birth control and have a clear bill of sexual health. You?"

"Yes to the clear bill of health." I nod.

"Good, then it's settled." She drops herself back to the mattress and widens her legs a little more. "No condom. Now fuck me. Please."

I chuckle at the tacked on please, but I don't make her tell me twice. I push into her in one thrust, and fuck, it's absolute perfection.

"Your piercing," she gasps out. "Holy shit."

I slap her ass and move faster, pressing my palm into her lower back to keep her steady. When she starts throwing back against me, I fold myself over her and snake one of my hands between her legs.

She hisses and shoots her own hand back, snatching mine around the wrist.

"Too sensitive," she breathes out. "It's too sensitive."

"Okay, princess. I'll go easy on you this time."

I slide in and out of her slowly and press a kiss to the middle of her back. I hit her as deep as possible and pulse inside her, feeling every single flex of her inner muscles. When I feel like I'm getting close, I pull out and put her on her back so I can sink into her while looking into her eyes.

She wraps her legs around my waist, threads her fingers into my hair, and kisses me deeply. Every inch of her is wrapped tightly around me. There's not a single part of our bodies that's not touching in some intimate way, and I'm reveling in it. In the connection and lack of space between us. Her skin hot against mine. Her breath on my neck. Her mouth on my mouth. I can feel her heart pounding in her chest from how it's pressed against mine. Our hearts thrum together, and I want to keep her here. Every heartbeat repeats it.

*Keep her, keep her, keep her.*

"I understand why this is your favorite now," she says against my lips.

I smile.

"Yeah? Why's that."

She tightens her hold on me and meets my slow thrusts, and what I see in her eyes makes my heart race faster. I know she can feel it.

"I like kissing you while you're inside me," she whispers finally, so I kiss her.

I kiss her slow and deep, so our kisses match our sex, until I'm certain we're not just fucking anymore. She asks me not to pull out, and when I come inside her, I have to bite my tongue to keep from saying what's at the forefront of my mind.

*I love you.*
*I love you.*
*I am in love with you.*

## TWENTY-ONE

*Sam*

I'm getting too comfortable waking up naked and wrapped around Chris Casper.

I know this, but right now, I can't bring myself to care.

Instead, I hold him tighter and snuggle further into him, wishing I could melt and be absorbed by him, so I cease to exist without him. The idea of never having to be alone again is intoxicating. The idea of always being with this man? It's too good to be true.

When my phone alarm goes off at five thirty, I hit snooze quickly, but Chris wakes up anyway.

"Why are you getting up this early?" he rumbles into my hair.

I kiss his chest before speaking.

"I have to go back to D.C. today." I try to hide the sadness in my tone. "I've got a lot of work to do."

He starts dragging his fingers up and down my side, the touch so soft and gentle that it makes my heart ache. I don't want to leave this bed.

"It's Saturday," he says. "You drove down even though you had to head back in twelve hours?"

I laugh, a little embarrassed, and nod.

"I just needed to get out of D.C. for a bit," I whisper.

My voice cracks, but he doesn't comment on it. He just wraps his arms around me and holds me tighter against his chest.

Memories of last night flash through my mind, and I swallow back the shame I want to feel. It doesn't matter that I trust Chris fully. It doesn't matter that he coaxed it out of me, that I felt safe enough with him to be honest. The idea of being vulnerable with a man fills me with immediate anxiety on instinct, and it's a trauma response I unfortunately can't unlearn overnight.

It's one that I probably will still need to rely on for a little while longer.

"Do you have to go back?" he asks hesitantly. "Is it that important?"

I clamp my eyes shut and breathe.

"Yes. Yes, I have to go back."

We fall back into silence, but he doesn't release me. I keep my head on his chest and listen to his heartbeat, strong and steady, just like him. I will my heart to follow suit, to mirror his, so that I can draw from his strength. Mine feels depleted.

"How long until you'll be back?"

"A couple of weeks, probably."

I take a deep breath and work on stacking bricks back on my mental wall. Not to keep Chris out, but in preparation for everything that's coming.

"My father has a big fundraising gala coming up, and we have to travel for a few campaign rallies. It's going to be exhausting."

My father is polling well. It's not a surprise. The media declared him the winner of the candidate debate last week, and while no one will admit it, it's because Ashton has been pawning off more responsibilities on to me and I was able to rework all of my father's talking points. I'm sure his upcoming rallies will be one big voter circle-jerk. At this rate, there's no doubt that he'll win the primaries.

If he makes it, anyway.

I try not to consider it. It will be a long, miserable campaign if things don't work out for me. Or maybe it won't be. I guess there's no reason to stick around if all my plans fall apart. And really, the idea of leaving it all behind and living in peace with the people I really care about is becoming more tempting than anything else.

Even if everything falls apart after today.

Even if I have to amend my end goals and accept a less than ideal outcome.

At least I'll still have Lennon. I think I'll still have Chris. And it won't be in a world where my father is president.

"You can call me, you know," he says, pulling me from my thoughts. "Or text. If you want to talk. I wouldn't mind."

"Okay." I try to calm my smile.

The idea of having phone dates with him makes me feel giddy. It makes the upcoming stretch of weeks in Washington seem a little less daunting. The promise of a moment of peace amid the chaos.

"When do you have to be on the road?" he asks.

"An hour."

He nods, then snakes his hand between us and rubs my clit. My breath hitches and my eyes fall shut at his touch.

"Then let's make good use of the time," he whispers, then takes my lips in a deep kiss that turns my blood molten.

Chris hikes my leg up onto his waist, and then slowly, he pushes into me. We both sigh, our foreheads pressed together. I'm ready for him. I'm always ready for him. I just refused to admit it to myself until now. I didn't want to acknowledge my want for him, so deep and insistent it borders on need, but it's impossible to ignore. It's always there, coiled in my chest, wrapped tightly around my heart, waiting patiently. Loyally. Waiting for him.

Slowly, he moves his hips, fucking me slow and deep in a way that makes me feel everything all at once.

Cherished. Special. Precious. *Loved.*

My heart thunders and my eyes sting.

I love him.

I love Chris Casper.

I only hope I get to keep him.

The crowd roars as my father speaks.

They clap after every sentence. They cheer at every pause.

It's just a large sea of HARPER FOR PRESIDENT hats and banners with his smiling face on them. I thought I would hate these people, but now I just feel sorry for them for falling for the lie.

The lie I've been feeding them.

When my father is finished speaking and he strolls off the stage, he claps his hand on Ashton's shoulder.

"Great job, Senator. They were hanging on your every word."

I want to vomit at the hero worship in Ashton's voice. Instead, I just smile and nod.

"It was amazing, Daddy."

My father pulls me into a hug, and I let him because I know there are cameras on us, and this is all just for show.

"Thank you, Samantha," he says before releasing me and turning to Ashton. "And thank you. The new speech writer you hired is working wonders. I don't think I've received that loud of an applause."

My father chuckles, and I wait for Ashton to confess to him that, actually, the new speech writer is none other than the broodmare he sired. He doesn't, though. He just lets my father praise him and remains confident I'll stand by and bite my tongue. I do. I only hope I don't choke to death on the pride I'm being forced to swallow.

I trail my father along the pre-mapped route back to our cars, stopping every few feet to shake a hand or smile for a picture or answer a question. By the time I slide into the back seat of one of my father's luxury SUVs, my face hurts from all the smiles I've faked. He's still chatting up voters and smiling for pictures, but I couldn't do it anymore.

Since the rally was in Maryland, we only have an hour drive back to D.C., and I'm grateful I get a car to myself.

Or I'm supposed to, anyway.

When the car door opens and Ashton slips in, I find my whole body tensing.

"Ashton." I give him a tight smile. "Aren't you supposed to be riding with Daddy?"

He buckles his seat belt, then turns to me.

"Your father had things he needed to discuss with Denise," he says brightly, "so I offered to ride with you."

I'm sure he did. More like my father wanted to fuck his finance manager after such a successful rally, so he booted Ashton from the car. I hum in understanding, and then I turn my eyes out the tinted window.

"I was wanting to speak to you, anyway, Samantha," Ashton says.

His fake casual tone belies his true intentions. I straighten my spine and face him. I raise my eyebrows and give him another smile.

"Oh? What about?"

He drags critical eyes over me, pausing briefly before speaking.

"I feel like I haven't seen you as much since your *bout of flu*. Shouldn't you be recovered by now? It's been weeks."

His words are skeptical. He doesn't believe I was sick with the flu.

"You see me almost every day, Ashton," I say, laughing lightly.

"You know what I mean, Samantha."

His tone is sharp, but I don't flinch. I know exactly what he means, but I give nothing away.

"I'm afraid I don't. Please, elaborate for me."

He holds my eyes again, and I make sure to keep mine blank as his narrow to cruel little slits. I half expect him to stick out a forked tongue.

"Let me try this another way," he says slowly. "What's in Franklin?"

I arch a brow.

"Daddy's house is there, Ashton. Surely you remember. I grew up there."

He chuckles and shakes his head, then pulls his phone out and types something into it.

"If you were going there to, say, spend time with your family, that would be one thing. But last I checked, your mother is in the South of France, and you haven't set foot in your father's house in over a year. You see, when you disappeared with *the flu*, no one could find you. No one could get ahold of you."

The skin on the back of my neck starts to crawl. It takes every ounce of restraint in me not to fidget under his scrutiny.

"What are you getting at, Ashton?"

He smiles.

"Of course, I was worried," he says. "When I brought it up to your father, he attempted to track your phone, but we found it discarded at your condo."

He waits for me to freak out, but I don't. I've known my father tracks my phone. I know he also has the whole house in Franklin recorded every second of every day. None of this is news to me, so I remain quiet. I keep my face placid, and when he realizes I won't react the way he wants, he continues talking.

These men love to hear themselves talk.

"So then your father—out of concern for you—activated the tracker on your car. For security, of course—"

"Of course," I agree with a nod.

He blinks.

I already knew they'd activated the tracker on my car, too. That's what Agent Sexton called to tell me while I was at the lake. It's what scared me so badly that I had to leave immediately.

They tracked my car to The Outpost's parking lot and one of my father's "security" stalked the place for two days. He stayed there until Lennon dropped me off, and then he tailed me back to D.C.

I've been ready for weeks with a lie for the moment someone asked. I was going to say that I stayed with my friend and she took care of me while I was sick. But no one has asked, and that's been more nerve-wracking than anything else.

I do not trust my father.

It's one of the main reasons I hadn't gone back to Franklin until this past weekend. Until I just couldn't take it anymore. And even then, I didn't stay long enough to raise alarm.

Or so I thought.

"Well, imagine how worried we were when we found you at the same bar on Friday night. You can't be going to seedy bars now that your father is a presidential candidate, Samantha. That's the kind of press we don't need. And this...."

He turns his phone and shows me a picture that makes my breath lodge in my chest.

It's of me and Chris from Saturday morning. He walked me to my car and kissed me goodbye before I came back to D.C. My blood boils in my veins, and I have to fight to control my breathing.

"You're having me followed." I flick my eyes to Ashton. "Did my father put you up to this, or are you finally showing ambition of your own?"

I'm so furious, I can barely see straight. He's smug. He thinks he's gotten one over on me. He thinks he's in control.

"Samantha, how do you think this would look if it got out?" he asks, his voice condescending. "Your father has made it very clear which outcome would be most advantageous for all of us."

"For all of us? Do tell me, Ashton, which outcome would that be?"

He grits his teeth and his nostrils flare. Then he leans into me slowly, eliciting flashbacks of the night in his car after my father's dinner.

"You are to be *mine*, Samantha, or have you forgotten? Do you know how this will make me look—"

I laugh, cutting him off, and he bristles.

"Now it makes sense. You're not concerned for my father. You just don't want to look like you got pl—"

Heat erupts in my cheek where his hand connects, and tears spring to my eyes because of the sting. On impulse, my hand shoots up and cradles the ache, my head rearing back in shock.

"You will not make a fool out of me," he seethes before I can even utter a word. "Especially not with someone who isn't even worthy of cleaning my fucking toilets. Do you understand? Do you understand me, Samantha?"

As he shouts, his spit lands on my face, but I don't flinch away. I breathe in and out through my nose, my teeth clenched so tightly I fear I might crack a molar. I let the pause fill the space before I finally address him.

"No. I do not understand," I say slowly. Clearly. I never break eye contact. "If you ever hit me again, I will ruin you. I will burn everything you fucking care about to the ground. You're lucky I deign to be seen with you, let alone allow my father to sell this bullshit story about us *dating*. You're a means to an end, Ashton, and you're fucking disposable. Touch me again, and you will fucking regret it."

His eyes rage as he stares me down. His smug grin is long gone.

"Do you even know who you're fucking, Samantha?"

I let a taunting smile stretch over my face.

"I know it's not you, thank god."

He jerks like he wants to hit me again, but he doesn't, and I don't flinch. I almost think I've won and he's going to back down, but then his lips turn up at the corners into something truly sinister, and my stomach clenches.

"Ask your father about Christopher Casper, Samantha. I'll admit, I didn't make the connection at first. Not until I ran his background. But what a surprise."

He's dangling the information in front of me, toying with me. He wants me to beg.

"C'mon, Samantha, aren't you curious? Don't you want to know?"

"I don't want anything from you," I sneer at him, and then I unlock the car door and climb out.

## TWENTY-TWO

## *Sam*

I walk to the road and order a car on my rideshare app.

It's going to cost a couple hundred dollars to have it take me back to D.C., but I don't care. I order a luxury vehicle and put it on my father's credit card.

When I'm dropped at my father's place, I let myself in with my key, then rearm the alarm behind me. Instead of waiting for him in the foyer, I go to his office and open the safe he keeps behind the portrait on the wall.

The contents are the same as they were last time, but I take more photographs, anyway. Cash. A gun. Stacks of spreadsheets. A black book of contacts. Bank statements.

When I was in high school, my father had a similar safe in our house in Franklin, only he kept drugs in it. Cocaine and pills, mostly. I used to steal them. I used to take them with Macon and our friends. But then a girl OD'd and died on drugs that Chase gave her, and my father cleaned out his safe. It wouldn't have mattered, though. I stopped using after that night.

I grab the black book and open it, thumbing quickly to the Cs, and my stomach drops to my feet when I see Chris's mom's name, along with her phone number, address, and birthdate. Then, under the listing, written in the margin as if it was added later, is a second phone number. I don't recognize the area code, so I take out my phone and search it.

New Mexico.

My heart thuds hard in my rib cage. I feel dizzy. I have to lean back onto my father's desk so I don't risk tipping over.

Before I can talk myself out of it, I dial the New Mexico number. It rings and rings before going to voicemail, and when the voicemail greeting plays, I almost vomit.

It's Chris's mom. She goes by a different last name now, but the first name is the same. It has to be her. I hang up without leaving a message, and I just stare at the wall. My father has Chris's mom's information in his personal book of contacts. Every man who has ever attended one of my father's bourbon and cigar parties is in that book. Every person he's ever owed or been owed a favor is in there. And every mistress he's ever had.

How did I miss this? How did I not see this name and zero in on it?

I already know the answer. I was focused on the men—on the monsters—and the mistresses were of no concern to me. There's a familiar sinking feeling in my gut, the one that tells me there's so much more that I don't know, and suddenly, I'm terrified of the truth.

I've never shied away from learning the darkest, ugliest things about my father. I've dug for them. I've searched and searched for them. But this? This connection between my father and Rebecca Casper? This feels different. This feels worse, and I'm not sure I want to know anymore.

When the alarm beeps, alerting me to someone entering the house, I put the contact book back in the safe, close it, and put the portrait back. I close the drawers and turn off the light as I leave, making sure my second cell phone is recording before making my way into the kitchen.

I work on my breathing. I clear my head. I wait.

I can't turn back now. There's no escaping this.

A few minutes later, I hear my father's voice, followed by the finance manager's voice before they're both stumbling into the kitchen attached at the lips and groping at one another.

I clear my throat, and they break apart, whipping bewildered eyes at me. My father looks furious. I skip over to him and narrow my eyes at the finance manager. She looks mortified.

"Barbara. Thank you for keeping Daddy company, but I would like to speak to him now, so you can go."

"Samantha," my father says sternly, "you don't have the authority in this house to send away my guests."

I laugh. His *guests*. And he's talking like I didn't just watch them sucking each other's faces. A consummate actor, this one.

"Fine." I sigh. "Barbara, you may wait in the foyer. When I'm finished speaking to my father, then you can let him bend you over the counter."

"Samantha," my father roars, and the finance manager's face turns bright red.

"Yes, Daddy?"

"That is completely uncalled for," he says. "Extremely disrespectful."

I roll my eyes.

"Daddy, I do not care which of the help you're fucking now. Honestly, I can't keep them all straight, but please stop insulting me by pretending like I don't know what's going on." I glance at the finance manager. "Your tit is out, Barb."

She gasps and moves to cover her chest, and I laugh a genuine laugh as she fixes the buttons on her blouse. My father releases a pained sigh, then turns his attention to the finance manager.

"Denise, would you mind waiting in the sitting room, please?"

"Oh, your name is Denise?" I say, acting shocked. "I'm so sorry. I just get all of Daddy's mistresses' names mixed up. Silly me."

She turns as red as a beet, then scurries out of the room. When I look back at my father, my small spark of good mood extinguishes.

"How did you get in here?" He growls, and I put on my best innocent face.

"It was unlocked."

He knows I'm lying. He'll probably change the locks and alarm code now, but I don't care. I just cut right to the chase.

"Did you have an affair with Rebecca Casper?"

There's a flare of recognition in his eyes before he stifles it, and that makes my spine straighten.

"Keep your voice down," he hisses.

"Did you?" I ask again. "Did you have an affair with her when I was in fifth grade?"

"Samantha, I do not have time for this. I am in the middle of a campaign. I do not need you digging up the past—"

"So you did, then? You had an affair with her sixteen years ago? You're the reason she left her family? Her *children*?"

The absolute apathy on my father's face fills me with disgust. No wonder Tiffany hates me. No wonder she thinks I'm evil. I'm the fruit of it.

"I did not make that woman leave her family. She chose to do that on her own when she learned I would not leave mine."

I shake my head, my jaw dropped. I shouldn't be shocked. I've known that he's a womanizing whore for years, but this is the first I've seen actual fallout. Not his, of course. Never his fallout. But that of his victims.

*She'd have left either way*, Chris said.

But is that true?

"Do you still talk to her?"

"No," he answers too quickly, and I know he's lying.

I know because I just saw her updated phone number in his contacts. I realize now that if I had flipped to the last name she's using now, I probably would have found her updated address, too. I *know* he's lying.

Suddenly, I almost feel bad for Barbara.

Almost.

"We are in a very delicate position right now, Samantha."

My father's voice pulls me from my thoughts, and when I look at him, he's frowning at me as if I'm the one who has done something wrong.

"Excuse me?"

He sighs.

"Our every move must be calculated and purposeful. We are in the public eye now more than ever before. We must be wary of how we behave. We must act with decorum."

It takes a moment for me to realize what he's saying, and when it sinks in, my jaw literally drops.

"You're fucking your campaign finance manager, and you're trying to lecture me on decorum?"

"Samantha, lower your voice."

"I will not," I shout. "I will not lower my voice."

"You will, or so help me, Samantha, you will regret it."

I know what he's implying. He'll cut me off. I'll no longer have access to his money. He'll take away my trust fund.

God, I don't fucking care. I'm so tired of pretending that I care about any of it. I'm so fucking sick of having to make myself into someone I hate—someone proud to wear the name Harper.

I bite my tongue so hard, I taste blood in my mouth.

"Appearances are the only thing that matters, Samantha, especially right now. I do not want to hear you bring up that family again. We do not air our dirty laundry in public. We do not need that kind of media attention. What's in the past needs to stay dead and buried, especially if you want to continue to enjoy the life of privilege to which you're accustomed."

I work his statement over in my head. He doesn't want me to bring up *that family*, but he's said nothing about the pictures of me with Chris. About my relationship with him.

Does he not know? Hope blooms in my chest.

Maybe Ashton was so concerned with looking foolish that he carried out everything himself. Maybe he hasn't actually told my father anything and my relationship with Chris can be left off my father's radar.

"What exactly are you saying?" I ask carefully, and he pins me with a glare so cold, I have to suppress a shiver. Not because I fear him, but because his blue eyes are like looking into a mirror, and it makes me hate myself.

"I'm saying stay away from that family," he repeats. "Stop having clandestine rendezvous with that boy. Put aside the fact that he is *beneath* you, that history is one that we do not want unearthed."

I pause. Scan his face. Run back through his words...

"This is more than just an affair, isn't it?"

He doesn't answer me. He just glares. He won't tell me anything else.

"I'm twenty-six," I say angrily. "You can't police who I date."

He arches a brow.

"Can't I?"

He straightens his tie and smooths the lapels of his suit jacket.

"One of our biggest donors is having a charity dinner next week. You will attend as Ashton's date. You will not see the Casper boy again. You will not bring up that family again. You will do as I say, and you will play by my rules, or you will have nothing left. I will stop paying for your condo. I will stop paying for your car. I will cut off all your credit cards. I will take you out of the wills. I will dissolve your trust fund. You will be destitute, and you will deserve it."

I narrow my eyes.

"How do you think cutting me off would look to your voters? Can't play the family man if you're not being supportive of your family."

He shrugs.

"You'd be surprised how easily I can smooth it over. Now if you'll excuse me. I have a meeting."

My father starts to walk toward the sitting room, but then he stops and turns around.

"Set the alarm on your way out, would you? It will have a new code tomorrow."

I listen as he greets his finance manager. They speak in hushed tones, and then she laughs airily as their footsteps disappear up the stairs toward his bedroom.

I let myself out like he said. Set the alarm. Walk several blocks, and then I pull out my second cell phone. I send the recording, and then I pull up Agent Sexton's contact and send two words.

**Me:** Rebecca Casper

---

I ORDER A LAVENDER LATTE AND A SCONE, THEN TAKE MY ORDER TO a table in the back corner.

This café is adorable. There are books everywhere, the soundtrack is a bunch of 2000s pop punk tracks, and hundreds of paper origami stars hang from the ceiling. The barista, a monster of a guy with a manbun, told me there's also an origami dinosaur hidden amongst the stars, but I can't find it. I scan the ceiling the whole time I sip my latte and wait.

My father has a rally today in Chicago, and another tomorrow in Northern Indiana. I managed to get a few hours of free time by saying I wanted to *go shopping*, hence the shopping bag at my feet, but I had to leave my phone in my hotel room since Ashton has taken to stalking my every move. I managed to snag a copy of Robert Frost poems off one of the *Leave a Book, Take a Book* shelves, though, so it's keeping me occupied while I wait.

The poems make me think of Chris.

He's been texting. He's tried calling. Since my run-in with my dad, though, I haven't responded.

What would I even say?

Oh, hey, my dad is the reason your mom left, and your sister is right to hate me?

I never find myself at a loss for words, so this is new for me. I don't want to hurt him. I don't want to cause him pain. I cannot stomach the thought of him looking at me differently when he learns the truth.

The truth about *everything*.

I just need to get through this. One day at a time. I need to get through it, and then I can worry about everything else.

I'm halfway through a poem about fences when the door

chimes, and I look up to find a tall woman with short-cropped red hair striding up to the café counter. I scan her body. Simple dress slacks. Simple light blue button-down. Simple black shoes. Simple black leather satchel. Everything about her is understated, but she still looks like a fucking badass.

As she orders, she flicks her eyes to me and gives me a subtle nod before turning back to the barista. She pays. She waits while the barista fills her order—large Americano with a dash of almond milk—and then she makes her way to me.

Surprisingly, instead of sitting at the table behind mine, she sits with me. When she notices my raised eyebrows, she shrugs.

"We're seven hundred and sixty miles from headquarters, and I've got a guy on the door. We can swing a little less cloak-and-dagger for today."

I release a small sigh of relief, and she smiles.

"Ms. Harper," she greets with a nod.

"Lynnette," I greet with a nod back.

I'm not allowed to call her Agent Sexton when we're in public. We usually barely interact at all because she doesn't want to blow my cover. My safety has been her top priority. Agent Sexton wants me to play it safe, and she really doesn't like that my safety is something I've always been willing to sacrifice.

"How are you holding up?" she asks, taking a sip of her coffee.

I shrug.

"I feel like I've swallowed a gallon of bleach and am bleeding to death from the inside out, but otherwise, I'm fine."

I laugh, but she knows I'm not joking. Her green eyes bounce around my face, and she purses her lips.

"Don't ask," I say before taking a sip of my latte. "The answer is still no."

Agent Sexton has been trying to convince me to see a Bureau-approved psychiatrist for the last year. I've refused. I told her that when I finally get my ass into therapy, it will be with someone I choose, who has zero ties to the government. Until then, I'm going to rely on my best friend reading me classic literary novels.

Agent Sexton nods and takes a sip of her own coffee.

"What's in the bag?" she asks, and I feel her foot knock the bag and box at my feet.

I smile.

"Jimmy Choo black velvet platform pumps with an open toe and a five-point-nine-inch heel."

She whistles.

"How much did that set your father back?"

My smile grows.

"A grand for this pair, but I also ordered some platform-heeled boots and a pair of sandals, so about five when you factor in shipping."

She shakes her head.

"You and your shoes."

I shrug.

"You can never have lips too red or heels too high."

Agent Sexton laughs and nods, even though I know she disagrees. I've never seen her in anything except loafers, and the woman is strictly a sunscreen-and-lip-balm chic.

I take another sip of my latte. She takes another of her Americano. Then she cuts right to it.

"I have an update," she says curtly.

"I figured. Must be something important to insist on flying to Chicago to meet instead of waiting for me to get back to D.C. in two days."

Her eyebrows pull together the tiniest bit, and that worries me. Usually, she's a blank canvas when we talk about business. She's ruthless and cutthroat with strategy, blunt when discussing risk and reward, but she rarely shows emotion.

"Okay," I say after a breath. "Tell me."

"We have a lead. It could be exactly what we've been looking for. And luckily, it's in Ashton Cartwright's possession."

I nod and think it over.

"What's the problem, then? You looked hesitant to tell me."

She pauses, but her eye contact doesn't waver.

"I'm worried about what you'll do to get it," she says finally, and then it's my turn to furrow my brow.

"We agreed. Whatever it takes," I say, and she arches a brow.

"*You* said whatever it takes. I agreed before I knew just how far you'd go."

We sit in silence for a moment.

Sometimes I forget that they often have someone shadowing me for security. That means every car screaming session, every back-alley breakdown, every anxiety pill refill, they know about. Briefly, I wonder if they also know about my destructive tantrum where I smashed every glass in my condo a few weeks ago, and then I realize they probably do.

If they don't, they at least know about the forced kiss and groping that took place in Ashton's car minutes before. That's probably part of the reason Agent Sexton was so freaked out when I disappeared, and my father's security started looking for me.

"What is it?" I ask finally, and she pulls a small picture out of her bag and slides it to me.

A small black external hard drive. I purse my lips.

"Ashton traveled to Richmond this past weekend," Agent Sexton says, and I nod, steeling myself for what she'll say next. "He had a meeting with his father. This was when the hard drive exchanged hands. We don't believe Ashton knows exactly what's on it. His father told him to hold on to it until after the fundraising gala."

When I glance at her, she's staring at me intently.

"You want me to steal it?"

She nods. "And replace it with a fake. If you're up to it, we'll get the fake to you when you return to D.C."

I'm agreeing before she even finishes her sentence.

"I'll do it," I say quickly.

She nods but doesn't say anything. She watches me. My heart starts to beat faster with nervous energy. I can't read her fucking face. I'm great with masks, but she's a master.

"What else?" I say finally.

She reaches into her bag and pulls out a folder.

She slides the folder in front of me, and I stare at it. I don't touch it.

"Is this about Rebecca Casper?" I ask, and she shakes her head.

"No, but it regards the Casper family."

I can barely hear anything over the rush of blood in my ears. My heart is beating so fast that I fear I might pass out, and I can't tear my eyes off the folder.

"You don't have to open it," she says. "It gave us good information, though. Alerted us to another offshore account we weren't aware of. It's another solid piece of evidence. It was good work, Ms. Harper."

My vision starts to go double, and I blink to refocus my eyes.

I swallow, trying desperately to wet my parched throat.

*Another offshore account we weren't aware of.*

I should just be glad we found it. It should make me feel better, but it doesn't. I can't see it as more evidence against him. Instead, it's just another taunting thing that proves there is likely so much more I haven't uncovered. So many more moves of which I'm unaware. So much I'm missing. Between the months I spent with Lennon in Paris and the four years I was in college, there is so much uncharted ground. There is so much I haven't done—so much I could have done but failed.

I tell myself this is Agent Sexton's job now. I tell myself that I don't have to do it all. It's not just my responsibility any longer.

But I'm lying to myself, and I know it.

I nod.

Then I reach for the folder.

## TWENTY-THREE

## *Chris*

"Eight ball, corner pocket."

Macon lines up his shot, takes it, and sinks it. He drops the pool cue to the table and stands, folding his arms across his chest.

"It's not even fun anymore." He shakes his head. "You're like playing with a zombie."

I rack the balls while he stares at me.

"I haven't beaten you at pool since we were sixteen, Casper. This is the third game you've lost in an hour."

I shrug. It's 4 p.m. on a Wednesday, so there's barely anyone at The Outpost, and Macon and I have been shooting pool since before Paul pulled the chain on the open sign. I don't usually work Wednesdays at the bar, but I don't work tomorrow morning at the garage. It's a weird mid-week period of time off that I wasn't expecting, and now I'm resenting it.

I have too much time to think.

"Maybe you're getting better," I suggest, and he lets out a loud laugh.

"Fuck that. I'm just as shit at this game as I've ever been. You're distracted."

I feel him staring at me, so I press my hands on the pool table and meet his eyes.

"Have you heard from Sam?" I ask, and he shakes his head.

"She go ghost on you?"

I furrow my brow as I take his pool cue, then stick his and mine back on the wall with the rest of them.

"I don't know," I say honestly, trying like hell to figure out if I'm being rational or delusional. "We don't usually talk when she's in D.C., but before she left this last time, we agreed to stay in contact."

I pick my beer up off the bar table beside me and take a drink. Macon does the same with his soda.

"She's not kept in contact, then?" he asks finally, and I sigh.

"She hasn't responded to a single text. They've all been read, though."

Macon whistles.

"Leaving the read receipts on but not responding? Harsh."

I chuckle and nod. It's definitely harsh. And on brand for her.

She's not been completely absent, though. Not out of the media, anyway. I've taken to internet searching her dad every night, and she's always in photos. Rallies in other states. Dinners at fancy restaurants. She's always dressed to the nines with her mask perfectly in place, and she's never far from Ashton fucking Cartwright. Last night, she was leaving a restaurant with him and had that fucking string of diamonds around her neck.

I'm not jealous, though. There's something else going on, and I can't figure it out.

"I'm worried about her," I say after a moment. "She's so different when she comes back from D.C. I think working with her father is fucking her up. She shows up, and she's like...drained. Miserable. She's here just long enough to regain some life, and then she leaves again."

I meet his eyes and find his brow is furrowed with concern, which only adds to my worry.

Sam and Macon have a complicated past. In middle school, they were close. In high school, they got closer, but then they fucked up their relationship with sex and drugs. For a while, it seemed like Macon was the only person Sam really talked to. She'd hang out

THE LOVE YOU FIGHT FOR

with us, but she only interacted with him. She only cared about him. Only trusted him.

Then Macon chose Lennon, and it caused a huge rift between Sam and him.

I still don't totally understand how Lennon and Sam became friends—especially when Sam used to hate Lennon for stealing all of Macon's attention—but now, years later, Sam and Lennon are best friends, and Sam and Macon are only acquaintances.

I know it hurt Sam deeply when Macon started focusing on Lennon. I remember seeing her spiral. Macon had always been a disaster, but she cared about him. I think she loved him in her own way. In the end, he couldn't love her the way she wanted, and he let her go.

The look on his face now, though. It tells me he still cares about her in some way, and he knows something worth being concerned about.

"What do you know?" I ask, and Macon flicks his eyes away before taking another drink of his soda.

I wait.

He swallows. He reaches into his fucking pack of licorice and tosses a stick in his mouth. He chews. Then he looks at me.

"You know how nasty Thom Harper is," Macon says slowly, and I nod.

I know better than most.

"Well, he's a shitty father, and he's allowed some things to happen to his daughter that would have gotten a less-connected man thrown in prison. And Sam is..."

He looks away, focusing on something on the floor behind me with his brows scrunched together.

"Sam doesn't just forgive and forget," he says finally.

I know this about her. My warrior princess. A vengeful fucking goddess. A reincarnation of Nemesis herself.

None of this is adding up.

"Then why is she actively working to get her father elected president?" I ask, more to myself than to Macon, but I see him shake his head, his eyebrows rising as he chews on his licorice stick.

"I don't think she is, man."

I let his words sink into my consciousness. *I don't think she is.* I roll them over in my head.

"Are you saying she's trying to sabotage him from the inside?"

Macon shrugs.

"I wouldn't put it past her. Her father and his friends? They're fucking snakes. A pit of fucking vipers. But Sam? She can don a snakeskin just as flawlessly as the rest of them. She's clever, and she's fucking vicious."

He looks at me finally, and I see the truth in his eyes. He doesn't know, not really, but deep down, he *knows*. And the more I think it over, the more I believe it, too.

Sam's not a reincarnation of Nemesis.

She's a modern-day Medusa, and she's seeking retribution.

---

It's an almost four-hour drive to Sam's condo in D.C.

I got the address from Lennon, and it's nearly eleven when I pull up to her building. It's hard to find parking in my truck, and I have to settle for a parallel spot a few blocks away before I can actually set foot in the building lobby.

"Can I help you, sir?" the man behind the security desk asks.

"I'm here to see Sam Harper," I say.

He looks me up and down with a blank face. I know how I look.

Worn blue jeans. Worn The Outpost T-shirt. Scuffed-up boots. Backward ball cap. Tattoos.

I'm probably the exact opposite of the kind of guy who typically calls on someone like Sam, but I don't let his scrutiny get to me. I don't give two fucks what he thinks. I'm just here to talk to my girl.

"Ms. Harper is not in at the moment, sir," the man says.

"I'll wait."

He arches a brow.

"Is she expecting you?"

His hand reaches to something on the desk, but he doesn't look down. This fucker is going to call security on me. I give him a smile.

"She is." I nod. "I'm a little early, though. I'll wait outside. Thanks for your help."

I don't give him a chance to respond. I just turn around and leave. I head down the street a few feet, so I'm no longer visible through the glass doors, and then I lean on a lamppost. Luckily, it's a nice night. It's warm and there's a nice breeze. Sam lives in a ritzy part of the city, so I'm not worried about gettin' mugged, either.

None of it matters, though, because I don't have to wait long. The moment a black luxury car turns onto her street, I know it's Sam. I stand straight and don't take my eyes off the vehicle as it drives past me and pulls up to the curb.

I watch as the back door on the driver's side opens and Ashton Cartwright steps out. He rounds the car to the other back door, then pulls it open and offers the passenger his hand.

Sam's hand.

She grabs it, then slowly she reveals herself to me. Her black platform heels are sky-high and buckle around her ankle. Her smooth legs follow before they disappear beneath the skirt of a tight red dress, and when she stands to her full height—taller than Ashton, I notice—her blond hair is cascading down her back in loose waves.

She's breathtaking, and I hate how my pulse spikes even when she's with another man.

When she turns, the light from the streetlamp glints off the diamonds in her ears, and I know they match the necklace. I know in my gut they're another gift from Ashton.

Jealousy and hurt swirl in my chest, threatening to suffocate my good sense.

Ashton presses his hand to her lower back, grazing his fingers over the curve of her ass. He lowers his face to her ear. He says something. Sam says something back, placing one of her hands lightly on his chest while the other holds a small black leather clutch purse.

He says something else, and she shakes her head, and then in slow motion, he brings his hand to her hair and sweeps it over her shoulder. I see the necklace seconds before he leans down and presses a kiss to her neck.

Every self-preservation instinct inside of me is calling for me to turn around and leave. To cut my losses before I find myself made into a complete fool. To avoid at all costs falling into another Sable relationship.

But instead, I zero in on the rigidity of her spine and the death grip she has on her clutch, and my feet move me forward until I am pulling Ashton away from her.

Sam gasps as Ashton grunts and flails his arms at me, but I've already put myself between him and Sam.

"What the fuck are you doing?" he barks at the same time Sam's hands dig into the flesh at my sides. "Who the fuck do you think you are?"

He takes two steps toward me, and I clench my fists.

"Back up," I command. "Don't come any closer."

I keep my voice calm, but there's no mistaking the lingering threat, and he takes a reluctant step back. I have to bite the inside of my cheek to keep from smirking.

"Chris," Sam says, her voice shocked. "What are you doing here?"

I don't answer her. I keep my eyes on Ashton. He's blustering, his face bright red, and he flicks his eyes from me to Sam and back.

"I'm calling the cops," he says.

"No," Sam shouts from behind me. "Don't call the cops. I'll handle this."

She puts her hand on my arm and steps up to my side, but I put my arm in front of her so she can't step any farther away. I hear the driver's side door open and shut as a man in a suit rushes up to Ashton, and two security guards come running from the building.

"It's fine," Sam says sternly, holding a hand up to the security guards, then nodding at the driver. "It's under control. You can go, Ashton."

Ashton's mouth opens in protest.

"You don't get to dismiss me, Samantha," he snarls.

He takes another step forward, so I do as well, and he freezes. I don't take my eyes off him, even though I'm very aware that the security guards have their arms raised and pointed in my direction, and I'm hoping they're holding tasers and not guns.

"Ashton. I told you already that you will not accompany me upstairs."

Sam's voice is clipped and firm, and a bloom of hope replaces some of the doom I'd been feeling just moments earlier.

"For fuck's sake, put those down or I will have you fired for attacking my friend," she commands, and the security guards obey immediately.

I throw a grin in their direction before looking back at the pretentious twat in front of me.

"Samantha, what would your father sa—"

"I will worry about my father, Ashton. You worry about yourself. Please leave before I have you removed."

Ashton's jaw drops, and the driver of the car puts his hand on Ashton's arm.

"Perhaps we should go, sir," the driver says.

Ashton darts his eyes between me and Sam.

"Go, Ashton. I will see you tomorrow. Go home."

When he drags furious eyes from Sam to me, I allow myself one small smirk, and I have to keep from laughing when his nostrils flare and his face turns redder. He looks back at Sam.

"Your father will be displeased," he says slowly, and Sam sighs.

"Yes, I am fully aware that you are going to tattle to Daddy that I hurt your feelings, Ashton. I do not care. Go fucking home."

Ashton huffs, then stomps toward the car and climbs through the open back door before slamming it in the driver's face. The driver flinches, then scurries around to the driver's side door, climbs in, and peels off.

I turn to the security guards.

"You may go too," Sam says to them. "Thank you for your quick response time. I'll be sure your boss is informed."

They nod their thanks, give me one last wary look, then head back into the building. When they're gone, Sam takes my hand and gives it a tug.

"Let's go, Rambo."

I chuckle, but she doesn't laugh. She's scowling as I trail her through the lobby and to a private elevator that requires her to punch in a code before we can take it to her condo. When the elevator stops, it opens right into her foyer.

And what the fuck.

Now I understand why she calls The Outhouse Penthouse a cave.

This place is massive, and my modern remodel can't compare to the luxury dripping from every surface. I follow Sam into a gourmet kitchen that looks like it's never been used, then she whirls on me.

"What the hell are you doing here?" Anger flares in her eyes.

I jerk my head back at the hostility in her tone.

"Why haven't you responded to any of my texts, Sam?"

Her jaw drops in an exasperated laugh.

"That's what this is about? Because I haven't texted you back?"

"Yeah, it is. And it's also about you just disappearing without a word. I'm fucking worried, Sam. You said you'd stay in contact, but then you went radio silent."

"I'm fine," she snaps. "I'm fucking fine, see? You wasted a trip."

"Oh yeah, you look fine. You looked real fine being felt up on the sidewalk by that rich dick in a suit, too."

She rolls her eyes.

"Don't be jealous, Christopher, it doesn't suit you."

"I'm not jealous, Sam, I'm pissed off."

"Why?" she shouts, and I toss my hands up.

"Because you're giving me fucking whiplash. Because I don't know where the fuck I stand with you. You spend the night in my bed. You scream my name, beg me to fill you with my cum, and as soon as we're done, you run back here to your castle and your butlers and your overdressed, overconfident lap dog of a suitor. Or whatever the hell he is to you."

I close the distance between us so we're just a foot apart, so I can clearly see every emotion pass over her face. She's angry. She's insulted. She feels guilty. But she's also sad. So I give her honesty.

"But mostly, because I'm worried about you."

She bristles and flicks her eyes away from me.

"I can take care of myself."

"I'm aware, Sam. Trust me. I know that you can take care of yourself. You don't need anyone's help. You can fight your own battles. You can handle all of it alone. But we went over this. You don't have to. I'm right fucking here. You said you wouldn't shut me out again. You said you'd let me be your peace."

She closes her eyes and breathes through her nose. When I reach up to touch her, she takes a step back, and I let my hand fall to my side.

"Did you know?" she asks, opening her eyes and meeting mine. "Did you know that my father had an affair with your mother?"

I flinch with surprise, but then I nod.

"I did."

"Why didn't you tell me?"

"Because it doesn't matter," I answer pointedly. "Because my mother was young when she got pregnant, and she was restless in our small town, and she always wanted something more than what we could give her. Because she would have left anyway and because it had absolutely nothing to do with you."

She narrows her eyes at me, and I brace myself for whatever she's going to say next. When her eyes start to mist over, I fist my hands to keep from reaching for her again.

"And when were you going to tell me about Michael?" she asks finally, and I'm consumed with shock.

When she sees my expression, when she knows for sure that I knew the truth and didn't tell her, her face crumples, and the first tear falls.

"My family has ruined yours," she whispers as tears stream down her cheeks.

I shake my head.

"My family isn't ruined," I say clearly. I mean it. "*You* haven't ruined anything."

She clamps her eyes shut and sucks in a shaky breath.

"You gave up your dream. You gave up everything to pick up the pieces of a mess my family caused, all while you watched Chase and my father and *me* get off without any consequences."

I step toward her, and she takes another step away. Her tears never stop falling. Her makeup is smudged. Her eyeliner is starting to run. She's still beautiful.

Beautiful and innocent.

"You didn't deserve any of the consequences. None of it was your fault."

"My brother almost killed your brother-in-law," she shouts. "My father is the reason your family hasn't gotten justice. Why you had to quit your dream job and move back to Franklin just to make sure everything didn't fall apart. *My family* did that."

"Yes." I nod. "Yes, your family did that. Not you."

She grits her teeth and glares at me.

"Do you know how much money he spent to make sure your family was fucked, Chris? How much he paid to make sure Chase got off scot-free while you all suffered?"

"I don't want to know." I shake my head. "It doesn't matter."

"Ten million dollars. Ten million dollars, Chris. He paid off cops. He paid off a judge. He paid off a fucking chop shop and a doctor. He paid to send my brother to South Africa on a fucking extended sabbatical, for fuck's sake, all while you guys were dealing with the fallout. All while your lives were irreparably altered."

I close my eyes and nod. I almost want to laugh. The bastard only offered my sister five hundred thousand to keep quiet. She told him to go fuck himself, that she was going to see him and his son put in prison for life, but in the end, there wasn't enough evidence. Just Michael's eyewitness account while on pain meds and some tire marks on the road. By that point, the car was nowhere to be found, and Chase Harper was gone. The story didn't even make it past the local news.

It's dizzying when you finally understand how much power money can buy.

It always leads to evil.

"Princess," I whisper, closing the distance between us once more.

This time, she doesn't step away, and I bring our bodies toe-to-toe. Gently, I reach up and put my finger under her chin, tipping her face up to mine. Then I slide my hand to the back of her neck and rest my fingers on her pulse point.

Her heart is thrumming rapidly, pumping warm blood through a human body, with weaknesses just like everyone else. Warm and real and breakable.

"None of it is your fault, princess," I say again.

She shakes her head slowly.

"Your sister blames me. Your father blames me."

"They're wrong." I rub my thumb over her jaw, then lower my forehead to hers. "None of it is your fault. None of it."

I say it and I mean it because it's true. I don't blame her for any of it. She's just as much a victim of his evil as we are. Probably even more so. It's daunting and thrilling to think that I've probably only grazed the surface of the dark well that is Sam Harper.

"I'm going to make him pay," she whispers, her lips ghosting over mine. "I'm going to burn it all to the fucking ground."

I smile. It's sad, but it's real.

"I know."

I'm scared for her. I'm fucking terrified. I want to wrap her in a cocoon and protect her from the world. From her father. From everything that's ever hurt her.

But I know she'd never allow it. That's not the woman I've fallen for.

Sam is a warrior. She's a fucking fighter. And I wouldn't be the man for her if I didn't respect that. If I didn't fight for her, for the woman she is, right alongside her.

It's a struggle. It's my natural instinct to take up arms for the people I love. To do everything in my power to lessen their burdens. But with Sam, I have to do that in a different way. I have to fight for her from the wings. I have to let her lead the charge. She wouldn't be okay with anything else.

"Let me be your peace, princess."

## TWENTY-FOUR

*Chris*

When Sam nods, my heart swells.

She twines her arms around my neck and kisses me, deep and slow. I almost tell her that I love her, but I don't. I hold it back but pour every ounce of it into this kiss, hoping she can feel it. Hoping she knows. Hoping that when she's ready, she'll welcome it.

She breaks the kiss and steps back against the kitchen island, her sky-high heels making her the perfect height to lift herself and slide onto it easily. Then she widens her legs slowly. Her dress rides up her thighs, just enough to show me her white-lace-covered pussy, and all the blood rushes to my dick.

She smirks, then runs her finger up and down her inner thigh.

"Should I leave the heels on or take them off?"

Fuck, this woman.

I stalk toward her.

"On. Definitely on."

I step between her legs and slide my hands under her dress, and she lifts herself just enough that I can slide it over her ass. Then I kiss her, this one more heated than before. Our tongues dance with one another, massaging and tangling. I let my hands rove up and down her body before moving lower and rubbing her pussy through the lace of her underwear.

"You and this lace," I say against her lips. "It's fucking torture."

She grins.

"It makes me feel sexy."

I nip at her jaw before kissing her neck.

"You would be sexy in a trash bag while covered in mud, princess."

She gasps and shoves at me lightly, but before she can tell me off, I kiss her lips again and slide my fingers into the side of her panties. She moans into my mouth as I swipe my fingers through her arousal, then rub her clit in small, tight circles. I kiss down her neck, then bite the swell of her breast through the fabric of her dress. She arches into me, eager and wanting.

I reach behind her with my other hand and find the zipper of her dress. When she realizes what I'm doing, she helps me tug the zipper down until it's loose enough to take off.

"Arms up," I say, and she raises her arms above her head.

I gather her dress and carefully take it off her before dropping it to the floor.

"Fuck me, princess."

I dip my finger into the cup of her white lace bra, the fabric thin enough that I can see her hard nipples through it, and I brush against her sensitive flesh. I pinch lightly and she whimpers. I slip the strap of her bra off her shoulder, then pull the cup down so I can take her peaked nipple between my lips and suck on it. Her hands go to my head, and she tugs on my hair.

I release her and she pokes out her lower lip in a pout. I smirk and kiss her.

"Lie back, baby. Let me look at you all splayed out for me."

She does, her hand roaming up and down her stomach before she cups her own breasts.

She's a gorgeous, heady sight.

"Look at you," I say, my dick straining against my jeans. "Laid out for me like my favorite meal."

I bend down and press a kiss to her stomach before moving to the apex of her thighs. I pull her panties to the side so I can see her wet pussy. I rub my knuckle up her seam before circling her clit.

She sucks in a sharp breath and her back arches. I will never get over seeing her like this. I will never not be in awe of her. Totally and completely under her spell.

"Do you want me to eat your pussy, princess?"

"Yes," she says. "I want you to eat my pussy."

I groan. I slip a finger inside her and use my other hand to palm my aching cock.

"Do you want me to eat it until you're writhing on me? Until my face is covered in you?"

"I do." She rises onto her elbows to watch.

I grin, then pull her panties all the way to the side so I can lick her thoroughly. I don't waste time. I tongue her clit and fuck her with my fingers. I suck on her until she's whimpering and begging me, and then I curl my fingers in the way she likes until she's coming on my face.

I stand and undo my jeans, pushing them to my ankles quickly and stepping out of them. I take my dick in my hand, move her panties to the side, and slide through her pussy lips once before pushing into her, slow and steady, until my pelvis hits her thighs. My head is foggy with need for her, my desire a pulsing, living thing inside of me.

"God, you stretch me so well," she rasps.

She moans as I move in and out of her. My cock becomes soaked in her arousal, and her pussy turns dark pink and glistens while taking me. I pull back until my piercing is out, then I push back in. Every time I breech her entrance with my piercing, she clenches around me as she moans again. These noises—the sounds I can draw from her—I will never get enough.

"I love watching you take me, princess. Watching your pussy swallow up my cock."

"I love taking you," she rasps, meeting my thrusts with her own. "I love feeling you stretch me. Feeling you hit me so deep."

I run my hand down her leg, then bring it up so I can press a kiss to her knee. I nip at the soft, smooth flesh on her calf, and then I wrap her legs around my waist and pull her up so I can kiss her. I want my lips everywhere on her, but I love when our mouths connect the most. Her sexy heels scrape at my lower back and ass, and it makes me harder. Makes my cock ache for release.

I speed up, pulling her to the very edge of the counter until all I can hear is the slap of our bodies together, the panting of our labored breathing, and her sweet fucking moans. I kiss her until I can barely breathe. I fuck her hard and fast until my thighs and glutes tremble with fatigue. When I'm close, I push my thumb into her mouth.

"Suck," I say, and she does. "Get it nice and wet for me."

I draw my thumb out of her mouth, then snake my hand between our sweat-slicked bodies, flatten it against her pelvis, and stroke her clit with my thumb. She gasps and quivers, and I rub faster.

"Oh fuck," she cries. "I'm going to come again, Chris."

"That's it, baby. Choke my cock while I fill you up."

She squeezes me so tightly, I see stars, and I swallow her cries when I take her lips for another kiss as I spill inside her. I thrust and thrust as I come, and she clenches through her orgasm. Then I pull out just enough to see our cum gathered on the head of my dick before pushing back in to the hilt.

"You are so beautiful when you come," I tell her, kissing her lips and forehead and jaw. "I'm fucking obsessed with the sounds you make. With the look on your face. You're gorgeous."

She kisses me for a long time, and we stay connected until we can't anymore. Then I help her down from the counter and kneel in front of her. I pull her panties down her thighs and bring my attention to her pussy.

"Clench for me, princess."

She does, and some of my cum leaks from her pussy. I groan. It's the sexiest fucking thing I've ever seen in my life. Sam, wearing black platform heels with her white lace thong at her knees, and her pussy so full of my cum that it's dripping from her.

I drop my head to her pelvis, drag my fingers through her, then shove them into her once more, putting my cum back where it belongs. I pull her thong back up her thighs until her pussy is covered, and then I pick her up and throw her over my shoulder.

She yelps and laughs, and I slap her ass cheek, making her laugh more.

"Where's your bedroom, baby? We've got twenty minutes and then we can go again."

---

AS MUCH AS I WANT TO STAY WITH SAM FOR THE REST OF THE WEEK, I have work, and she has campaign bullshit to deal with.

I don't ask her what she's doing. Don't ask what her plan is. I want to trust her, and I resolve to be whatever she tells me she needs.

Our kiss goodbye turns into a heated make-out session in her foyer when she ends up dry fucking my thigh, and I almost come in my pants. She laughs when I tell her that, and then she tells me to think of her on her knees for me when I fuck my hand in the shower later.

My smile lasts half the drive back to Franklin before my mood inevitably backslides. I'm so in love with Sam that it's terrifying, and even though I try like hell to ignore it, I can't avoid the reality.

She's unpredictable, and my loving her doesn't mean she'll love me back. It doesn't mean any sort of relationship with her would be possible, either. We're opposites in almost every way. I value peace, and she's the embodiment of chaos. I wear my heart on my sleeve, I always have, but she keeps hers locked up tight, and that is what scares me the most.

What if she never lets me in?

What if I bare myself to her, only to get denied time and time again?

Am I fucking delusional in thinking there is something real between us? Am I fighting a one-sided battle? She said she'd let me in, but do I believe her? *Should* I believe her?

Sam's past behavior suggests I should be prepared for her to disappear on me again. This has become a pattern. She comes around, lets me in just long enough to sleep with me, and then she leaves again. Just when I think I've gained ground, she throws her walls back up, and I'm left standing alone with my heart in my fucking hands.

She puts off this illusion of perfection, but I've seen enough to know it's all a lie, and I'm addicted to it. I'm addicted to her truth, to her messy, complicated interior, and it's got the potential to ruin me.

I know I love hard. I know I deserve someone who loves me back in the same way. I want a resilient, fearless, timeless kind of love. The kind people write books about. The kind people fight battles over. The kind of love that guides and grows and never wavers.

I want a *true north* kind of love.

Am I a fucking idiot for thinking I can have that with Sam? For *wanting* it with her?

I've all but told her that I'm in love with her. Anyone who knows me can probably tell. I don't try to hide it. I don't know if I could, even if I wanted to. I might even be toeing the line between love and infatuation at this point because Sam consumes my thoughts. I'm aware of how dangerous this could be for me.

If I'm wrong about her...

I grip my steering wheel until my fingers turn white. I think of how she is with Lennon. How she was with Macon before everything between them went to shit. Sam loves hard, just like me, but she doesn't love freely.

The desire to be someone who is lucky enough to be loved by Sam Harper is overwhelming. The fantasy of it is damn near intoxicating.

When I run back through all my memories with her—every

caress and whisper and intimate moment—something in my gut tells me I'm *not* wrong. I just have to be strong enough for her.

The love I could have with Sam is the kind you fight for.

It's the kind you don't give up on.

I know it.

I just need her to realize it, too.

It's around five p.m. when I pull my truck into Tiffany's driveway.

Over the privacy fence, I can see water shooting high into the air, so I know the twins are probably running through the sprinkler in the backyard. I climb out of my truck, make my way up the front porch, and let myself into the house.

The television is on, but no one is in the living room to watch it, and when I walk into the kitchen, it's empty too. I grab a soda from the fridge and head out back.

I was right. The twins are running through the sprinkler. I don't see Cheyenne, but my dad is already here and chatting with Michael. My sister is sitting in a lounge chair and looking extremely uncomfortable.

"Chris," she says when she sees me. "You made it."

"Of course." I smile. "Only a few more weeks of family dinner before there's a new diaper to change. I'd rather skip those."

She sneers in my direction and Michael laughs. I take a drink from my soda and stifle my grin. They know I'm kidding. I'll be first in line to babysit the new baby. I can't wait to hold him.

"Have you thought more about naming him Chris?" I ask, and Tiffany groans.

I've tried to get her to name all her kids after me. I even told her she could name the girls Gabriella since my middle name is Gabriel. She refuses. I open my mouth, and she throws a palm up.

"If you threaten to run away, I swear I will throw my shoe at you."

I smirk. "Can you even reach your shoes right now?"

"Chris!" she shouts.

I laugh. "Okay, okay, I'm sorry. I was just kidding."

"Where have you been?" my dad asks, and I fight against the way my shoulders want to tighten.

"What do you mean?" I ask with a shrug. "I've been here."

"You were gone yesterday, and then today Tiffany said you texted that you'd be late. She thought you wouldn't make it. Just wonderin' what you've been up to."

I pause for a moment. Briefly, I consider lying but then decide against it. If I want it to work in my favor, I have to meet it head-on.

"I was driving back from D.C.," I say clearly. "I was visiting Sam."

Tiffany whips her head toward me.

"Christopher, please tell me you haven't gotten yourself tangled up with that family," she snaps.

The authority and disappointment in her tone reduce me to about two feet tall, but I hold my big sister's gaze as I speak.

"I've been seeing Sam," I say, careful not to stumble over the words or let my own uncertainties show. Are we dating? Is it a relationship? The truth is, I don't fucking know, so I stick to the facts. "We've been hanging out for a few months, and I'm very fond of her. I want to see where it goes."

Tiffany's jaw drops.

"You can't be serious," she says incredulously.

I nod. "I'm serious."

"Are you sure that's a good idea, son?"

I glance at my dad. His eyebrows are scrunched and there's nothing but concern on his face. I don't see anger, not like I saw from Tiffany. He's just worried for me, and that makes the tight bands of anxiety around my chest loosen a bit.

"I do, Dad. Trust me."

Tiffany laughs. It's sardonic and low, and it makes my stomach clench. She opens her mouth to speak, but I cut her off calmly.

"I have an idea of what you're about to say, Tiff, but I'm going to ask you not to. I know you don't like the Harpers. I know you think you know everything you need to know about Sam. I know you think I'm naïve and a hopeless romantic, and you don't trust my judgment after Sable, and that's fine. You can think those things. I won't tell you what to think. But as your brother, I'm going to ask that you bite your tongue. Nothing you can say is going to change my opinion about Sam, so just don't say anything."

She shakes her head and purses her lips. Her eyes run over my face, no doubt noting the determination there. I don't go against her often, but I will if I have to.

"She's going to break your heart," she says finally. "You can't trust her."

"Maybe. Maybe not."

She scoffs.

"You would choose a Harper over your family?" she asks.

"Tiffany, don't," my dad says in warning.

"No, Dad. No. He has to know the full extent of what he's doing," she snaps at our father before looking back at me. "You start something with her, you let a Harper into your life, and you will be choosing her over us. You know what they did to us. To Mom. To Michael. I can't allow you to do that. I can't let you do that to yourself."

I take a deep breath and shake my head.

"It's not your decision, Tiff, and you're wrong. You're wrong about Sam. I know it—"

"You only think you know because—"

"I *know*, Tiff! I know you're wrong. I know because I know Sam, and I need you to trust me here. I've always been there for you, okay? I've always done what you've asked of me, and I've never expected anything from you. I've always made our family my top priority, and I don't regret that, but I am asking you to fucking trust me now, okay? You aren't wrong about the Harpers, but you're wrong about Sam."

My sister grits her teeth and her nostrils flare. I knew this wouldn't be easy. She's as stubborn as they come, and she's always been fiercely protective of me.

"And when she breaks your heart?" Tiff says. "When she ruins your relationship with your family?"

I shake my head once.

"That won't happen. I'm right, Tiffany. I know I am. You'll see."

She glances away without another word. She refuses to look at me. Refuses to budge even an inch. I sigh and turn to Michael and my dad.

"I'm going to head out. I'll see y'all later."

Michael nods and shakes my hand. My dad gives me one of those sympathetic smiles. I don't say anything else to Tiff. I just head back through the house, dropping my soda can in the trash on the way.

When I reach the front door, Chy comes bounding down the stairs with one of those little portable hamster balls in her arms.

"Uncle Chris! You're here!"

"Hey, Punk." I ruffle her hair and give her a smile. "I actually have to leave, but I'll see you soon, okay?"

Her face falls and she shrugs. "Okay. See ya."

It fucking hurts, but I can't be here right now. I give her a quick hug and walk to my truck. I drive to my house and park. I take out my phone and send Sam a text along with a picture of the lake from the boat dock.

ME

Thinking about that Blue Ridge gator.

I wait for five minutes, but she doesn't respond. I force away the dread forming in my stomach and pull up my text thread with Macon.

ME

Want to box?

Macon replies immediately.

MACON

Loser buys diapers.

I laugh.

> How does that benefit me if I win?

Like you're going to win.

He's such a dick.

> See you in 5.

## TWENTY-FIVE

## *Sam*

I make the drive back to Franklin when I know Chris is working at the garage.

I avoid the main road that drives past Franklin Auto Body and the community rec center that Lennon and Macon run and live above. I leave my phone in my condo in D.C. and rent a car with my personal credit card.

I make it all the way to Tiffany's block, and then I take a Valium.

I lay my head back on the seat headrest and breathe. I think of Lennon reading me *Jane Eyre*. I think of Chris and the lake. I think of his words. *Let me be your peace.*

I don't deserve him. I don't deserve any of them, but I will.

When I'm certain I'm not going to have a panic attack, I open the car door and walk up the sidewalk to the house. I hear giggles and kids shouting through the door, and it makes me smile despite my nerves. I knock and no one comes. I wait five minutes, and then I ring the bell.

The door opens immediately, and I come face to face with Michael.

It takes all my strength not to start crying and fall on my knees to be forgiven. The smile he gives me makes it worse.

"If you're selling Girl Scout cookies, you're out of luck." He grins. "We have a freezer full of them from the spring."

I force a smile and shrug.

"Guess I'll try again next year," I say, and he laughs.

It's full and good-natured and so very *not* ruined. It gives me hope and bolsters my confidence.

"Can I maybe talk to Tiffany?" I ask quietly, and his smile grows softer.

Still kind. Still real. But a little sad.

"Sure," he says. "Do you want to come in?"

I shake my head.

"Don't want to push my luck," I say with a half-hearted smile, and he nods.

"I'll get her."

He shuts the door, and I wait. I wait five more minutes. Then the door opens, and Chris's sister steps out onto the front porch before pulling it closed behind her.

"You wanted to see me?" she says curtly.

I nod and scan her face. She looks tired. Her face is a little swollen, and she stands with her hand on her back like it's hurting. She's probably due soon, and I'm overwhelmed with the desire to see her baby. To hold it. To be a part of something that isn't cold and corrupt.

"Do you want to sit?" I gesture to the porch swing.

She shakes her head.

"That thing is more uncomfortable than standing."

"Okay. I'll, um. I'll make it quick, then."

She arches a brow and looks me up and down, but she doesn't shut me down. I take that as a good sign and continue.

"I wanted to come and tell you that I didn't know...what my family has done to your family. I didn't know about your mom and my father, and I didn't know about Chase and Michael. I had no idea until two weeks ago."

She looks a little shocked, but she recovers quickly.

"Did Chris tell you?"

"No," I say quickly. "Someone who works for my father said something, and then I did some digging."

"Okay. Is that all?"

"No."

I take a deep breath and make sure not to break eye contact. I make sure I'm mask-free so she can see every ounce of honesty on my face.

"I know there is nothing I can do or say to undo the damage and pain that my family has caused you. I know that no apology from me will fix it, but I am sorry. I am sorry, and I want you to know that I'm going to make him pay. Not just for what he did to you, but for every single thing he's done. I'm going to make sure he burns for all of it, and I won't stop until he's ruined."

Her eyes widen, then fill up with tears. She nods slowly.

"I hope you do," she says.

"I, um, I also want you to know that I'm in love with your brother. I know I don't deserve him. I don't deserve your forgiveness either, but I'm going to earn it. I'm going to be someone who is worthy of him."

Tears of my own start to fall, mirroring hers, and fuck, my heart hurts. Feeling something this strongly fucking hurts, but I'm welcoming it.

"Does he know that?" she asks, and I shake my head.

"Not yet. But I'll be ready to tell him soon."

We stand there and stare at each other for a moment. Both of us crying, neither of us moving, until someone screams "MOM!" through the door. I force a laugh.

"I should go. But I wanted to tell you that. I wanted you to hear it from me."

She nods again, but she doesn't say anything, so I tell her goodbye, and then I head back to my car. As I'm opening my door, Tiffany calls out to me, and I freeze.

"Thank you for not trying to throw money at us as a quick fix," she says, and I can't help but laugh.

"Honestly, if I thought you would accept it, I would have."

She laughs, too, and I feel lighter as I wave and drive away.

I check the clock on my dash. My next meeting is on Main Street in thirty minutes, so I take the long way to stay hidden and park several blocks away. I wait in my car for twenty minutes, then make the walk to the empty building nestled between the grocery store and a flower shop.

I push through the door and the bell chimes above me. A woman standing in the middle of the space looks up from a clipboard and smiles.

"Ms. Harper. Right on time."

---

It's 7:15 p.m. on the dot when I step out of my building and onto the sidewalk.

Such an obedient little pet.

Ashton's car is waiting, and his driver opens the door for me so I can climb inside.

"Samantha," Ashton greets without glancing up from his phone.

"Ashton."

Finally, he looks up at me with that slimy, predatory grin. Genetics. He gets it from his father.

"You look beautiful," he says.

He scans his eyes over me, lingering on my lips, then on the curve of my breasts before falling to my hemline. I'm showing cleavage tonight, which I never do, and my dress is shorter than usual. I feel like a high-end prostitute.

He slides his hand onto my thigh, and I don't remove it. I will my body to relax, to settle into the Valium. Ashton goes back to his phone, and I replay Lennon's voice reading me *Wuthering Heights* from last night in my head.

I called her in preparation. I called her because I was scared.

I *am* scared.

But I'm going to fucking succeed.

We pull up to the restaurant fifteen minutes later, and like he's been doing recently, Ashton commands me to wait while he gets out and walks around to my door so he can be photographed helping me out.

I'm almost certain he's been setting up these photoshoots. I can't imagine anyone would care about what I'm doing enough to have paparazzi on my tail, but it works in my favor anyway. The more attention these days, the better. I hate every minute of it.

Ashton orders my dinner for me as he's apt to do. I allow myself two sips of the wine, despite the Valium. My nerves have me wanting to down the whole glass, but I don't. When our dinner comes, Ashton reminds me to only eat half.

*The portions here are too large for you. Wouldn't want all that Pilates to go to waste.*

I smile and do as he tells me to, and I decide to eat an entire cheesecake tomorrow.

As he drinks, he gets more handsy, and this time, I let him. I don't halt his fingers when they slide under the hem of my dress and massage my inner thigh. I don't turn my head when he leans in to press a kiss to my jaw. With every inch of leeway I give him, he grows bolder. The only thing keeping me from punching him in the nose is the constant reminder that I am in charge. I am in control. My moves are calculated and purposeful, just like my father said they should be.

He'd be so proud.

When dinner is over, after I slide back into Ashton's car and he is situated beside me, I turn to him.

I smile.

"I've been thinking about what you said and what Daddy said."

He arches a brow, his eyes glassy. When he speaks, his breath smells like bourbon, and I want to vomit. Somehow, the scent is different on his lips than it is on Chris's. Ashton smells like his father.

"And?"

I shrug and lower my eyes before glancing up at him from my lashes. I act shy. I pretend to be submissive. And he buys it.

He's a moron.

I've spent the last few months degrading him. Insulting him. I've even bought shoes just to be taller than him. He's truly so pompous that he thinks I can be bought. It almost makes me excited for what comes next.

"And, well, you were both right. I'm twenty-six. It's time I start thinking rationally. Logically. I need to stop being so emotional. Daddy is always right, after all."

He smiles and nods slowly. He closes the distance and plants a kiss to my lips.

"You should let me come up tonight." He slides his hand higher on my thigh.

"I was actually hoping we could go to your place."

Ashton goes still and quiet. I pull back to look at him and his eyes are narrowed at me. The hair on the back of my neck stands up, but I put my hand lightly on his and give him a saccharine smile.

"I want you to be comfortable." I bat my eyelashes and bite my lip like a fucking harlot.

It works. Of course, it does.

"Take us to my place," he calls to the driver, and then he slides his hand farther up my thigh until he's probably only an inch or two from my underwear.

I keep my hand atop his, but I don't stop him. I have to bite the inside of my cheek to keep from screaming. Thankfully, his brownstone is closer to the restaurant than my condo, so I'm out of the stifling car before he tries to kiss me again.

With years of fucking men I loathe under my belt, you'd think this would be easier, but I can't seem to ignore the guilt swirling in my stomach. It's creeping up my throat. As Ashton unlocks his front door and lets me in, I can taste the bitterness of it.

For a moment, I question myself. For the first time in years, I consider backing out. I find myself wondering if it's all worth it.

But then I remember Tiffany. I remember the look on her face when I promised I would bring him down. I remember the stabbing pain I felt when I read over the files Agent Sexton showed me in Chicago.

And then I remember Judge Cartwright.

I steel my spine, push every doubt to the back of my mind, and step over the threshold into his house. Shoulders back. Mask on. *Whatever it takes.*

I look at him over my shoulder.

"If you show me where your bourbon is, I can make you a drink."

The smile that spreads over his face is enough to make me almost feel bad for him. I don't. But I almost do. He leads me through the foyer and into the kitchen before taking me farther into the house.

I've never been this far into Ashton's house before. He's always cut me off at the kitchen when I drop off his dry cleaning, his groceries, or his latte order. He leads me past a sitting room and a living room. A bathroom. A library. A den.

And then he opens the door to his bedroom.

I blink.

"You keep your alcohol in your bedroom?" I say with a laugh, and he shakes his head while he shrugs out of his suit jacket.

"I thought you could leave your shoes and purse in here."

He disappears into a closet to hang up his coat, then comes out with the top buttons of his shirt undone and his tie missing.

I suppose I did tell him I wanted him to be comfortable.

He glances at me.

"Well? Take off your shoes, Samantha."

Without stepping foot into his bedroom, I toe off my heels and nudge them to the side of the door, but I keep my clutch in my hand. When I stand, he's in front of me. He puts his hand on the small of my back, then slides it to cup my ass. He squeezes it hard, then smirks like he's won something.

"This way."

He brushes past me, and I turn and follow. He leads me back past the den, library, and bathroom, then stops in a small sitting room. He grabs a remote and turns on the fireplace, despite it being summer and hot as hell outside. Then he sits down on the sofa, arms draped over the back and legs spread wide. I remain standing.

"The drinks?" I ask.

He gestures back down the hallway.

"There's a bar cart in my office. Three fingers of bourbon. Use the open one, obviously, and you can make something for yourself as well."

I nod.

"Be right back."

I pad down the hallway and go into the den—his office—and straight to the bar cart. I make his drink quickly, making sure to stir until the bourbon is clear and thanking whoever the fuck is watching over me that I'm able to do it without Ashton breathing down my neck.

When I step back into the living room, he's leering. His eyes are stickier than they were before. He's shameless as he stares at my cleavage. He even licks his lower lip, and I have to stifle a gag.

Then he sits up and pats the seat cushion next to him, so I hand him the drink and lower myself onto the sofa. He takes a long pull, swallowing back half of the bourbon before setting it on the table in front of him. I can't help but draw comparisons between this scenario and the one in Chris's house during the rainstorm. It makes the guilt surge again.

I close my eyes and breathe through it.

I love him.

When I open my eyes, Ashton pounces.

He's not gentle. There's no caressing. No tenderness. He bites at my lips, forcing himself onto me, gripping my chest. I turn my head, and he moves to my neck, his hands like pythons between my legs and down my dress.

"Slow down." I press onto his chest, pushing enough that I hope he gets the memo.

He doesn't.

"I've gone slow for months, Samantha," he says between slobbery kisses. "You said it was my way now, remember?"

Fuck. I focus on my breathing. When his fingers graze the crotch of my panties, I jolt backward. Instead of backing off, he uses the opportunity to invade more of my space. I clamp my legs shut, and he grunts.

"Don't play coy, Samantha."

He kisses me again. I don't kiss back. My dress rips at the neckline as he shoves his hand down the front of it into my bra. He digs his fingers into my breast until his nails cut into my skin, then he pinches my nipple so hard that I whimper. I feel him smile against me.

"A fucking corpse," he says, mimicking his words from that night in his car. "We'll fix it."

"Slow down, Ashton," I say again, shoving harder on his chest.

He ignores me, pushing me down onto the sofa. My dress hikes up my thighs, and I try to climb out from underneath him, but he presses his forearm to my collarbone.

I can feel his erection on my thigh. He's hard. I want to kill him.

He bites my lip, frustrated that I've clamped my teeth together. He presses his forearm down harder on my collarbone, then inches it up so it's on my throat. He thrusts his erection against my thigh, and my fear finally erupts from me.

It wasn't supposed to get this far.

"Ashton," I cough out. "Get off. Stop."

Pushing at his chest, I buck against him, even though I can feel his hard penis digging into my leg. Even though he groans like he enjoys it. I dig my nails into his chest so hard that one of them breaks off.

He laughs and presses onto my throat harder. Until I can only take sips of air. Until my esophagus aches and scratches, and I imagine it crushing altogether, and I have no choice but to freeze.

"Samantha Harper," he slurs. "Not such a mouthy bitch now, are you?"

He shoves his hand up my dress and grabs me between my legs. He squeezes so hard that it hurts, and on impulse, I draw my knee up so hard and fast that it collides with his hard penis. He roars and bows, releasing me long enough that I manage to crawl out from under him.

Not fast enough.

His hand closes on my hair and yanks me around, and then he backhands me with so much force that my vision sparks and I cry out in pain. He lets go of me, panting like he just ran a marathon, and zeroes in on my lip. It's split. I can taste blood. My dress is ripped. My left breast is exposed, almost falling out of my bra cup, and it aches like he's bruised it or cut it.

If I had a knife, I'd stab him in his throat and watch him bleed out on his Tom Ford dress shirt.

He grits his teeth as he stares at me. He pants and snarls like some kind of rabid animal. He blinks slowly, then narrows his eyes at me. He leans into my space once more, and my heart starts to thunder.

"You're not in charge anymore, Samantha."

I CREEP OUT OF ASHTON'S HOUSE, HOLDING MY DRESS TOGETHER, and walk a few blocks down before I order a car.

The driver looks at my disheveled appearance. My torn dress and ratted hair. My bruised cheek. My fat lip. He asks if I need some help. If I want him to take me to the police station.

I tell him no. Then I give him the address to my building. He takes me there in silence.

When I get up to my condo, I text Agent Sexton, and then I shower for a long time. An hour, maybe more. Until my fingers and toes are wrinkled from the water. Until my skin is bright pink and scrubbed raw.

I close my eyes and pretend I'm at the lake in the outdoor shower with Chris. I pretend my breast doesn't have half-moon cuts from some other man's aggressive hold. I pretend my lip isn't split, my cheek isn't bruised, and I still have my fucking dignity.

I turn off the water and climb out of the shower. I change into a pair of Chris's joggers and his T-shirt. I blow-dry my hair. I curl it. I put on a full face of makeup and my brightest red lipstick. I leave my cell on my bed, then walk to my long-term rental car.

I do it all on autopilot. I don't feel. I don't think.

When I pull up to the address an hour south of D.C. that Agent Sexton texted me, I find a quaint little twenty-four-hour diner and Agent Sexton waiting for me in the parking lot. I climb out of the car and walk to her, and I hold out the reusable shopping bag that contains the hard drive.

"What the hell happened?" Her face falls as she looks over mine.

Guess my full face of makeup isn't that effective.

I close my eyes and shake my head.

"If this doesn't have what we need, we move forward with what we have," I say.

I open my eyes and stare at the neon open sign in the diner window. It looks just like the one at The Outpost. I force a smile, then look back at Agent Sexton.

"It will have to be enough," I tell her, and then I get back into my car.

I drive another hour before the tears start. Slow and steady at first, and then I'm wracked with sobs. They turn so violent that I have to pull off the road so I don't crash.

I cry, and I cry, and I cry. And then I scream.

Everything washes over me in a rush. The disgust. The guilt. The fear. The anger. The bone-deep, exhausting sadness. I see him on top of me. I feel his arm on my throat. His hands on my body. Between my legs. His lips on my skin. His face and voice and hands morph into someone else. Someone older. Someone even more cruel. Someone even more forceful. Then I climb over the center console, throw open the passenger door, and vomit into the ditch.

I throw up everything in my stomach. My throat burns and my head aches. Even my eyes hurt by the time I'm finished. Then I sit with my head between my knees, and I think of *Walden*.

## TWENTY-SIX

*Chris*

A KNOCKING ON MY DOOR WAKES ME.

When I glance at the clock on my nightstand, it's after three in the morning. I check my phone, but I have no missed calls or texts.

Quickly, I get out of bed, throw on a pair of shorts, and head to the front door.

When I open it, I lose my breath.

"What happened?" I ask.

My fear and anger are obvious. I gather Sam into my arms and hold her to my chest. I smooth back her wet hair and run my hands up and down her back.

"What happened, baby?"

I move back so I can look at her. Her cheek is sporting a light bruise. Her lip is swollen. Her eyes are red-rimmed, her left one displaying a burst blood vessel. I feel terror and rage. Terror to think of what the woman I love has been through, and rage for whoever caused it.

"Can I come in?" Sam asks, her hoarse voice barely a whisper, and it spurs me into action.

I steer her into the house and take her to the couch, then I kneel in front of her and survey her some more. I brush her hair back off her face and run my thumb lightly over the bruise on her cheek. Her eyes flutter shut, and she leans into my touch.

"What happened?" I ask again, and her face falls.

It's like a dam breaks.

She hiccups on a sob, tears flooding her face in a steady stream.

"You're going to hate me." She squeezes her eyes shut and shakes her head. "You're going to hate me."

She drops her head in her hands and sobs.

"I'm sorry. I'm so sorry, Chris. I'm so sorry."

"No." I rub her back. "I could never hate you. I could never hate you, princess."

"You don't know what I did," she says.

She won't look at me. She won't open her eyes. Her body wracks with another sob, and my heart breaks. My heart shatters for her.

"I don't care what you did," I say honestly, and she shakes her head again. "I don't care, Sam. I don't care."

She cries harder, and all I can do is gather her to my chest and rock back and forth. She feels so small. So fragile. She feels broken, and tears spring to my eyes, too.

"Who did it, Sam? Who did this to you?"

She buries her face in my neck. Her tears gather on my shoulder, trickling down my bare chest. She doesn't stop crying.

"I'm so sorry, Chris. I'm so, so sorry."

I don't know what to say. I don't know how to fix it. All I can do is hold her.

"It's not your fault," I whisper into her hair. "It's not your fault. I don't hate you. I would never hate you."

"He kissed me," she sobs. "He kissed me. He touched me. He ripped my dress."

My heart thunders so hard in my chest, echoing in my head. My blood rushes in my veins, carrying my rage through my extremities. I want to kill him. I want him dead.

"It's not your fault," I say, and I mean it.

"I drugged his drink. He passed out before...before...but he..."

She chokes on more words, but she can't get them out. The

shame and guilt I hear in her voice are so heartbreaking that the tears welling in my eyes finally fall.

"Shhh, baby. It's not your fault. You don't have to tell me."

"I'm so sorry," she whispers again.

"You don't have to apologize. You didn't do anything wrong."

"I did. I did. I went to his house. I wore the low-cut dress. I let him…I made him think…but he went too fast. He wasn't supposed to do that. He was supposed to drink the drink. He was supposed to fall asleep before…before…"

She hiccups on another sob. She holds on to me like a lifeline. Like she thinks I'm going to kick her out. Like she thinks I'm going to hate her.

"Princess, listen to me. I could never hate you. I do not hate you. I'm not angry with you. I don't blame you. You did nothing wrong here, okay? This is not your fault."

"What if it doesn't work?" she says through her tears. "What if I did all of it and it was for nothing? What if I've wasted years of my life, whittled myself down to raw nerves, and it was all pointless?"

I don't know what to say. I don't know how to answer that.

"I'm here," I tell her. "We'll figure it out together. I'm here. Just rest, okay? Just rest."

She starts to calm, her sobs growing quieter until it's just soft sniffles, but her tears don't stop, and her hold on me doesn't loosen. I don't let her go, either. I don't stop rubbing her back or smoothing down her hair. I don't stop whispering to her.

*I'm here.*
*You're safe now.*
*I could never, ever hate you.*
*It's not your fault.*

When her breathing evens, I think she might have fallen asleep, so I stand gently and carry her to my bedroom. I lay her on the bed and pull the comforter up around her, and then she opens her eyes.

"I don't think I can do it anymore," she says, her voice shaky. "I don't think I can go back there."

Her will is broken. Her spirit is shattered.

"I'm so sorry, Chris. I'm so sorry."

I climb into the bed next to her and hold her against me.

"You can be done, Sam. It's okay. It's okay to be done now. You don't ever have to go back."

*Stay with me. I'll take care of you. I'll keep you safe.*

"Thank you," she whispers sleepily. "Thank you for being my peace."

---

Sam startles awake an hour later.

I'd been watching her. I watched her, and I seethed. She was restless. She whimpered in her sleep. Whispered *no* over and over. Then she sat straight up in bed with a gasp so loud that I jumped.

She looks around the room like a terrified child running from a monster, but when she sees me, her whole body deflates, and I pull her against my chest.

"It was a dream," I tell her. "It was just a dream. You're safe here. You're safe with me."

She nods rapidly against my chest.

"Just a dream," she whispers. "It was just a dream. Just a dream."

She whispers it to herself, but her body doesn't relax. She stays tense, her heart thudding so fast I can feel it through her back. I give her time to catch her breath, but when she doesn't, I speak.

"What can I do? Are you hungry or thirsty? Do you need some ibuprofen or anything? What can I do?"

She's quiet for a moment, and I wonder if she'll answer.

*Lean on me,* I want to say. *Let me help.*

"Will you..."

She starts in a whisper, but then she stops. Fidgeting with the comforter, she takes three deep breaths with three slow exhales before she speaks again.

"Would you mind reading to me?"

Her voice is so small. So childlike. So unlike the strong, sassy woman I love. But I love her this way, too. I love her vulnerable, and I love her strong. I love all of her.

"I would love to read to you." I give her a small smile.

I slide out of bed and go to my bookshelf.

"Do you have any requests?"

"Fiction. Something with a bit of romance. Something with a happy ending. I need to know there will be a happy ending."

I smile and nod, then select a novel.

"How about *Pride and Prejudice*?"

Her smile is the fucking sun, her happy little laugh the most beautiful song.

"You own *Pride and Prejudice*?" she asks.

I arch a brow.

"Do you still not believe that I can read? Perhaps I just memorized those passages in *Walden*?"

She laughs again and shrugs. I narrow my eyes playfully.

"*Pride and Prejudice* is my favorite," she says finally, so I smile and bring the book back into bed with her.

I settle back into the pillows, and she snuggles up to my chest. I kiss her head once, then open the book to the first page and start to read.

---

I CALL OUT OF WORK FOR THE NEXT TWO DAYS AND STAY HOLED UP IN my house with Sam.

I cook for her. I read to her. I tell her stories of my summers at the lake.

Eventually, she tells me the whole truth of what happened the other night with Ashton fucking Cartwright, and I determine that he is the worst kind of man. The worst kind of human. She cries, and I cry, and I hold her again. I reassure her that I'm not angry with her. I don't hate her. It is not her fault.

Even if she'd covered herself in whipped cream and lain down on his kitchen table, that still doesn't excuse what he did.

Does it make me fucking livid that he touched her? That he *hurt* her? Yes.

Does the idea of her using herself as bait for whatever nefarious scheme she's carrying out make me sick to my stomach? Yes.

Do I tell her any of that? No.

I don't tell her because I can tell she already knows. She feels the same and saying it out loud will accomplish nothing good. She needs unconditional support. She needs zero judgment. She needs peace. I give her all of that and more.

Every hour, she starts to look a little better. A little less broken. A little more rested. Every hour, she looks a little more like herself, and I do my best to ignore the fact that it also brings us that much closer to when she might leave again.

In the middle of lunch, Sam's purse chimes with a notification, and she pulls out a phone I've never seen before. She clicks it on and reads a message, and the color drains from her face. Her body goes rigid. Her brows shoot toward her hairline. When she looks at me, there's an apology in her eyes.

"Don't go," I say quickly. I fucking plead. "Don't go, princess. Stay here with me."

She closes her eyes and breathes as she straightens. Steels her spine. Pulls her shoulders back. Her face is wiped clean of every emotion except determination. It's like I've witnessed a transformation in her, and it takes my breath away.

When she speaks, I hear the words I've been dreading.

"I have to. I have to go back."

"You don't have to." My voice rises despite my attempts to stay calm. Anger and fear spike my heart rate, and my temper rises with it. "You don't have to go back there, Sam."

She shakes her head and stands. Starts to clean up her plate. She doesn't look at me.

"Don't ignore me." I stand and move to the kitchen.

Stepping in front of her, I tilt her chin up so she looks at me. I'm met with fierce determination that fills me with as much dread as it does pride.

"Those people, that place, it's fucking killing you. You're a shell of yourself when you come back. You look like someone used you as a punching bag, and you want to go back there? To them? To *him*? Nothing is worth that, Sam. You, your safety, it's all worth more than whatever it is you're trying to do."

She grits her teeth, then turns her head so my hand falls from her face.

"It's not. This is the only thing that matters."

She goes back to cleaning off her plate, the lunch I made for her now discarded into the trash.

"Goddamn it, Sam. Stop for one second and think about this. Think about—"

"I have!" She whirls on me. "It's *all* I fucking think about. It's all I've thought about for *years*, Chris. You think I don't know what I'm doing? That I don't know the risks? You think I haven't agonized over it a hundred times? Because I have. I have, and I've made my fucking decision, and I'm doing this, so move out of my way and let me go."

She brushes past me, and I follow her into the living room.

"You're going to let this fucking revenge plot or whatever it is ruin you. You're letting them win—"

"Don't," she shouts. "Don't say that. They will *never* win. If I have to fucking die trying, they will not win. If I have to burn with them, then so be it."

"No." I step in front of her. "How the fuck can you say that? *So be it*? You're so driven that you're fine with ruining everything—"

"Yes! Yes, I am, and you have to be fine with it too. This is my decision, my life, not yours. I'm not your possession. You can't just order me around."

"I don't want to *possess* you, Sam. I want to *protect* you."

"I can protect myself," she snaps, her eyes narrowing, daring me to bring up the bruise on her cheek and her swollen lip.

I can see the challenge in her eyes. She's already formulated an argument against it. She's prepped and ready for fucking battle, but

I don't want to be another man she has to fight. I don't want her to battle with me. *Never* with me.

"And what about me, Sam?" I question, my voice softer. "What about us?"

She shakes her head and clamps her eyes shut.

"Don't do that." Her voice breaks. "Don't make this about us. It's not about you. I have to do it, Chris. I have to, but I promise I'll come back. Just trust me, okay? Just trust that I'm informed and aware and that I know what I'm fucking doing. I'm not some damsel in distress who needs you to come out and save me. I've got this fucking covered, and if you can be okay with that, I promise you I will come back to you. But if you're going to try and jump in here, manipulate me or give me an ultimatum so that my behavior becomes something that you feel comfortable with, then we will never work. I have had enough of those men in my life. I refuse to fall victim to another."

Her last statement takes my breath away. That is exactly the opposite of what I want to be for her. The exact opposite of who I am.

"I would never do that. I would never manipulate you or give you an ultimatum."

"Then let me go and trust me to know what's best for *me*. And believe me when I say I will be back. But I have to go."

The finality in her tone doesn't fill me with pain the way I expect, and I realize that's because I was expecting it. Deep down, I knew it was coming. She was always going to go back.

My girl doesn't give up.

I've seen the truth in the determined glint in her eyes.

I've heard it in her tired laugh.

She's going to see this through to the end, whatever it is, and I'm going to be there with her through it all.

"I'll come with, then."

She shakes her head.

"No. No, you stay here. I just have to get through the fundraising gala, and then I'll let the chips fall how they're meant to."

The fundraising gala sparks recognition in my mind, and I remember Sable's words a few weeks ago.

*Supposed to be huge.*

*Five thousand a chair.*

*Anyone who's anyone is going to be there.*

"You don't have to do this," I try again. "You don't have to go."

She gives me a sad smile.

"I do, though. I couldn't live with myself if I don't see it through."

I close the distance between us. I cup her neck. I focus on her pulse. I drop my forehead to hers.

"Come back to me," I whisper over her lips.

I feel her smile.

"Always."

I stand on my porch and watch as Sam drives off in her rental car.

I wait ten minutes, staring down the street long after her taillights have disappeared. And then my feet move without my prompting.

I go to my bedroom and dig through the bottom dresser drawer until I find what I'm looking for. A heavy, black velvet box. I slip it into the pocket of my jeans, and then I jump in my truck and head to the pawn shop.

I won't let the woman I love fight her battles alone.

Never again.

## TWENTY-SEVEN

### *Sam*

I look at myself in the mirror with a critical eye.

My lip has healed, and the bruise on my cheek was easy enough to cover with makeup. It helps that my shimmering gold eyeliner and bright red lipstick steal the show. No one will be looking too closely at my cheeks.

My long blond hair is in an elaborate updo. Pieces frame my face, but they don't hide the jewelry adorning my ears. My earrings, rose gold snakes with emerald eyes, dangle from my earlobes. The emeralds catch the light, and they seem to glow. I smile at them, then run my finger over the matching bracelet on my left hand.

I smooth my hands down the emerald dress, the pattern giving the illusion of snakeskin. I had a local designer custom-make it. It fits like it was painted on, with a long slit on the side and a hemline that teases my platform stiletto heels. My favorite part, however, is the back. I turn and look over my shoulder in the mirror, and the smile that curls my lips is nothing short of predatory.

I grab my shawl, black silk and lace, and lay it delicately over my shoulder blades, draping it over my forearms, and then I walk to my dresser. Instead of grabbing the diamond necklace from the drawer, my fingers find the compass necklace from Chris. Carefully, I bring it to my neck, do the clasp, then adjust the compass so it falls perfectly on my collarbone.

The feel of it there calms my nerves. It fills me with strength. With purpose.

"I can do this," I whisper into my silent bedroom. "It's time to burn it all to the fucking ground."

At 7:10 p.m., I slide into the back of the car I ordered. As my driver pulls away, I peer out the back window as Ashton's driver pulls up. I smirk and turn back around. I wonder how long it will take him to realize I'm standing him up. I'm only sorry I won't be able to see his face.

During the drive, I go over everything Agent Sexton has said. Go over my plan, over my words. I close my eyes and breathe. My fingers itch to take a Valium, but I don't. I want to feel all of this. Instead, I focus all my attention on the compass necklace, on the weight of it as it rests against my collarbone. The way it has warmed with my skin. How it feels like it's always been a part of me. Like it's where it belongs.

*For your true north*, he'd said.

I breathe.

When we get to the event space, I take note of the luxury vehicles lining up for valet parking and the men and women dressed for the formal affair. I recognize many of the faces. I hate them all.

Honestly, the opulence is disgusting and embarrassing. My father is acting as if he's already won. He's flaunting his money, his connections, shamelessly. It turns my stomach thinking about how carefree he is at this very moment. Despite everything he's done and all the skeletons he's got stashed in his grand walk-in closet, he still thinks he can get away with anything.

Truthfully, if it weren't for me, he probably would.

My driver puts the car in park when we're at the large steps. He climbs out and rounds to my door, offering my hand once the door is open. I take it. I let him help me out, and then I nod my thanks. I'm too full of nerves to speak.

I make my way up the large staircase that leads into the event space with my chin up and my shoulders back. I ignore the flashes of cameras. I don't take my eyes off the entrance.

No one asks for my ticket as I approach. Instead, I receive meek, shaky greetings from the volunteers and staff. I don't respond, but as soon as I step through the doors, I want to laugh out loud.

It's even worse than I thought.

The only plans for tonight that I had eyes on were the speaker lineup. Everything else is a surprise. There's a fucking ice sculpture, for god's sake. In *August*.

Crystal chandeliers hang from the ceiling. Soft piano music plays. There are servers in black slacks and white button-down shirts whisking around trays of hors d'oeuvres and champagne flutes. I snag a glass off one of the trays when it's offered, but I don't drink it. I just wander around the perimeter of the banquet room and observe. Several times, I see Father interacting with someone, a glass of bourbon cradled in his hand, but he doesn't notice me. He's completely oblivious, which confirms what I thought.

Either Ashton doesn't know I drugged him and stole the hard drive, or he's too ashamed to tell my father. My guess is the latter, but it doesn't take long for me to know for certain.

I spot Ashton before he sees me. He walks through the front doors, visibly agitated. Wondering how long he waited for me, I resist the urge to roll my eyes. The fact that he even thought I would be waiting for him is a testament to his pig-headed arrogance. His gaze sweeps over the sea of people, so I walk slowly into the center of the room, directly in his line of sight, and wait for him to find me.

The moment he sees me, his eyes flare with anger, and he practically storms toward me.

Well. I guess he knows.

I take a small sip of my champagne and watch with a pleasant smile as he closes the distance between us.

"You bitch," he snarls under his breath the moment he's within arm's reach. "You lying, thieving snake."

I raise my eyebrows and bat my eyelashes.

"Hello to you, too, Ashton. Is something wrong?"

He leans into my space, reaching for my arm, but I halt him with a single finger.

"Ah, ah, Ashton. You don't want to make a scene on Daddy's big night."

*That pleasure will be all mine.*

He drops his hand to his side, nostrils flaring as he pants. He grinds his teeth together. I take another sip of my champagne.

"You drugged me," he seethes, and I cock my head to the side.

"Are you upset that you weren't able to rape me, Ashton? Mad you didn't get as far as you wanted before you passed out?"

His nostrils flare and his eyes dart from side to side, movements much more alert than they were in his brownstone once the sleeping meds kicked in. At first, I was worried I didn't use enough, but when he finally passed out, I thought maybe I'd killed him.

Bummer he's still alive.

"Shut up," he snaps. "Where is it? Where the fuck is it, Samantha?"

I furrow my brow.

"Where is what?"

"Don't play dumb, Samantha. Where the fuck is it?"

He whisper-hisses at me through his teeth, leaning so far into my space that if I step back, he might topple over. I release a small laugh at the mental picture, and his face flares red.

I smile. When I speak, I don't lower my voice. I keep it conversational, but if anyone around wanted to hear, they could without trouble.

"If you mean where my underwear is, Ashton, the answer is in the trash can. I had no use for it after you ripped it while forcing yourself on me."

His eyes dart around the crowd.

"Shut up, Samantha."

"Or perhaps you mean your human decency? I couldn't tell you. You certainly didn't have it when you tried to choke me, or when you forced your fingers into my vagina."

Someone gasps off to the right. Ashton lunges for me before

halting abruptly, as if being yanked back by a leash of self-awareness because we now have an audience. He scowls at someone next to us, then gives them a strained smile.

"She's had too much to drink," he says, then turns his beady, wild eyes on me.

He steps up until he's inches from my face, and he forces out a strangled threat. "If you don't behave, I will have to speak to your father—"

I laugh, cutting him off. "Yes, Ashton, do run and tattle on me to Daddy. I'd love to hear what he thinks about whatever it is that you've lost."

He glares daggers at me. I bring my champagne to my lips and take another small sip.

"You won't get away with this," he threatens.

I sigh. "I already have."

I brush past him, making sure to bump my arm into his side, and do another serpentine lap through the crowd. All the while, I watch the clock. After the cocktail hour, we'll sit for dinner, but before dinner, there will be welcome addresses and blustering speeches blowing smoke up my father's ass.

How fun.

To kill time, I wander along the edge of the large banquet room. I study the paintings and ornamental mirrors on display, following the long wall until I spot a hallway leading to the restroom. I go in. Check my second phone. Apply fresh lipstick. Practice my detached stare in the mirror. Then I walk back into the hallway.

I make it halfway to the banquet room when someone turns down the hall and heads straight to me. I recognize the shape of his body. I recognize the sound of his gait. As he gets closer, I recognize his smell.

Cigars mixed with the exact same expensive cologne he's always worn.

My body locks up. I knew he would be here. I knew I would run into him, but my knees still wobble. My heart still races, my throat tightening until my vision blurs on the edges.

"Samantha, honey," he croons. "It's been a long time."

I stand and stare. Clenching my teeth, I breathe through my nose and force a smile. I have to fist my traitorous hands to keep from trembling.

"Hello, Judge."

He chuckles. It's a weak, dying sound, and he uses his dry, aged fingers to trace the neckline of my dress. I hold my breath.

"Judge? You should be calling me Andrew now. You're not a young girl anymore."

He toys with the compass on my necklace, and I dig my nails into my palms to keep from slapping him away.

"We will be family soon, I hear," he says.

He steps closer. He's shorter than Ashton, but they have the same eyes and nose. The same vulturine grin. The same self-important attitude.

"I have missed you, honey."

When he dips his fingers into my neckline, I take a step back. I shake my head.

"You don't get to touch me anymore, Judge. I'm not someone my father can sell anymore."

He arches a gray, perfectly shaped eyebrow.

"Is that right? Then how do you explain your future betrothal to my son, honey?"

I shake my head. "It's never happening."

He smiles. "You always did think you had more say than you do." He chuckles. "Good. I like the fight in you. I like to collar it."

I narrow my eyes and step forward, back into his space. His eyes flare.

"You are a sick, twisted, fucked-up old man, and you deserve to burn for what you did to me. If I could get away with gutting you right now, I would."

His eyes widen with shock, and I force myself to smile through the overwhelming urge to vomit. I lock my knees to hide the way they want to wobble in his presence. It only makes me angrier. Over a decade, and I'm still terrified of him.

"You deserve to burn, Judge," I say again, "but I'll settle for seeing you humiliated and shamed in front of everyone."

I go to push past him, but he grabs my arm. His skin is cold and clammy and familiar. My stomach lurches. My eyes burn.

"Let go, or I will scream."

He drops my arm immediately. I shake my head in disgust. So much more worried about *appearing* decent instead of actually *being* decent.

"Fuck you, Judge Cartwright. I'll see you in hell."

Quickly, I rush to the end of the hall and turn into the banquet room. I skirt the edges, running my hand along the wall for stability. I gulp oxygen into my lungs. My eyes go blurry. I'm going to cry. I'm going to spiral.

I zero in on the exit, then a body steps in front of me and I collapse into a hard, warm chest. I freeze for seconds before I melt.

*Pine trees. Lake water. Laundry detergent.*

Clean and fresh and as natural as breathing.

*Home.*

I bury my face into his neck, breathing deeply, as his arms wrap around me.

"Hey." He chuckles, pressing a soft kiss to my head. "Are you happy to see me?"

I nod. Then I laugh. I close my eyes and fight back the tears.

"Why are you here?" I ask, pulling back to look up into his grinning face.

He traces his knuckle gently over my cheekbone before sliding his hand to the back of my neck. I lean into him and gaze into his beautiful brown eyes.

"I couldn't let you do this alone, princess. Your battles are my battles now. I'm fighting with you."

My eyes fall shut as my heart aches and swells. My stomach erupts with butterflies. He's perfect. I don't deserve him. I don't deserve him, but I love him, and I'm selfish.

"Thank you." I open my eyes and meet his once more. "I didn't know how much I needed you here until I saw you."

His smile stretches wider, all warm and charming and adorably happy.

"Well, I'm here now, and I don't plan on leaving until you do."

I press my thumb to his lower lip.

"I want to kiss you, but I can't mess up my power red." I gesture to the lipstick on my mouth, and he laughs.

"I'll take an IOU, princess." He makes me laugh too before my smile falls.

I sigh.

"Things are probably going to get pretty fucked up soon," I warn him, and he nods.

"I figured." He smirks. "My warrior princess. I'll watch the destruction you cause with pride."

My lips twitch with the need to smile wider, but I shake my head slowly instead. I open my mouth to speak, but then a server pops his head into our bubble and tells us it's time to start the dinner.

I flare my eyes. "Showtime."

Threading my fingers through Chris's, I lead him to the table I'll have to sit at with my family. His hold tightens on me, but he doesn't say anything else. I've all but laid my cards on the table with him, but I just have a few more hurdles to jump before I can put all this behind me. Just a little bit longer, and then I can wash my hands of all of it.

My father and mother are already seated, but Chase is noticeably absent. That's probably for the best. I sit down and pull Chris into the chair next to me. My father raises an eyebrow.

"There is a seating chart, Samantha," my father says, dragging his eyes between me and Chris. "Ashton is supposed to be sitting there since he is your plus-one."

"If it's all the same to you, Daddy, I'd rather not sit next to Ashton since he attempted to rape me."

"Samantha," my father threatens.

I shrug.

"Wouldn't want me to make a scene. Especially not with the live camera crew you've brought in." He doesn't say anything, so I gesture to Chris. "Daddy, you remember Chris Casper?"

My father's nostrils flare. He doesn't speak. He just glares at me.

"No? Well, let me reintroduce you. Daddy, this is Chris Casper. Chris, this is my father."

When I glance at Chris, he's stone-faced. He nods at my father.

"I would say it's a pleasure, Thom, but my father taught me that honesty is the best policy."

I swallow back a laugh, and my father turns his rage-filled eyes on me.

"Samantha, I don't know what kind of bullshit you're p—"

"Careful," Chris says, his voice low and stern.

My father stops midsentence, and Chris drapes his arm around my shoulders.

"Speak to Sam with the respect she deserves or keep your mouth shut."

A thrill skates down my spine at his tone. At how sternly he delivered his command. It's even more exciting because my father *hates* it.

"I don't know who you think you are, *son*, but this is none of your business."

My father squirms a bit in his chair. He's so pissed. Tonight was supposed to be all about him and now he wants to throw a tantrum while my mother sits quietly beside him, sipping her champagne and probably daydreaming about her lover.

"It *is* my business because Sam is my business. You speak to her with respect, *Thom*, or you don't speak to her at all. If you can't do that, then I will be the one to make a scene. And with the shit I know about you? I don't think you want that on the nightly news."

My father bristles. He huffs and puffs. He turns a delightful shade of puce. He opens his mouth once to speak but snaps it shut again when Chris leans forward, as if trying to hear him better.

The whole scene is so enjoyable that it's almost enough to make me forget about what's to come. I don't. But I *almost* do.

"Mother," I say, dragging my attention off my father, "this is my friend Chris."

My mother smiles and nods.

"Very nice to meet you, Chris. I always love meeting friends of Samantha's."

I resist an eye roll at my mom's lie, her airy tone giving away her inebriated state. She's drunk, high, or both, and she's never met a single friend of mine. My mother needs to live her life of delusion, though, so I bite my tongue. It's the least I can do for someone who has had to be married to my father for over three decades. I owe her nothing, I know, but I think a small part of me feels bad for her. Or, rather, I feel bad for the woman she used to be before my father ruined her.

"It's my pleasure," Chris says to my mom, and I slip a hand under the table to rest it on his knee.

When the lights dim over the tables but brighten on the stage set up at the back of the banquet hall, a hush falls over the crowd, and my muscles stiffen. Chris takes my hand in his and gives it a little squeeze. He leans over in his chair and presses a kiss to my temple, and I relax into him.

My peace. Amid the chaos, he is my peace.

"Light the match, princess," he whispers into my ear, and I laugh lightly before I stand from my chair.

I let my black shawl fall from my shoulders and drape it over the back of my chair. Chris chuckles, and it shoots straight to my core. I grin down at him and give him a wink, then walk toward the stage.

## TWENTY-EIGHT

## *Chris*

Sam weaves her way through the tables, and I marvel at her.

The back of her dress is open, stopping just above the curve of her ass, exposing the entirety of her Medusa tattoo. Excitement, pride, and fear war in my gut, but I make myself stay seated. These people have no fucking clue what they're in for.

Just as Sam steps behind the podium and the crowd hushes, her father starts whispering frantically.

"What the fuck is she doing? What the fuck?"

He stands abruptly, but I turn and catch him by the lapels. His eyes widen, and I smile as I push him back down into his seat.

"Sit the fuck down, Thom. Give your attention to Sam. She's here for you, after all."

He glares, but I look away from him. I don't care what he has to say. Instead, I zero in on my girl as she smiles out into the crowd.

"Good evening," she says smoothly. "Thank you so much for coming out tonight to celebrate my father, Senator Thom Harper."

Everyone applauds. She nods, and no one but me notices the slight tremble in her fingers or the almost imperceptibly harsh slant of her eyebrows.

"Thank you. Thank you."

She puts up her palm, and the applause slows until everyone is quiet once more.

"As most of you know, I am Thom's daughter, Sam, so I've gotten to know him pretty well over the last twenty-six years."

Laughter ripples through the crowd.

"Doesn't she look pretty," Sam's mom whispers, almost dazedly, but her father doesn't acknowledge her.

He doesn't look away from Sam.

"When my father decided to run for president, I remember thinking, *Wow, what would the nation become with someone like my father at the helm*? Once, when my brother Chase and I were younger, my father tried to take us sailing and we almost died, so needless to say, my confidence was lower than it probably should have been."

More laughter from the crowd. People at neighboring tables lean over to throw playful barbs at the senator. He smiles and plays along, but his responding laughter is forced. His eye is twitching. If he could order her off that stage now without everyone watching, he would.

"But then, I remembered everything my father has done for Chase and me over the years, and my confidence shifted. He's always been a meticulous businessman. A powerful friend to powerful people. An assertive and self-important patriarch for our family. He does what needs to be done to keep us on top. He told me recently, *Samantha, our moves must be purposeful and calculated*, and I couldn't ignore advice from my father."

People around us start to murmur. The laughter has turned nervous. The playful barbs from moments earlier have turned to suspicious side-glances. The senator laughs it off, but even his performance is lacking.

"That's why I thought it would be nice to share some personal anecdotes with you," Sam says with a feline grin.

My heart starts to race, and I fist my hands on my lap under the table. I don't miss the way her father has gone stiff as a board beside me.

"When I was fourteen years old, Chase was arrested for reckless driving while under the influence of drugs and alcohol. Boys will be boys, right? My father—in his infinite love for power and prestige—sold my virginity to the Honorable Judge Cartwright in exchange for Chase's...*innocence*."

The crowd gasps and Sam's father jumps to his feet.

"Samantha," he calls, "you st—"

I grab him by the arms and shove him roughly into his seat.

"You will listen," I growl at him.

I half expect to be rushed by security, but no one touches me. No one steps in to help him, and I have to breathe deeply to keep from tearing into him. He's a fucking monster.

Sam laughs into the microphone, the sound soft and menacing.

"Innocence for innocence. How clever." She turns her glare on her father as her smile drops from her face. "Thankfully, when I was fifteen, he reimbursed me for my abortion."

"She's lying," her father says, struggling against my hold.

I see movement from the corner of my eye, the hum of the crowd gets louder, but I don't take my eyes off my girl. I don't let go of her father. My grip tightens to painful, and when he tries to struggle, I give his arm a jerk.

"You're lucky I'm not giving you the beating you deserve," I seethe through my teeth. "Sit still and keep your fucking mouth shut."

This man was supposed to protect her. He was supposed to keep her safe. Instead, he's been the cause of all of her worst nightmares.

"And how *kind* of him," Sam says, her voice rising over the clamor from the audience, "for always looking out for my brother. Sending Chase to rehab after his drugs killed a girl when I was eighteen. Sending Chase to South Africa after a near fatal car accident that he caused. Lucky, Senator Harper has all those campaign funds at his disposal. Lucky, he has all those connections. Lucky, his daughter is a meek, fearful woman who would never, ever expose him."

Her father vibrates with anger and fear. I can hear his teeth grinding as he glares at Sam. She glares right back.

And then she smiles.

"So sorry, Daddy. Maybe Chase will still visit you in prison."

Two hands come down on my shoulders and I jump, but a woman's voice stops me from fighting back.

"Step aside, sir. We have a warrant."

I release Sam's father, then stand and step to the side. A tall woman with close-cropped red hair towers over the senator.

"Thom Harper," she says smoothly, "you're under arrest."

Sam is quiet as I follow the agent's car through the city.

I keep glancing at her out of the corner of my eye. Keep waiting for her to give some sign that she's okay, but her cold, detached demeanor is still in place.

I reach over and take her hand in mine. She gives me a soft smile, but she still doesn't speak, so I follow her lead, keeping my mouth shut and my face blank. The time to ask questions will come, but right now, my only role is to support Sam.

I follow the agent into an underground garage and park. Sam's father is taken through a set of doors, then the tall, red-haired agent turns toward us. When Sam opens her door, I do the same, and silently, we walk toward the woman who arrested her father.

The agent smiles at Sam, then at me, and Sam smiles back.

"Agent Sexton, this is Chris. Chris, this is Special Agent Lynnette Sexton of the FBI."

Agent Sexton nods at me, so I nod back, and then she turns to Sam.

"How do you feel?" she asks Sam, and Sam shrugs.

"Strange. Good, I think, but strange. It's almost like I don't know how to feel."

Agent Sexton lets out a light chuckle and raises her eyebrows in understanding.

"That often happens when a multiple-year-long project comes to an end. I've experienced it a few times as well. It always helps to find something new to focus on. Get a hobby, Ms. Harper. Go to therapy."

The agent says the last part almost teasingly and Sam rolls her eyes and sighs before glancing back at the agent with a smirk. Then her playful smirk turns into a genuine, soft smile.

"Thank you for letting me do this tonight. I know it's all against protocol, but I really appreciate it."

The agent smiles again, and this time it's wide and real, almost proud, and she laughs.

"You'd have found a way to have the last word either way. At least the live-televised portion will help the case against him."

Sam shrugs but doesn't deny it, and Agent Sexton nods at the doors.

"Ready?"

Sam takes a deep breath, her fingers tightening around mine, and then she nods. We follow Agent Sexton through the doors and into an elevator as she scans a badge, and then the elevator moves. When the doors open, we step into a nondescript office-type waiting area.

"This way," Agent Sexton says, and we follow her down a hall before stopping outside a black door. "He's in there. You sure you want to do it? You could just leave it here and be done with it."

Sam shakes her head, but she doesn't let go of my hand.

"No, I need him to know. I'll be fast."

"I have to leave someone in there. You can't do it privately."

"It's fine. None of it is a secret anymore." Sam looks up at me. "Would you come with me?"

"I'm with you for as long as you want me to be," I tell her honestly, giving her hand a squeeze.

I mean it. I'm here as long as she needs me. As long as she wants me, I'm by her side. She smiles and holds my gaze for a few breaths, then looks back at the door.

"Okay. I'm ready."

The agent reaches up and knocks twice, then a security officer opens the door wide, and I follow Sam into the room. It's plain and white, just like the rest of the office has appeared. There's a table in the middle with a single chair, and on it sits Sam's father with his hands in handcuffs.

When he sees Sam, he sneers.

"You have a lot of nerve coming in here after the stunt you pulled," he says, his voice low and menacing.

Sam smiles.

"But, Daddy, you always said how important it is to follow through on all your endeavors. I thought you'd be proud."

"It won't work," he snaps. "No one will buy any of your little tantrum tonight. It's only served to make you a pariah. No one will touch you now. You're done. You're cut off. You'll be on the street for this. No one is going to believe a word of it."

Sam's eyes scan over her father in the silence. He's panting and sweating with nerves, but she's calm. Her brow furrows slightly, and then she tilts her head to the side.

"You think I did this on a whim? You think you're here because I *threw a tantrum?*"

She takes two steps closer to him, and he leans back in his seat like what he sees on her face scares him.

*Good.*

He should be fucking terrified. It's about time he recognizes her for what she is. A fucking queen.

Sam puts her palms on the table across from him and leans in.

"Father, you are never beating this. The evidence they have on you? It's iron-clad. It's *beyond* damning. It's ruinous. I know because I keep *meticulous* records, and I've been collecting them on you for a decade."

Goose bumps rise on my flesh as she speaks, at the raw power emanating from her. I'm in awe, and all I can do is listen as she lays waste to her enemies.

"Everything, Father. Every *single* thing. Your tax records. Your bank statements. Your wires overseas. Your clandestine cigar parties with other sick, lecherous, twisted fucks like yourself. I got all of it. Every bribe. Every payoff. Everything. All of it. What you did to me is terrible. Horrible. I hope you burn for eternity because of it, but it's not even a fraction of the shit they're about to throw at you. You, Judge Cartwright, and probably ten of your other buddies? You're all fucked."

Sam's father's face is ghostly pale—a sickening shade of white and gray—as he stares at her with wide, shocked eyes.

"But I'm just a scared, fragile, helpless little girl, right? I'm no one to worry about. I'm only good for selling and breeding and being used. Isn't that what you said? I couldn't possibly be a threat, right? Right, Father?"

She stands back to her full height and looks down her nose at him. She waits for him to respond, and his mouth drops open twice before he finally speaks.

"You bitch," he forces out, his voice shaking. "You conniving little snake. You're a fucking monster."

She huffs a small, satisfied laugh and nods.

"Yes. That's right. How does it feel to be ruined by your own creation?"

She grabs my hand once more and glances at the guard. He lets us out of the room just as her father starts screaming profanities at our backs.

"That sounded like it went well," Agent Sexton says with an arched brow as we step back into the hallway.

Sam takes a deep breath and closes her eyes. She leans into my side, so I release her hand and pull her under my arm.

"Yeah," she says. "I guess you could say it went well."

Agent Sexton escorts us back to my car, then tells Sam she'll be in touch before we're sent on our way. Sam asks me to take her back to her condo, so I do, and when we step into her foyer, I find a single suitcase waiting.

She smiles at me.

"I probably only have a few more hours before they realize my father's accounts are frozen, and I'm evicted."

She grabs the handle of the suitcase, but then I raise a playful brow and take the handle from her. She laughs and rolls her eyes.

"Will you come back for the rest?" I ask, and she snorts.

"Fuck the rest. I already took the shoes. Everything else, they can box and donate. I don't care."

I follow her back to the elevator.

"Your car?"

"It was in his name, so I'm car-less for now."

Then, I stop in my tracks.

"That's why you got the apartment above The Outpost," I say, and she shrugs.

"Yeah. Everything that is in his name is about to become government property. I had to be prepared."

"And your writing? That was to make sure you had income?"

She nods.

"It's also something I really enjoy doing, so it was a good outlet on nights when I felt like I was drowning in Senator Harper's bullshit. Which, you know, was almost every night."

I look her over. She's still in her emerald dress. Her hair is still swept up in an elaborate, fancy updo. Her lips are bright red, and her heels are sky high, and you'd never know from looking at her that she's worked tirelessly for ten years to build a case strong enough to put her corrupt father in prison.

"You're something else, you know that? I've never met anyone like you before."

She gives me a real, genuine smile full of mischief and humor and winks at me.

"And you never will. I'm one of a kind."

## TWENTY-NINE

*Sam*

I pull into the parking lot of The Outpost and groan when I see the car behind me follow.

It's way too early for this to be a bar patron. I park in my usual spot and my suspicions are confirmed when a man in a suit parks beside me. We both get out of our cars at the same time.

"Ms. Harper, can I have a word?" the reporter asks, and I grit my teeth and take a deep breath.

"This is private property."

I try to sidestep him, but he steps with me, blocking my path to my apartment.

"I want to talk to you about the charges that have been brought up against your father," he says, ignoring my comment. "Many people are curious about the things you said at his gala. You've got a lot of people demanding the truth, Ms. Harper. I'd just like to talk."

I glare at him and hope he feels the heat of it through my dark sunglasses. My apartment has been swarmed by reporters almost every day for the last two weeks, and it got bad enough that Chris had to call the state police. The reporters have mostly been staying across the street now, but this one seems to be *ambitious*. Or stupid.

"No comment," I say flatly, just like Agent Sexton and the lawyers advised me. "Excuse me."

I move to sidestep him again, but he follows me again, not letting me pass. I swallow back the urge to kick him in the balls and release a small sigh of relief when Chris's truck pulls into the lot. I glance up at one of the new security cameras he installed last week. He gets a notification on his phone anytime a car enters the lot outside of business hours now.

Protective ass was probably watching me.

"I'm sorry to disappoint you, Mr...."

I raise an eyebrow and the reporter fills in the blank for me.

"Roberts," he says quickly. "Chad Roberts of the *Houston Sun Times*."

Damn. These assholes are just flocking from all over the country. Chris pulls up behind Chad Roberts of the *Houston Sun Times's* car and parks, then he hops out of the truck and heads behind the building without saying anything to me.

"I'm sorry to disappoint you, Mr. Roberts," I continue, "but you'll have to wait for the trial like everyone else. I'm afraid this was a wasted trip."

This time, instead of sidestepping him I take several giant steps backward, making plenty of space for Chris as he opens fire on the reporter with the water hose. Chad Roberts screams and shouts profanities, then runs to the other side of his car to take cover. Chris follows, dousing the guy until he climbs into his car for shelter. The reporter is absolutely soaked, and I'm sure it's not a pleasant feeling since the hose has the gun attachment that is used for spraying out the trash cans.

"Hi, baby." Chris presses a kiss to my head just as a tow truck pulls into the lot. "Give me just a minute, yeah?"

He sends me a wink, then jogs to his truck and pulls it out from behind the reporter's car so Chris's coworker from the garage can hook the car up to the tow truck.

"What the fuck," the reporter yelps, jumping out of his car. "You can't tow me. I have a right to be here!"

Chris walks back to me and slings his arm over my shoulders, then points to the sign posted in front of the reporter's car.

*Private Property. Parking for The Outpost Customers Only. Towing Enforced.*

"I did tell you it was private property," I tell him with a shrug.

Chris's coworker ignores the reporter's blustering and goes about his job, hooking the car up to the tow truck.

"Your car will be taken to Franklin Auto Body," Chris tells Chad. "You can square the fine away with them. Come here again, and I'll call the cops on you for trespassing, and then I'll press charges."

Without another word, Chris turns us around and leads me up the stairs to my apartment.

"Are you okay?" Chris asks once the apartment door is shut behind us.

He runs his hands up and down my arms and scans his eyes over my body. His movements are jerky, his jaw tight, and he's visibly agitated.

"I'm fine." I sigh. "How did you get here so fast?"

Chris shrugs.

"It's a two-minute drive from the garage. I was on the way as soon as that fucker pulled into the lot."

"And the tow truck?" I ask with an arched brow, and he smirks.

"I had Andre follow me with it just in case."

I shake my head.

"So you stalk the security cameras now?"

"Yes." He nods unashamedly, folding his arms across his broad chest in a show of defiance. "And I'm not going to apologize for it. I told you. I'm here. I'm not letting you go through any of this shit alone. If that means stalking you on security cameras and following you around with a hose and a tow truck, then that's what I'll be doing. Gladly."

I close my eyes and tilt my head to the ceiling, gritting my teeth against the urge to lash out. My impulse is to argue. To tell him to back off and let me handle it. My instinct is to push as hard as I can against it. But then his warm hand wraps around my neck, his calloused fingers brushing over my jaw and resting on the pulse point below my ear. His lips press to my forehead, and like magic, the tension bleeds from my body, and all I want to do is melt into him.

"That's better," he whispers. His lips drag over my skin as he speaks and kisses me again. "Don't push me away. Let me do this with you."

I breathe him in, picturing a small cabin on a lake surrounded by pine trees, and then I nod. When he wraps his arms around my body, I let myself relax into him and thread my hands around his waist. I rest my head on his chest, listening to his inhales and exhales, to his steady, strong heartbeat.

"Okay," I say after a moment. "Thank you."

I wonder how long it will take me to get used to this—to having someone else in my corner besides Lennon. To trusting a man with my whole heart.

It goes against everything I've ever known.

I have twenty-six years of experience-based instincts directly revolting against the idea of being vulnerable with him, but fuck, my body wants it. My heart wants it. I just have to get my head on board.

When Chris tilts my chin up with his fingers and takes my lips in a soft, reassuring kiss, I know for certain he'll wait patiently for me. He'll be here. He'll show up, time and time again, until I've worked through all my demons. He'll take me exactly as I am, and it will be more than enough for him.

Not for the first time, the words dance on the tip of my tongue, but I don't say them.

Not yet.

"When do you have to get Lennon's car back to her?" he asks after he releases me.

"She said I can borrow it as long as I need it, but I'm going to brunch with her tomorrow, so I'll make her take it back then."

Chris strides to the window and checks the lot.

"Andre took the trash out." He grins. "How about you come work on your articles at the bar and I'll make you lunch before we open?"

I smile. This has become something of a routine in the last couple of weeks, and I've found comfort in it. From the way Chris smiles back at me, I think he knows it.

"Okay, Chef," I say. "Lead the way."

---

"So, what about your mom?"

Lennon takes a sip of her mock Bellini and watches me from across the table. Of all the brunches I've shared with Lennon, this is the most enjoyable. This is the first one where I feel like myself.

"She'll have to do a deposition, just like me, but her name isn't on anything. My father would never include a woman in his plans. She'll be fine. Her boyfriend is some French aristocrat or something, so she'll probably move to France permanently, and I'll never see her again."

Lennon doesn't try to soothe me, or apologize, or act like losing my mom in this mess is any sort of hardship. She knows I don't care. She knows I'm glad to be rid of all of them.

I didn't even realize until days later that my mother left the gala in the middle of my speech and flew back to France. Her absence never even registered in my mind. My mother wasn't even on my list of priorities. Chase will likely never come back from South Africa, or wherever he is, and once my dad is found guilty, I'll never have to see him again either. It's only too bad they won't bulldoze my old house here in Franklin. That would be the cherry on the sundae.

"I still wish you had come to me after that bullshit with Ashton. I'm your best friend, Sam. I should have been there for you."

Lennon is frowning at her drink, and I can tell she feels like she let me down. Like she thinks I went to Chris because I didn't think I could trust her.

"Well, first of all, you're six months pregnant," I say, and Lennon huffs as if that's just a minor detail. Her belly bump suggests otherwise. "You were already losing sleep from my middle of the night phone calls. I wasn't about to burden you with the Ashton bullshit."

"It's never a burden, Sam," Lennon says, and I can hear the honesty there.

I can hear the hurt, too. I reach over and take her hand in mine.

"When your dad got worse a few years ago, who did you call? Who did you run to?"

Lennon's eyes dart to mine and her face falls. I smile.

"You went to Macon, not to me," I say softly. "At the time, I'll admit, I was jealous. Hurt that you didn't come to me. We'd been all the other had for nearly four years. It was jarring to finally see you let someone else in."

"I'm sorry," Lennon whispers. "I didn't know."

I smile and shake my head.

"You don't have to apologize. I'm not mad. I don't hold it against you. I get it now, actually. I get it why he was the first person you wanted to find comfort in."

Lennon's lips tip up into a small smirk.

"Because you feel that way with Casper now?" she asks, and I shrug, then nod, then laugh.

"Yeah. I don't know when or how it happened, honestly. But I do. When I felt my most lost, he was where my body led me. He was who I needed in that moment."

Lennon screws up her lips, and I laugh louder.

"Don't be jealous," I tease.

She rolls her eyes.

"You're still my best friend," I say honestly. "You'll always be my person, but now I think I've got two persons, and Len, it feels really fucking good."

After years of having no one, then years of having only Lennon, it feels good to let someone else in. It's new, and it's difficult at times, but I like it. I'm learning to like it. Lennon's grin breaks through and she nods.

"It does feel good, doesn't it?"

I knew she'd understand because that's how it is with her and

Macon. I know I'm her best friend, that I'm her person, but Macon is also that for her, and I finally understand it now.

"Well, for what it's worth," Lennon says, "I'm proud of you. You're a badass with a great ass, and I'm honored to be your best friend."

I let out a laugh, and then Lennon laughs until we're both laughing like fools at the brunch table. It feels refreshing in a way it never has before, and I realize it's because I feel lighter. Healthier. Rested and loved and safe.

*Happy*.

Really, truly happy, with no other emotions trying to take control, and I've never actually felt that before.

I've never been wholly, completely, incandescently happy, and the realization makes me start to cry tears of relief. I never thought I would get to this point. I thought I would have to fight until my dying breath. Instead…here I am.

Laughing. Happy. *Free*.

Lennon puts her hand on mine, and when I look at her, her eyes are shimmering with tears that mirror mine. She squeezes my fingers and smiles.

"I love you, Dagger." She smirks, referencing our matching tattoos.

"I love you, Daisy," I say back, and then we fall into more laughter.

We laugh until our tears have stopped and the table beside ours has to ask us to be quiet. Then we laugh periodically throughout brunch and the rest of the day, until we're collapsing on the couch in my cave for a sleepover later that night.

She's so cute with her little pregnant belly. She props her feet up on my coffee table and rests her hands on her bump. Every once in a while, her baby will kick, and it's the weirdest, most fascinating thing. She lets me plaster my hands to her stomach so I can feel it.

"Damn," I say. "Does that hurt?"

He kicks again and I laugh.

"Sometimes," she says. "I swear he likes to use my bladder as a trampoline, and that's annoying. And sometimes it's like he's practicing kickboxing moves in there, and I could definitely do without that. He's very active at two in the morning when I'm trying to sleep."

"Fuck." He kicks again and my eyes widen. "Can he hear me? Should I not be cussing?"

Lennon laughs.

"He can hear you."

I press my face to her stomach.

"Hey, kid. I'm your auntie Sam. I'm going to spoil you rotten, okay? But you have to make sure you love me more than your uncle Chris. Maybe even more than your daddy, and definitely more than that bitch, Claire."

Lennon laughs loudly, and the baby kicks in agreement. I grin.

"He understands," I tell her, and Lennon shakes her head with a smile. I put my face back to her stomach. "I love you already, you little monster, but you have to quit beating up your mom because she's my best friend. If you hurt her, we're going to have words."

Lennon chuckles.

"Macon's already tried that. This baby does what he wants."

I snort and push myself to standing.

"Yeah, well, Macon isn't an alpha." I grin. "I am."

I pop us some popcorn and turn a movie on the television. Just as we're settling in, Lennon's phone chimes. When I glance at her, she's frowning at the screen.

"Is Macon being needy again?" I tease and she laughs but doesn't respond as she types something on her phone before setting it down on the couch beside her.

"It's Claire," she says.

My jaw drops, and I pause the movie.

"I'm sorry, what? Did I hear you right? That was *Bitchface Claire*? *Dysentery Claire*? Your evil ex-best friend and current evil stepsister? *That* Claire? That's who texted you?"

Lennon laughs and rolls her eyes, but she knows how much I hate Claire.

"Yeah, that Claire." Her smile falls off her face again.

"I didn't know you were on speaking terms."

"We're not," Lennon says with a flare of her eyes. "But she got kind of cagey after she moved to New York. She's working for that big company, you know? And every once in a while, I'll get a weird, random text."

I snort.

"She wants so badly to be a main character that it's embarrassing. She needs to just give up and accept the fact that she'll never be more than the repulsive side-character everyone loves to hate."

Instead of laughing like I expected, her brow furrows again, and she stares at her phone.

"I'm kind of worried about her," she says finally, and I scoff. "No, seriously. Are we friends? No. But do I want something *bad* to happen to her? No."

I raise a brow.

"Pregnancy is making you soft."

She waves a hand at me in dismissal.

Lennon knows I vehemently disagree with her statement. I wish all bad things on Claire. Honestly, if we found out today that a cab she was in accidentally drove her into the Hudson and they couldn't find her body, I wouldn't even be a little sad. I have to stop myself from smiling at the thought, actually.

"I think she's fucking her boss," Lennon says, and I almost choke to death on a mouthful of popcorn.

"You what? Why?"

Lennon shrugs.

"A hunch? Stuff she'll post on social media. I can't explain it. I just...I think she is."

I let out a whistle.

"Makes sense. She does have textbook daddy issues." I wink. "I would know."

Lennon laughs, and I reach for the remote to push play on the movie just as the key turns in my door and it swings wide open, revealing Chris and Macon.

They walk right in, don't even wait for an invite, and they're holding reusable shopping bags. I can already smell something delicious wafting from the bags—something with oregano and tomato sauce—and my excitement spikes with my hunger, but I keep my face blank.

Chris looks at the coffee table in front of us and shakes his head in mock disgust.

"Popcorn and Reece's Pieces are not dinner," he says.

I narrow my eyes.

"We're eating them at dinner."

He smirks and holds up his shopping bag.

"So I guess you don't want the lasagna I made?"

Lasagna. So that's the heavenly smell. I glance at Lennon, and she gives me a little nod, so I sigh dramatically and wave my arms toward my small kitchen.

"Fine. We'll eat your food if it will make you happy."

Chris grins, then leans down and gives me a kiss.

"Thank you, princess."

My eyes follow him into the kitchen and Lennon bumps my arm with hers.

"Jeez, Sam, take a breath," she teases, mocking my statement from The Outpost a few months ago, and my cheeks heat.

"Shut up," I tell her, and we both laugh.

Macon and Chris fix plates and bring them to us. Lennon and I never have to leave the couch. Chris takes a seat on the couch next to me, and Macon drops himself at Lennon's feet, taking one of her legs over his shoulder so he can massage her foot and calves. It's fucking adorable, and it makes me happy that they have each other. Macon dotes on Lennon the way she deserves, and that's the only reason I've forgiven him for being such a dumbass in high school.

Those two quotes from *Walden* filter into my brain, but this time, they bring me comfort. They give me hope, and that's how I know that I'm going to be okay.

*Things do not change; we change.*
*Rather than love, than money, than fame, give me truth.*

We eat lasagna and watch a shitty movie, and it's a relaxed and uneventful evening. It's really fucking nice.

In the weeks since my father's gala, I've seen these three people every single day. The media attention has been annoying, and I know that if I had a phone, I'd be fielding calls from reporters, but I haven't had to go through any of it alone. My friends have been like my very own security blanket. They've been like the family I wasn't lucky enough to be born into.

I reach my hand to my neck and trace my fingers over the compass necklace. I wasn't lucky to have them back then, but I have them now.

Chris places his hand on my knee and squeezes. When I look down at him, he's watching me.

"You okay?" he mouths.

"Yeah," I mouth back with a small smile. "I'm okay."

I'm better than okay. I'm finally happy.

## THIRTY

*Sam*

"Are you nervous?"

I glance at Chris in the passenger seat. The blindfold he's wearing is actually a pink sleep mask that I found in one of my suitcases. He looks cute, all rugged and masculine. Even if he has that dumb camo hat sitting backward on his head.

His full lips curl into a smirk. "No. I trust you to drive my truck."

He can't see me, but I smile, and then I release the brake so we roll forward a little before I slam back down on it. Our bodies rock forward and Chris yelps, and I can't help the laugh that erupts from me.

"Not cool, Harper," he says, panting. "Not cool."

"Sorry."

I'm not sorry.

I put his truck in drive and drive him around town for five minutes, taking random side roads and cutting through neighborhoods until I'm certain he has no fucking clue where we're going, and then I head back to Main Street. I parallel park his monster of a truck right in front of the vacant building, and then I cut the engine.

"Okay, we're here, but you can't take the blindfold off yet."

He nods. "Okay."

"I have something important I need to say, and I'm just going to say it because I'm a lot more nervous now than I thought I would be, so it's probably just easier for me to say it while you're wearing the blindfold."

My words come in a rush, and my heart starts to speed up. My hands get clammy, and I rub them on my jean shorts. This shouldn't be so hard. Why is this so hard?

"Okay." I nod even though Chris can't see me. "Okay. I'm just going to do it, okay?"

Chris chuckles and blindly reaches for my hand. When he finds it, he squeezes gently and rubs his thumb back and forth over my knuckles.

"Okay," he says again. "Take your time."

I nod again. I nod some more. And then I just do it.

"I love you," I blurt, and he smiles immediately, which makes me smile despite the tears prickling my eyes. "I am in love with you, and I wanted to tell you that. You're my peace and my comfort, and I love you."

My voice breaks on the last word and I clamp my mouth, but my cheeks hurt from trying not to grin like an idiot. Crying and smiling. I'm so gone for him.

"Can I take the mask off now?" he asks, and I reach up and pull it off his face with a laugh.

He meets my eyes with his, and all I see is love. Love and acceptance, and I feel all of it.

"I love you too," he says, then leans in and kisses me.

It's the softest, sweetest, most loving kiss in the world, and I nearly melt. I almost forget entirely why I'm here in the first place. My tears fall more quickly, and I have to pull back to stifle a whimper.

"I'm sorry," I whisper, wiping at my eyes. "I'm sorry. This should be happy and I'm ruining it."

"You've ruined nothing." He cups my face and rubs his thumb gently over my cheek. "You can cry."

"It's just...I'm just..."

"It's scary," he finishes, and I nod, grateful that he gets it.

"I love you. I love you so much that it physically hurts sometimes, and I'm just...I'm just not used to that. You're terrifying." I groan. "Fuck, I'm messing this up."

He presses his lips to my forehead, soft yet firm.

"You scare me, too," he whispers. "It's terrifying to realize that someone has so much power over you. You've got my heart in your hands, princess, and I'm drawn to you. Your moods. Your desires. Your pains and dreams. Even the darkest, most private parts of you. I'm drawn to every part of you. You own me, and it's a risk to be so vulnerable with another person. It's scary to be at their mercy."

I nod, but I can't speak. I swallow back another whimper. He gets it. I should have known he'd get it. It relaxes the swirling vortex of my thoughts to know he feels it too. He feels it for me.

"Can you open your eyes for me?" he asks, so reluctantly, I do.

His warm brown irises are shimmering, and there are tear tracks on his cheeks, leading into his scruff. I laugh lightly and wipe them away gently.

"I've never loved anyone the way I love you, and it's scary, but there's no stopping it. I just have to hold on tight and enjoy the thrill because there's no talking my heart out of it. It wants you, Sam. So even if you hurt me, at least I know I had you for a while. At least I know I gave it my all."

"I'm not. I'm not going to hurt you." I lean forward and kiss him again. "God, I...you're one of the best people I know. I won't hurt you. I love you. I love you so much."

"I know. I believe you. I trust you." He grips my neck with both hands, his thumbs gently caressing my jaw as he holds my gaze. "I promise to be careful with your heart, princess. I swear it. It would be an honor to be loved by you, and I promise that your heart is safe with me. *You're* safe with me, okay?"

"Okay," I whisper through my tears. I kiss him again, then press my forehead to his. "I love you. I'll be careful with your heart, too."

He chuckles. His lips move into a smile, and I smile, too. I know he means what he says, and I know he'll keep his promises. I trust him, and the realization is like an anvil lifts off my chest. It's been so, so long since I've trusted anyone other than Lennon, but my heart is ready. I'm ready.

I'm ready to love him and to let him love me.

I pull back and swipe the lingering tears from under my eyes. I take a deep breath, and then give Chris a small but excited smile.

"Okay, so I have a gift for you."

He narrows his eyes. "It's not my birthday," he teases.

I arch a brow. "Well, I'm broke now, so this might have to do for your next few birthdays."

He barks out a laugh and shakes his head. It's not totally true. I'm not broke, but my personal bank account looks a hell of a lot different than the one I shared with my father. Way, way, way less zeroes, but I'm okay with it. Better than okay with it.

"Stay there," I say, then hop out of the driver's seat and round the truck.

I open the passenger door and offer Chris my hand with a flourish. He takes it with a chuckle and climbs out of the truck onto the sidewalk.

"You crushed parallel parking this thing," he says, surveying the tires and their distance from the curb.

"I know," I say proudly, then snap my fingers. "Pay attention, please."

"Right, sorry. Where's my gift?"

I try like hell to tame my smile, but it just won't be tamed. I want to start giggling, but I swallow that back and turn to the side, waving at the building behind me.

"Ta-daaaa!"

Chris looks at the building, trying to keep the utter confusion off his face. He's never been good with masks.

"Princess, this is the old Italian restaurant," he says slowly, looking back at me with a raised eyebrow.

I smile and nod, then wave my hands at the building again.

"Taaaa-daaaaa!"

He bounces his eyes from me to the vacant building and back. Slowly, the confusion gives way to surprise and then denial.

"No way," he whispers, and I bounce a little on the balls of my feet.

"Yes way."

I take the key out of my pocket and slam it in his palm. He stares at it. He looks from the key to the building, then back at me.

"But how?"

"I figured I'd do something good with my father's money before the accounts were frozen. I also pre-paid for five years of school lunches for all the students at the elementary school and bought all new art supplies and pottery wheels for the rec center."

He blinks at me. He doesn't speak. I think I broke him.

I start to worry that I did the wrong thing. That I was impulsive or maybe I insulted him. The men I'm used to would have hated a gift like this from a woman—they'd have found it emasculating.

Shit.

Maybe I didn't think this through.

"It doesn't have to be a restaurant," I say quickly. "It doesn't have to be anything, if you don't want it to be. The whole building is yours, but you can sell it. You can rent it out. It's paid off, but you don't—"

He kisses me. He cups my face in his hands and kisses me breathless, then he scoops me up and spins me in a circle until I'm giggling before setting me back on my feet.

"Does that mean you're not mad?" I whisper against his lips, and I feel him smile.

"I'm not mad at all. I'm thrilled. Thank you, but I need you to know that I don't need this. You don't have to do this for me. My love isn't conditional. You d—"

"Shush!" I press my finger to his lips, silencing him. "Shush. I didn't do this for any reason other than I wanted to do something kind for you. I love you, and I read somewhere one time that you're supposed to do kind things for the people you love, so this is me doing that."

He presses a kiss to my fingers, still pressed to his mouth, and then pulls my hand down.

"So this wasn't because you feel guilty about me leaving my culinary career and working at the Franklin Auto Body garage?"

I scrunch up my nose and my ears heat.

"It might be a little bit that," I confess. "But most of it was just that I love you, and you deserve something like this. You're talented, and you should have a way to share your talent with others, and I love you. And I wanted to do something nice for you. And, you know, I love you. Did I say that already?"

Chris nods, then leans down and kisses me again.

"You can say it as many times as you want. I'll never get tired of hearing it."

"Good. Because you also might need to give me a job," I joke. "I don't think I can sustain my shoe addiction on freelance writing. I might need to take up bartending."

Chris smiles.

"You're hired."

I laugh, then turn around and let us into the building. He gets more excited the more he sees. The kitchen, the dining area, the bar. He starts talking about remodeling. About menus. About everything, and in all of it, he includes me. He talks like it's *our* future and a dream that *we* share, and the more he talks, the more I realize that it is.

Chris Casper is my future, and for the first time in forever, it's a future I can't wait to experience. It's not daunting. It's not precarious. It's just...us. Us, and love, and dreams.

After a few hours, we lock up with plans to come back tomorrow.

I kiss him in front of the building, and I'm seconds from leaning back and telling him I love him again, for probably the hundredth time today, when I hear a gasp. We break the kiss and I look up to find Chris's ex-girlfriend staring at us.

She's just standing in the middle of the sidewalk on Main Street, staring at us with a gaping mouth. I thread my fingers through

Chris's and nod in Sable's direction. I'm grateful when Chris squeezes my hand, and I lean into his side a little before smiling at our uninvited guest. She drops her eyes to our linked hands and her brows furrow.

"Sable," Chris greets. "Did you need something?"

She drags her eyes to his face and forces a smile.

"Saw your truck. Thought I'd stop and say hi."

Chris nods.

"Hi. We're actually leaving, though."

"Of course," she says awkwardly, the slight hitch in her voice betraying her shock before she flicks her eyes to me. "Samantha. I'm so sorry to hear about your dad. I'm sure it's been hard, what with all the bad press."

She's not sorry. I shrug.

"I expected it when I turned him in," I say. "I was prepared."

"So it's all true, then?" she asks, eyes wide. "And his accounts and properties are gone, too? They've all been frozen? Did you know that would happen before you said what you said at the gala? It's all over the internet. Everyone is saying you're"—she swallows hard and whispers the final word—"*broke*."

The laugh that escapes me startles everyone, me included. I can't even hide the derisive tone in my voice when I respond.

"There are some things more important than money, Serena. Now, if you'll excuse us. We have somewhere to be."

I turn toward the truck and Chris follows.

"It's Sable," she says, and I roll my eyes.

"I don't care."

Chris's stifled chuckle makes me have to bite back my smile, but Sable narrows her eyes, proving she heard it. She takes another step toward us and glances at Chris.

"So are you dating, then?" she asks. "Are you together?"

Chris's thumb runs gently over my wrist as he responds, "We are."

Her brows furrow even more until they're almost touching and her jaw tightens. I sigh.

"We really need to go, Serena," I say, making sure she can hear my feigned pity. "It was nice to... Well, goodbye."

She doesn't take the slight well. I didn't think she would. This woman has always had issues with me. I suppose she was right to.

"He *proposed* to me," she snaps. "You know that, right? It was me first."

It takes all my strength not to jab her in her store-bought nose. Instead, I give her a smile that says speaking to her is beneath me, it bores me, and I'm ready for it to end.

"Yes, I'm aware."

I let go of Chris's hand and thread my arm through his instead. I smile up at him, making sure every ounce of what I feel for him is readable on my face. When I speak, I don't look at her, I look at him, and I say what I've been thinking ever since that night of the thunderstorm in Chris's house.

"Thank you for turning him down. You did me a favor."

She gasps, and when I glance at her, her jaw is dropped, and her eyes are wide. I want to laugh, but I feel bad for her, so I don't. I head toward the truck, and this time, she doesn't try to stop me. When I'm in the passenger seat and Chris is behind the wheel, he turns toward me.

"Jealous, princess?"

I huff.

"I'd never be jealous of someone like her. She's an idiot. I'm just glad she didn't see what she had before she let you go."

I can feel his eyes on me, and when I finally look back at him, his smile makes me smile.

"Have I told you I love you?" he asks, and I laugh.

"Yes." I lean across the bench seat and kiss him. "But I can always hear it again."

# THIRTY-ONE

## Chris

"You don't have to be nervous," I say, swallowing back my laugh.

Sam nods and wrings her hands in her lap.

"I know."

She doesn't look at me.

"They want you here. You were invited."

She nods again. Hands still wringing together as she stares out the windshield.

"I know."

I reach across the bench seat and take her hand in mine.

"Look at me," I say, and reluctantly, she does. "They want you here. You're important to me, so you're important to them. There's no bad blood here. They don't blame you for anything. They want you here, okay?"

"Okay," she whispers. "What if they hate my gift?"

I smile.

"They won't. I promise."

She studies me a moment longer, and then she takes a deep breath and nods.

"Okay, I'm ready."

Sam and I climb out of my truck and make our way up the

sidewalk until I'm opening the door to let her into my sister's house. Immediately, Luke and Lucy tackle us. Drive-by hugs and hellos before they bound up the stairs and disappear in a flurry of giggles.

Sam blinks up at me in surprise and I laugh.

"You'll get used to them," I tell her, then usher her into the living room.

"Hey, guys." Michael comes up to pull me and then Sam into a hug. "I'm glad you could make it. Tiff and the baby are in the kitchen."

"Thank you for the invite," Sam says, and Michael smiles down at her.

He takes her hand between his and squeezes, looking right into her eyes.

"You are welcome here anytime, Sam. We're happy you're here."

Fuck, the smile that stretches over her face. The way her eyes mist over. I want to pull her into a hug and never let go. Michael means it. He's sincere, and I know she can tell. I'm so grateful for him in this moment because Sam's shoulders relax for the first time since we got the invite to come over for brunch three days ago.

"Thank you," she whispers. "Um, this is for you guys."

She holds out a large gift bag full of diapers and onesies and baby board books, and Michael takes it with a smile. He thanks her and gives her one last smile before looking at me.

"Your dad isn't here yet, but he's on the way. Head in the kitchen and I'll grab Chy."

Michael heads up the stairs, and I lead Sam into the kitchen. The moment Tiffany sees us, she turns off whatever she's cooking at the stove and rushes toward us, wrapping her arms around us both.

Sam freezes for a second, then she wraps her arms around my sister, and they hug. Sam sniffles, then my sister pulls away and swipes some of her own tears away. She smiles at me first, then looks at Sam.

"I'm sorry I haven't had you over sooner," Tiff says. "It's not that I didn't want you over—"

"No, it's okay." Sam shakes her head. "I imagine it's been pretty crazy with a new baby."

Tiffany laughs and nods.

"It's been a little crazy," she confirms, then pulls Sam in for another hug. "But I'm glad you're here now."

I've only been over a few times since they finally brought the baby, Brock, home. Tiffany was recovering from the cesarean and Brock was in the NICU for a week with unstable blood sugar. I kept the kids and the hamster for a few nights while Tiff and Michael were in the hospital, but Sam stayed at her apartment. She said she wanted to respect my sister, and I didn't push.

Since Brock and Tiff have been home, I've swung by to drop off food and do a few loads of the kids' laundry, but Tiffany and Michael are pros and have everything pretty much covered. They don't need my help, but I give it anyway.

"Do you want to meet him?" Tiffany says, and I want to laugh at the mix of excitement and fear that passes over Sam's face as she nods.

"Yes," she says, and Tiff leads us to the swing where Brock is sleeping in the corner.

"He's beautiful," Sam whispers as she takes him in.

He's a cute little thing. Kind of resembles an adorable old man with his bald head and chubby cheeks. He's sleeping now, but I know he's got these giant brown eyes and thick black eyelashes, and a set of lungs on him that don't give out. I told Tiffany he might be an opera singer when he grows up.

"He loves this swing," Tiffany explains. "Once he wakes up, you can hold him if you want. You can feed him, too."

Sam's eyes widen and she looks at Tiffany, then at me, then back at Brock.

"I'd like that," she says.

Tiffany goes back to the stove. She's making pancakes, a stack of them already sitting on a plate on the counter, and I can smell bacon wafting from the oven. I glance back at Sam. She's still staring at the swinging, sleeping Brock. I take her hand in mine and give it a squeeze.

"Lennon's baby is going to be here soon," she whispers. "You think he'll look like that?"

I tilt my head to the side and study Brock.

"I think Lennon and Macon's baby is going to have a head full of unruly curls," I say decidedly, and Sam laughs.

I feel a body step up to stand next to me, and I glance down at Cheyenne.

"Hey, Punk." I wrap my arm around her shoulders and glance down into the pocket of her shirt. Sure enough, her little fluffy hamster is curled up in there. "You're breaking the rules again."

She looks up at me with narrowed eyes.

"Don't tattle," she says, and Sam laughs.

Sam leans around me to glance at Cheyenne.

"Don't worry, Chy. I won't let him snitch."

Cheyenne grins, says thank you, and then disappears into the living room.

My dad shows up and greets Sam the same way Tiffany and Michael did—with nothing but love and acceptance—and my heart fucking soars.

My family has accepted the woman I love with open arms. They finally see her the way I see her, and it fills me with joy. It makes me glad I never stopped fighting for them. This family, this love, this life. It was worth the struggle. It was worth the fight.

When I look down at Sam and find her smiling up at me, I know she feels it.

I know she knows.

*Sam*

## EPILOGUE

One Year Later

I HOIST GABE ON MY HIP AND CARRY HIM BACK OUT TO THE DOCK.

I brought him to the cabin to do a diaper change, but he's got his little swim diaper and floaties back on, and I know if I set him down, he'd take off stumbling down the path and jump right into the water. Ten months old and the little shit is fearless. I don't know how Lennon does it.

"Quit squirming, Gabe, we'll be at the water soon enough."

I laugh at the way he pouts, looking just like Macon with his curly hair hanging in his eyes. I kiss his chubby little cheek and he giggles. Gabe is thoughtful and pensive like Lennon, but he's bold like Macon. He's got all their best qualities.

The first time we got him in the lake, he wasn't sure what he thought of it. He furrowed his brow and studied the water. Kicked his feet slowly and tested it out. Now that he's decided he likes it, though, we can't keep him out of it. He's been out here every day this week. As soon as he wakes up, he asks to swim. It's adorable and exhausting.

"Mama," Gabe yells, gesturing wilding to the water as soon as he sees Lennon. "Mama!"

Lennon laughs and glances at us from where she's sitting on the dock. She's not even out of her first trimester yet, but she's already got a little baby bump with this one.

We were all shocked when Lennon told us she was pregnant again, but I don't think anyone was as shocked as Lennon. This pregnancy has been really uncomfortable for her. Morning sickness that lasts days. Insomnia and fatigue. She's had to put a hold on all of her painting commissions, and I've been keeping Gabe a lot just so my best friend can rest while Macon is working at the rec center.

This week at the cabin has helped, though. That's why I suggested it. The cabin makes everything better.

"C'mere, little man," Chris says from the water. "We'll let you swim."

Chris holds his hands out for Gabe and he nearly jumps from my arms and into Chris's. Macon lets out a loud laugh, and I flare my eyes at Lennon.

"He really loves the water." I sit down next to her and dip my feet in the lake. "How are you feeling?"

Lennon smirks.

"You don't have to ask me that every five minutes," she says playfully. "But I feel okay. I haven't thrown up yet, so I'm hoping that means I'm getting to the end of the worst of it." She nudges my shoulder with hers. "How are *you* feeling?"

I purse my lips and think it over while Chris and Macon splash around in the lake with Gabe. They're laughing and having fun, and I want to soak up the sound. I don't want to forget it. It's a kind of happiness I never thought I would experience, and I never want it to end.

"I'm good," I say after a moment. "I've done everything I need to do. The lawyers say I probably won't have to set foot in the courtroom because I've recorded everything. The media attention will probably pick up again once the trial starts next week, but I'm ready. I've got the restaurant opening to focus on, and I've got you guys. They think it will probably be a quick trial, and once it's over…"

I shrug.

Once it's over, it's over, and I don't have to worry about any of them again. Not my mom, who filed for divorce days after my father's gala and moved permanently to France, and not my brother, who has so far ignored his outstanding subpoenas and will likely be arrested if he ever sets foot on American soil again.

I wish Ashton Cartwright had gotten some sort of legal repercussion, but the public disgrace and arrest of his father, paired with the loss of his family fortune was a pretty decent punishment. Ashton hasn't taken well to the rapid change of social status and tax bracket, and I find it amusing. He hates me but fuck him. I hate him, too.

I hate them all, and they can all burn. I'll be glad to never think about any of them again once this is all over.

Lennon takes my hand in hers and squeezes.

"I'm proud of you," she says. "Are you proud of you?"

I smile and nod.

"Yeah. I think I am."

I rest my head on her shoulder and we're quiet for a moment as we watch the boys swim in the lake.

"There is one other thing," I say slowly, and Lennon hums.

"Hmm? What's that?"

"I had a missed call from Lynnette when I went to the house to change Gabe. She said to call her back because she had news, so I did."

Lennon sits up straighter and stares at me.

"And?" she asks, and I shrug.

"They unfroze my trust fund. They didn't find any suspicious activity, so it's mine again under the same terms. I get all of it when I turn thirty or get married. Whatever comes first."

Lennon's jaw drops, and I smile. I wasn't expecting to ever see that money, to be honest, so this news came as a surprise. I'm still processing it.

"I don't even know if I want it," I say idly.

Lennon shakes her head.

"You take that money, Sam Harper. It's yours. You fucking earned it."

I laugh lightly at the vehemence in her tone.

"That's exactly what Lynnette said," I say, and Lennon nods in agreement. "I'll probably have to talk about it in therapy for a year before I finally make a decision, but that's fine. I have time."

Lennon tilts her head to the side and studies me.

"Are you going to tell Casper?"

"I don't think so," I say on an exhale. "Not yet, anyway."

"You're not…You're not worried that he'd—"

"No, no. It's not that. I know he wouldn't care about the money. I trust him. But I don't know…if he ever proposes, I want it to be as pure as possible, if that makes sense. I don't want him to do it because he thinks *I* want that money. It took us months before he fully accepted that I didn't *need* a life of luxury, you know? Hell, I don't even want one."

I glance down at my hand still wrapped in Lennon's. I lift my arm to inspect our nails.

"I sometimes miss having a good manicure, but it makes me feel better that your nails are just as trash as mine."

Lennon gasps and elbows me lightly with a laugh. I'd say I was kidding, but I'm not. Her nails *are* trash, and so are mine.

"If he proposed, would you say yes?"

"Yes." My answer comes immediately, without any hesitation. "I've thought about it a lot in the last year, and I would absolutely say yes if he proposed, but I'm not in any hurry. I've only just moved in with him. I like our life how it is right now. I want to enjoy every day and take it all as it comes."

Lennon laughs, and when I look at her, she's smiling brightly.

"What?" I ask, my grin stretching to match hers. "What's so funny?"

"I just love you, is all. I love seeing you happy." She shrugs and glances out at the water where the guys are swimming with Gabe. "He's been good for you, and you've been good for him. You're good for each other, and I'm really glad everything worked out the way it did."

I narrow my eyes in jest.

"You're just glad that you can go on double dates with your babysitters," I say, and Lennon grins.

"That, too."

We fall back into silence, and my eyes wander to Chris's newest tattoo, right where his neck and shoulder meet. My lips, bright red and impossible to miss. I can't look at it too long, otherwise I'll get turned on and will have to drag him to the cabin for a quickie.

He used the lipstick print I'd left on the *Hellfire* note over a year ago and had it permanently inked onto his skin. I was surprised that he'd been carrying the note in his wallet all this time. Even more surprised when he told me he was going to get it made into a tattoo right after I'd moved in with him.

But now that it's done? I'm obsessed with it.

I might be a little obsessed with him, actually, and he knows it.

Later in the day, we take the speed boat to the marina for lunch. We listen to the live band, and everyone laughs at the way Gabe tears up the dance floor. We close out the night with a small campfire at the cabin, and it's an absolutely perfect day.

As I curl up on Chris's chest in our bed, I don't think I could be any more content.

I didn't know it at the time, but I think this was what I was fighting for all along. This is what I always wanted. I just wasn't ready to admit it to myself. A love like ours. The family we have. The life we're building.

It's better than I ever could have imagined.

"Hey, babe," I whisper, pushing up on my elbow so I can look at him.

God, he's beautiful.

"Yeah, princess?"

He reaches up and runs a strand of my hair gently through his fingertips, the soft touch making me shiver. I press a kiss to his tattoo of my lips, and he hums low in his throat.

"I've found my true north," I say softly. I can feel his heart beating under my palm. Can feel his light inhales and exhales on my naked skin. "It's you. Our family. Our life. That's my true north. I get it now. I understand."

Chris wraps his arms around my body tightly, and I snuggle into him. He presses a kiss to my head.

"I knew you would," he says, and I smile.

He did. He knew even before I did. I think back to our conversation the first time he brought me to this cabin, when I was warring with myself daily, fighting desperately for a future I couldn't yet fathom.

*What if I don't have a true north?*

*You have one, princess. You just have to let yourself find it.*

"Thank you for being patient with me," I say as he runs his fingers up and down my back. "I love you."

"I love you, Sam. My warrior princess. My fearless queen. My true north."

*Sam*

## EXTENDED EPILOGUE

One More Year Later

I CAN TELL IT'S LATE MORNING WHEN I OPEN MY EYES.

I shoot upright and check my phone, briefly worried I missed my alarm before I remember it's Monday. The Princess is closed on Mondays. But still, we're usually there by now. We've got inventory and grocery shipments and payroll. Chris needs to finalize the menu for the week, and I need to look over our reservations list, which is about a mile long and scheduled two months out.

The responsibilities don't end, and I love it.

I furrow my brow. No texts. No sounds coming from the house. I'm alone. It confuses me until I glance at Chris's side of the bed and find a single red Gerbera daisy and a note. I smile as I reach for it, but then my heart starts to race.

*come find me* ♡

I read it three times, my eyes growing wider each time before I finally tell myself to stay calm. This could just be a fun a little game. It's probably not what I think it is. I'll probably find him on the deck outside with fresh coffee and something delicious for breakfast.

That's all.

This is probably *not* a proposal.

I force myself to move slowly. I put on a pair of shorts and tank top. I throw my hair in a ponytail, but just before I leave the bedroom, I head back to the bathroom and put on some mascara and red lipstick. *Just in case.*

"Babe," I call into the house as I walk through the house. "Cute note. Where are you?"

I force my voice to be light, but I can't hide the slight excited waver in it. It's just breakfast. It's just coffee. *Calm down.* I don't know if I'm trying not to get my hopes up or if I'm worried I'll jinx it, but I'm still hyper-alert as move toward the kitchen.

I don't smell coffee or breakfast.

I don't hear movement. I peek out the sliding doors to the deck, but it's empty.

The moment I step foot into the kitchen, I see a pink Gerbera daisy by the coffee pot. The pot is empty, but my travel mug from the local café is next to it, and I almost trip over my own feet as I rush to it.

There's no note this time. Just the flower and the mug, so I snatch both and hurry to the driveway. I'm flinging open the door to Chris's truck when I realize I didn't put on shoes, but I don't have to worry. My sandals are sitting on the bench seat right next to Chris's truck keys and my handbag. I laugh out loud as I grab the sandals and slip them on before climbing into the cab of the truck.

It's hard not to speed through town, and even though it's less than a ten-minute drive to the café, I barely breathe. My hands are gripping the steering wheel so tightly that my knuckles are white, and my cheeks hurt from the wide smile I'm fighting.

"Calm down, Sam. It's just coffee. It's just coffee."

I repeat it over and over, but I can't help it.

I want it to be *more* than just coffee.

I think it is.

I park, probably poorly, in the lot next to the café and force myself to walk through the doors even though every part of me wants to run. The barista smiles the moment she sees me.

"Morning, Sam," she says, holding out her hand. "I'll take that."

"Good morning, Shelly," I say slowly, confusion lacing my tone as I hand over the travel mug.

I watch as she takes the mug to the espresso machine and gets to work making my drink. I smile as I watch.

A lavender latte.

Something about the barista in our small-town café knowing my drink order before I place it fills me with warmth. Sure, Chris likely called ahead, but Shelly knows my order on her own. She starts my drink the moment I step through the door, and it always succeeds in making me smile. I grew up in this town, but it never felt like home until I was free from the Harper family name. Until I was able to shed all the baggage and be *just* me. Just Sam.

I never had a home until I finally let Chris love me.

I take a deep breath and will away the prickle of tears I feel in my eyes. I focus on Shelly as she puts the lid on my latte, then takes a slice of quiche from the case and heats it up. The quiche is from The Princess. Chris's recipe. We have a standing order to provide them weekly for the café. This week is one of my favorites: spinach, sun dried tomatoes, and pancetta.

I can smell it even before Shelly sets the plate and latte in front of me, and my stomach growls despite the rush I'm in.

"I have something for you," Shelly says, setting a napkin and fork next to the plate, "but I'm under strict orders not to give it to you until you've eaten."

My jaw drops, and for a moment, I consider arguing, but then I decide against it, reaching for the quiche and prepping to shove the whole damn thing in my mouth at once.

"Ah!" Shelly says on a laugh, halting my movements.

She grins as I stand frozen, then gestures to an empty table.

"You have to *sit* and eat it." I frown and she laughs again. "*Strict* orders, Sam. We don't want to go against the man that feeds us."

I sigh and give her a small smile.

"Okay. Fine. Thank you."

I take my latte and quiche to the table and make myself enjoy it. I chew thoroughly before I swallow. I let my latte cool before I drink it. I push down the need to rush, to hurry, to get to the end goal. When I finish the last bite, I do feel better. Less jumpy. More grounded.

I laugh. Fucking Chris and his insistence on me eating actual meals. I'll never tell him that he's right, but he is.

I take my empty plate back to the counter and Shelly gives me an excited smile. I wait impatiently as she brings the plate to the back, and when she returns, she sets another flower on the counter in front of me—this one a pink rose—and…a wrench.

I raise an eyebrow.

"He left this for me?" She nods. "Did he say anything?"

She shrugs, her wide smile still fixed to her face.

"Just to give you the wrench and the flower after you've eaten."

I furrow my brow for a second, and then it dawns on me. The garage. I turn to leave, then stop myself.

"Hey, Shell, can I get a large to-go cup filled about halfway with water? For the flowers."

She grabs it for me, tells me goodbye and good luck, and I'm out the door within seconds. I put the three flowers in the cup of water and put the cup into the cupholder of Chris's truck before cranking the engine and pulling onto the road. In a matter of minutes, I'm parking in the lot of Franklin Auto Body.

I see Andre waiting for me even before my feet hit the pavement. He's standing out front with a wide grin and a sprig of what looks like baby's breath. When I get to him, he pulls a paintbrush from behind his ear and hands it and the flowers to me.

"Lennon?" I ask quickly.

My heart is galloping in my chest, and I can't fight the way my voice squeaks when I speak. I'm excited and terrified and so damn impatient that it's taking all of my restraint not to run at a full sprint.

Andre shrugs.

"Probably?"

I rush back to the truck, shouting my thank you over my shoulder. He laughs out loud, and the last thing I hear through the open truck window is him shouting *don't speed* as I pull out of the lot.

I'm knocking on the door to Lennon and Macon's house three minutes later. It's Macon who opens the door.

"Took you long enough," he drawls with a smirk. "I was expecting you hours ago."

I arch a brow.

"Not all of us are up with the sun."

He opens the door wide and lets me in, and I note the house is strangely quiet. It's never quiet at Lennon's. Charlotte and Gabe are loud little monsters. Sweet, amazing, beautiful monsters—but loud.

"Where is everyone?"

Macon just shrugs and leans on the door with a grin.

I raise both brows.

"Well?"

"Well, what?"

"Don't you have something for me?"

He looks at the ceiling as if he's trying to remember, and I sigh loudly.

"Kitchen counter," he says finally, and I run to the kitchen, jumping over some kids toys as I go.

I find another flower, something beautiful and purple, and a menu for The Princess.

"Thankyoubye," I say as I rush past Macon and out the door. I don't look back. I keep the menu on my lap until I'm pulling up to our restaurant.

"Chris," I shout as I unlock the back door and run inside. "Babe? You here?"

It's quiet. I walk through the kitchen, the office, and the back dining room, but there is no one here. It's not until I step into the front where the bar is that my fingers start to tremble. Sitting on the bar top next to a yellow flower is Chris's compass and his copy of *Walden*.

The cabin.

The drive is long. Longer than usual. Every few minutes, I flick my eyes to the clock on the dashboard. Every few minutes I remind myself to stay calm. To drive responsibly. To not start freaking out.

But if the to-go cup of flowers and the cute scavenger hunt tell me anything, it's that this is almost definitely, probably, *hopefully*, a possible proposal.

The man has romance in his blood, though.

He could have just planned a small weekend getaway for us. We've been working nonstop since the restaurant opened, and while we love it, Chris has mentioned several times recently that we should take a vacation.

I'm three hours into the four-hour drive when I finally break down and call Lennon. She answers on the first ring.

"Hey." I can hear the smile in her tone.

"I'm freaking out. I'm freaking out, Lennon. Do you know anything?"

She's quiet for a moment, and in the silence, I know that she knows. Whatever is happening, she knows.

"Take some deep breaths," she says finally. "How are you feeling? Is it good or bad?"

"Good." A giggle bubbles out of me, and I have to blink away tears. "It's good. It's a good feeling."

She laughs with me.

"Good. Just drive safely. Do you want me to read to you?" A door opens and shuts on her end of the phone, and I hear something shuffling when she speaks again. "I've got some Robert Frost poems, *On the Road*, and…oh, *Emma*."

"Definitely *Emma*."

The final hour of the drive is better. I listen to Lennon read Jane Austen, and I do what she told me to do. I focus on my breathing. I drive safely. By the time I'm pulling onto the small gravel road that leads to the cabin, I'm almost calm.

I interrupt Lennon's reading.

"Okay, I have to let you go. I'm here. I'll call you later."

"Love you. Tell me everything later."

"Love you. Thanks, Len."

"Always."

She hangs up as I pull into the driveway. There's no car out front, but I don't take the time to check around the side of the cabin where we sometimes park. Instead, I just gather the cup of flowers, the coffee mug, the wrench, the paintbrush, the menu, the book and the compass into my arms and bolt inside. I don't know if I even shut the door to the truck. I rush through every room of the small cabin and make sure it's empty before heading out the back door and down to the lake.

The moment I see Chris on the dock with a bouquet of beautiful flowers, I start to run. Or jog, really. Awkwardly. I move as fast as I can in my sandals down the uneven path to the lake with my arms full, and when he smiles at me, I start to cry again.

I stop a few feet in front of him, and he chuckles.

"You brought all of that?"

He gestures to the items in my arms, and I shrug.

"I didn't know if I'd need it."

He closes the distance and trades me—the gorgeous bouquet for all of my scavenger hunt souvenirs—then sets the collection on the dock by his feet. When he rises again, his hands cradle my face as his thumbs wipe at my tears.

"Hi, princess."

His voice is a whisper as he searches my tear-filled eyes. I know what he finds. Excitement. Vulnerability. A hint of anxiety. Immense, endless, unconditional love.

"Hi."

He presses his forehead to mine.

"You found me."

"Of course," I rasp. "I'll always find you. You're my true north."

His lips brush over mine as they fold into a grin. He kisses me softly, tasting my tears.

"Good. And you're mine."

"I'm your what?"

His breath ghosts over my face, cooling my tear tracks as he laughs lightly.

"My everything," he says, then he moves his hands from my face and lowers himself to his knee before me.

I hiccup on a sob, taking my free hand to cover my mouth as the other clutches my bouquet of flowers. This is everything I've ever wanted. He is better than I ever could have dreamed. Our love is so much more than I ever thought I deserved.

I blink, trying to clear my eyes of tears so I can see him better. So I can commit this moment to memory so I never, ever forget. Chris, the man I love, on his knee in front of me with a beautiful diamond ring in his hand. His smile. His loving, tear-filled gaze.

He is perfect.

He is perfect for me.

"Sam Harper, I love you so much. Each day, I wake up excited to spend another day with you, and each night, I fall asleep feeling grateful to have you in my arms. I feel so damn lucky to be the one you love, princess. To be the one who gets to *see* you, all of you, and I swear I will never take that for granted. I will love you until we're old and wrinkled. I will love you until this life ends, and then I will love you into whatever comes after. You're all I want, now and forever. Will you marry me?"

I nod and stick my hand out for him.

"Yes. God, yes, I will marry you."

Chris slides the ring on my finger, then stands and takes my lips in another kiss. Soft at first, then deeper, until I'm breathless and completely engrossed in him. I tighten my arms around his neck and laugh when he lifts me up and spins me in a circle. I'm happier than I can ever remember being.

"I love you," he says as he sets me back on my feet.

I don't release him. I hold him tightly.

"I love you so much," I say back, and then I close my eyes and breathe him in.

I rest my head on his chest and listen to his rapid heartbeat. It's as familiar as my own at this point. I open my eyes and pull back to tell him as much, but then movement from the end of the dock catches my attention.

I laugh when I notice Lennon standing there with her phone in her hands. She smiles and holds the phone up.

"Congratulations! I got it all," she says proudly. "The whole thing."

"Good thing you said yes, Harper." My eyes move to the shore and find Macon leaning on a tree. He must have drove here the moment I left his house. His phone is out, too. "Would have been a real bummer of a video if you hadn't."

I roll my eyes on a laugh and look back at Chris.

"It's on video?"

He nods. "Pictures, too. It was Lennon's idea. She thought maybe you'd want to have them as a keepsake."

It's perfect. It's all so perfect. I glance at Lennon and mouth *thank you* before looking back at Chris. At my fiancé.

"I love you," I repeat. "Thank you for being everything I didn't know I needed."

He smiles. "Back at you, princess."

Then I kiss him again.

**THE END**

**Want more Sam and Chris?**
Keep flipping for a bonus chapter showing the beginning of their love story—that first night in his truck that started it all!

**Claire's book is coming!**
Yes, you read that correctly. Claire IS getting a book. Yes, *that* Claire. To make sure you don't miss it, please join my newsletter at https://authorbritbenson.com/newsletter/

# *Chris*

## BONUS SCENE

Approximately 1.5 years before chapter one

"Don't go," Sam's says, her brow furrowed.

"I'm sorry, I have to. I'm exhausted." Lennon's statement is punctuated with a yawn and a sleepy smile. "You're staying over though, right?"

Sam rolls her eyes and smirks.

"No way in hell am I crashing in your sex pad. Ever since you moved back, you two have been attached at the genitals. I can't handle it."

Lennon's jaw drops on a laugh, but she doesn't argue. It's true. I'm pretty sure Macon and Lennon spend every spare moment alone fucking, and when they're in public, they're rarely not touching or kissing or making sex eyes at each other.

It doesn't bother me, but I'm getting the impression Sam's jealous. I just don't know who she's jealous of—Lennon or Macon.

I wipe down the bar and finish closing duties while pretending to not be eavesdropping on my best friend's girlfriend and his ex-fuck buddy. Their relationship confuses the hell out of me.

"What are you going to do, then?" Lennon asks. "You can't drive back to D.C."

## BONUS SCENE

Sam shrugs and takes a sip of her red wine.

"I'll stay at the house."

"No. You hate it there. Just come back with me. I'll make Macon sleep on the couch."

Macon sighs, and when I glance at him, I can tell he does *not* approve of that plan. Lennon ignores him, but Sam narrows her eyes in his direction while she responds.

"It's fine, Len. It's one night, and I'll see you for brunch in the morning. Go get some sleep. You look like you're about to pass out."

"Are you sure? I don't mind. I'd rather you be with me than at your father's house."

"Positive. He's not even in town. Go. I'll see you in the morning."

There's a pause in their conversation that has me glancing back in their direction. Lennon and Sam are frowning at each other, some sort of weird silent conversation, and then finally Lennon sighs and wraps her arms around Sam in a hug. As they say goodbye, I look at Macon.

"Boxing tomorrow?" I ask, and he nods.

"Bright and early," he says with a grin.

Being in the Marines has made Macon an early riser. Despite his discharge, it hasn't changed. He's up with the dawn. It's fucking annoying.

I slap his hand in a low five, give Lennon a smile, and then they're walking out the door leaving me with Samantha Harper. I glance at the princess and find her scowling at the door.

"Your jealousy is showing, princess."

She narrows her eyes in my direction. She hates that nickname, but she'd never let herself tell me that. It would show weakness, and Harpers don't show weakness.

"I don't trust him," she says, and my shoulders tense, ready to defend my best friend.

"You should," I say flatly. "He's more than earned it."

"Not from me." She arches a brow. "If he hurts her again, I can have him murdered."

My lips twitch and I nod. I believe it.

"He won't."

She doesn't respond. She just takes another sip of her wine and stares bullets at the door, so I leave her to it.

When I finish my closing duties and get the okay from Mackie to clock out, Sam is still sitting at the end of the bar nursing her drink. I study her carefully. She's got her eyes on her phone and worry lines between her eyebrows, and Lennon's comment before she left filters through my mind.

*You hate it there.*

*I'd rather you be with me than at your father's house.*

Sam must really not want to go home.

Without thinking too much on it, I round the bar and lean next to her stool.

"How about a game of pool, princess?"

She glances up at me slowly, face blank, and arches an eyebrow.

"I've never played before," she says, and I grin.

"I'll teach you. C'mon."

I turn and head to the pool tables without glancing behind me. I can tell she's following me, though. I can feel her stare on my back.

Luckily, one of the pool tables is empty, so I grab two cues from the wall before finally turning to face her.

"This is a pool cue," I say, handing it to her.

She rolls her eyes.

"No shit."

I laugh and shake my head. She's so prickly, and it just intrigues me. I want to poke her some more.

"Okay, so here are the basics," I say.

I run her through the *for dummies* rules of eight-ball pool, and she listens intently. Nodding like a good little student with her red lips pursed in concentration.

When I'm finished, I model how to hold the pool cue.

"Now you do it," I say, and reluctantly, she fumbles through maneuvering the cue to the table.

I take my hat off and run my hands through my hair before

BONUS SCENE

putting it back on my head, her eyes sticking to the motion as she tries to get the pool cue situated in her hands.

"Not bad," I tell her, walking around the pool table to stand beside her. "Can I?"

She tilts her head to the side, eyes flicking from my face, to my backward ball cap, and back.

"Can you what?"

I grin.

"Can I help you with the pool cue? I'll have to stand next to you, put my arms around you. It will be close. I just want to make sure you won't be uncomfortable."

She blinks at me, her face going slack with surprise for the briefest of moments before she wipes the expression away, and I'm left wondering if I saw anything at all. She nods.

"That's fine," she says, so I close the distance.

Nerves racket in my chest, catching me off guard, as I position myself behind Sam. She smells like flowers. Some light, feminine perfume that's probably a designer brand and expensive as fuck. It's intoxicating. I find myself wanting to take gulps of it, filling my lungs with the scent.

You get what you pay for, I suppose.

I make sure not to press my body against hers, keeping our proximity respectful, but I'm still taken aback by the way her soft, pale arms look next to my larger, tattooed ones. With the sleeves of my flannel rolled on my forearms and the worn leather band of my watch on my wrist, we couldn't be more different. The delicate gold bracelet and the dainty rings on her perfectly manicured fingers are a direct contrast to my large, calloused, suntanned hands and grease-stained nailbeds. I'm bombarded with the sudden desire to wrap my hand around her two delicate wrists and hold her against me. To hold her body against mine and revel in the feel of her.

I bet she'd be eager. I bet she'd feel like heaven and hell all at once.

I breathe lightly through my mouth to avoid her scent and focus on her grip and stance.

## BONUS SCENE

"Legs a little wider," I say, using my booted foot to nudge her stilettos to widen her stance. "Bend down a little."

My voice comes out rougher than intended, but she does as she's told.

"Good. Hold this hand at your hip," I tell her, tapping the hand holding the end of the cue. "And relax these fingers but keep these firm." I tap on her fingers that are currently pressed to the table with her pool cue resting on top. "Think of making a bridge with your hand to balance and guide the end of your stick. Your cue should never touch the table felt—only the cue ball, okay?"

"That's the white one?"

I don't miss the way her voice is breathier than usual. Quieter. Whether that's due to the proximity or something else, I don't know. I try not to think about it.

"Yeah. The white one."

I move my hand to her arm that's holding the back of the pool cue, and I almost groan when I finally close my fingers around her wrist.

I can feel her pulse thrumming rapidly under my fingers, and for a second, I don't move. I just stand behind Sam with my arm wrapped around her body and her wrist enclosed in my fingers. It's not until I hear her breath hitch that I snap out of it. I move her arm back and forth, mimicking taking a shot.

"You'll want to set your bridge about six inches from the cue ball, and keep your grip relaxed but controlled when you take your shot." I release her and take a giant step back. "You ready?"

She nods and tells me to take the break. She's stripes, and I'm solids, and it takes all my strength not to laugh at how terrible she is. I have to readjust her stance twice before she finally starts to appear comfortable with the cue, but I still wipe the fucking floor with her.

"This game sucks," she says, eyes narrowed on me. "Let's go again."

I laugh.

"It's not easy to master, but you're not doing too bad."

She rolls her eyes and props a hand on her hip.

"Let's go again," she repeats, "but I need a drink first."

I grab a bottle of the red wine she was drinking and two glasses. I pour us both a generous amount, then set the bottle and the glasses on the little drink ledge behind the pool tables.

I set the balls up again and take the break, and then watch as Sam grows more infuriated every time she fails to sink a ball. I'm not surprised to find that Samantha Harper is a sore loser, but damn is she sexy when she's mad.

"You did better this time," I say with a smile as I rack the balls again. "You knocked in four. That's two more than last game."

She practically growls as she takes a drink of her wine. If her eyes could shoot lasers, the pool table would be in flames.

"One more game," she says finally. "One more."

I sigh and shake my head.

"Are you sure? You seem agitated. Maybe we should take a break." She turns her glare on me, and I throw my palms up. "Whoa, okay. Forget I suggested it. One more game for the princess."

Her nostrils flare, but she says nothing as I take the break. I knock in three before it's her turn, and then she sinks a ball on her first shot. The smile of triumph that takes over her face is one that makes my stomach flip on itself.

"Atta girl," I say with a grin. "See? You're getting it."

She misses her next shot, but I notice a change in her body language. The tense irritation is gone, and it's replaced with a competitive edge I've never seen in her before. She's lighter, and at first, I think it's because she's finally getting the hang of the game. When it's her turn again, though, I realize my mistake.

She's not lighter because she's finally gotten comfortable with the game.

She's lighter because she's stopped *throwing* the game.

Sam cleans the table of the rest of her balls without breaking a sweat. She sends me flirty little smirks after every ball she sinks, and all I can do is stare with a stupid lopsided grin on my face. When it's down to the eight-ball, she leans her hip on the table and smiles sweetly at me.

"Eight-ball, side pocket," she says.

Then she takes the shot and sinks it.

I laugh and shake my head.

"You're a pool shark," I say.

"Beginner's luck." She shrugs nonchalantly. "Let's go again but make it more exciting."

"Oh no," I say. "I'm not betting against you. I'm not fooled."

"Scared?"

The way she blinks innocently at me, all bright blue eyes and red pouty lips, sends a thrill down my spine. I'm being taunted by a fucking angel, and I'm falling right into her trap. She's toying with me, and I don't even care.

Fuck. I *want* to be toyed with.

"Fine. Twenty bucks says you can't do that again," I say, and she smirks.

"A hundred says I can take the break and beat your ass without you ever touching your cue."

My jaw drops.

Jesus Christ, I've never been so turned on in my life. Before I even take the bet, I know I've lost. I don't care. I'd light twenty hundred-dollar bills on fire just to watch her hand me my ass.

"You're on," I say, and then I stand back with my arms folded across my chest and watch as she does exactly what she said she'd do.

She beats my ass, and I never even touch my pool cue.

She calls every ball she sinks, prowling around the table with a feline grace that gives me chills. I've found a new kink, and it's watching Samantha Harper hustle me out of money while wearing six-inch designer heels. I should just slap my wallet on the table right now and tell her to have at it. I could watch this forever.

"Eight-ball, corner pocket," she says, and then she sinks it with a grin.

BONUS SCENE

She plucks the hundred-dollar bill off the table and puts it into her pocket.

"Again?" she says, and I laugh.

"Sam Harper," I say in awe, shaking my head. "Who the fuck are you?"

She smirks.

"Wouldn't you like to know."

I would. I really, really would.

"Want to get out of here," I ask before overthinking it, and she nods without hesitation.

"Yes."

She turns and walks out, and I follow, watching her hips sway confidently in her tight pants. They're probably bespoke; that's the only way a pair of pants could mold on an ass like that so perfectly. I've never been an ass man, but I suddenly want to take a bite out of hers.

She leads me through the parking lot, straight to the back corner where my truck is parked, then leans on the front bumper. Her chic attire looks so out of place next to my old blue truck, but I find myself wishing I could snap a picture. Her black high heels next to my muddy tires. Her pressed designer clothes in a pile on the tailgate...

I clear my throat.

"Where to?" I ask, opening the passenger door for her.

She brushes past me and climbs onto the bench seat before turning and grabbing the edges of my unbuttoned flannel shirt.

"Here's good," she says, and then she tugs me to her.

I don't hesitate. I just kiss her like I'm starved. I plunge my fingers into her hair and hold her closer, kissing her deeper, and run my other hand down her back so I can grab her ass and pull her against my body. She scoots back and tugs on the hem of my white shirt, so I climb into the cab with her. She wastes no time straddling me the moment I'm seated, and I groan when she lowers her body to mine.

"Fuck," I growl, grabbing her hips as her hands roam under my flannel, pushing the shirt down my arms. She grinds down on my now hard dick and my hips buck. "Fuck, Sam."

Her lips drag from my mouth to my ear to my neck. Her nails scrape into my biceps and shoulders. Her hot heat rubs on my erection with every move of her hips, and all I can do is fucking hold on tight. I grasp on to every part of her that I can, squeezing and testing the feel of her under my palms. I kiss every inch of skin I can reach. Her lips, her jaw, her collarbone. I'm spurred on by the sweet way she whimpers and her harsh, ragged breathing.

She's like an entirely different person, and I don't want it to end. I clamp my hands on her hips and guide her movements, making her grind down on me harder and faster. A steady, torturous rhythm that threatens to make me come in my fucking pants, but I don't care. Seeing her like this? Lipstick smeared, hair mussed, eyes wild. I want more.

I want her messy.

I want her real.

"That's right, baby," I say, dragging my teeth along the sensitive skin of her neck as she tosses her head back. "I want to see you come undone. Let me see you."

I take her lips in another kiss, desperate for another taste of her, but her hips stop, and the kiss cools. She puts her hands on my shoulders and pushes me back against the seat, then removes my hands from her hips. I let her, breathing heavily and confused.

"This was fun," she says politely as she climbs off me and opens the truck door.

On impulse my hand shoots out and wraps around her arm.

"Stay," I say quickly, almost pleadingly, but the look she shoots me has me dropping my grip.

"Thanks for the pool lessons," she says, all business, and I nod.

"Sure."

And then, she just leaves. She climbs out of my truck, shuts the door, then walks to her flashy custom-luxury car. I watch her silently until she's in the car and pulling out of the lot. It's not until her car is out of sight that I realize I should have driven her—or at least asked if she was okay to drive. She'd only had two glasses of wine all night, but I still should have checked.

I worry about her until the next day when I find out from Macon that Sam met Lennon for brunch. Then, I think about her nonstop for two weeks straight. I watch the bar door like an eager puppy. I listen like an obsessed person for her name in conversation. By the third week, I start to accept that what happened with Sam and me was a one-off. A fluke.

Whatever I thought happened, didn't. She played me, and the truth is, I enjoyed it.

We'll just leave it at that.

# SNEAK PEEK

## BETWEEN NEVER AND FOREVER

Levi

A high-pitched scream wakes me, and I shoot upright in my bed.

My heart is in my throat and my breath is straining my lungs when I hear it again. Another high-pitched scream. *Brynn*. My feet hit the floor just as a chanted stream of *oh my god* begins, and I sprint down the hall toward her room.

I have never known fear like this.

For these few seconds, terror turns my blood to ice, and the need to protect overpowers everything else. Logic, reason, self-preservation—they all disappear in the seconds it takes me to cross the house. Only the primal instinct to protect, to defend, remains.

I shove through the bedroom door at the end of the hall with my fists raised, ready to fight. Ready to kill, if necessary. When I find Brynn sitting cross-legged on her bed, alone, my eyes immediately dart around the room to find the threat.

The closet door is open, displaying clothes on hangers. The second-floor window is closed tight. Everything seems as it was hours earlier when I hugged her goodnight.

"What's wrong?" I say, my voice urgent. I glance back at her and find her staring at her tablet with her hand covering her mouth. She doesn't answer.

"Brynn?" I say again, rushing to her bed and dropping to my knees, reaching for her shoulders while scanning her body for injury.

She jumps with a gasp as her eyes shoot to mine.

"Dad!" she shouts. "Oh my gosh!" Her hand splays over her chest. "What the heck? You scared the crap out of me!" She takes off her headphones and lets out a laugh, her eyes wide. "Oh my gosh, Dad, you look like a ghost. What's wrong? Are you okay?"

My jaw drops, and I suck in a breath. Possibly the first one since being jarred awake.

"You screamed," I say. "I thought something was wrong! I thought you were...that something..."

I can't stop my eyes from scanning her features, my sleep-fogged brain still not grasping that fact that Brynn is fine. She is not hurt. She's not in danger. I don't need to beat the life out of an intruder. She's safe in her room.

I consciously unclench my fists.

"Oh," she says sheepishly. "I'm sorry I scared you."

"Brynn," I breathe out, dropping my head to her mattress and trying to get my heart to calm down. "Jesus Christ, Brynnlee."

"Sorry, Daddy."

We sit in silence for a minute, and when my chest no longer aches with panic, I bring my eyes to hers and raise a stern brow.

"Why the hell are you screaming in the middle of the night? You know you're supposed to be asleep, and you're not allowed to be on your tablet after 7 p.m."

"I know," she says a smile stretching over her face. "I was asleep, I swear, but then Cameron messaged me and—"

"Cameron messaged you at—" I check my watch "—three in the morning?"

"Yes, because—"

"Why were you screaming?"

"*Ohmigod*, Dad, I'm trying to tell you," she says with a roll of her eyes. "Cameron messaged me because Sav Loveless is coming here!"

My shoulders tense again, but Brynn doesn't notice. Her voice rises in pitch with each word as she bounces on the bed, speaking quickly.

"She's coming here, Dad! Here! Here to our dumb, boring town. Nothing good ever happens here, and she's coming, like, right here. Maybe I can meet her? Maybe I can actually get her autograph? Can you take me to meet her? And get a photo or a hug or—"

"I thought that band broke up?" I say calmly, trying to ignore the pain in my hands as my fingers curl back into fists.

I *know* that band broke up.

Brynn has been sobbing about it for two weeks, and I've felt terrible. I'd planned to let her go to one of their shows on the next tour, but now she won't get the chance. They announced that their current tour will be their last, and there are only three shows left, all at the Garden in NYC. They're sold out, and of course, now with the news, scalped prices have skyrocketed.

Brynn's only just stopped tearing up every time one of their songs comes on the radio, and their songs come on the radio constantly.

"Actually, Dad, they didn't *break up*," Brynn corrects, a slight edge to her voice. "The Hometown Heartless is *on a hiatus*, and now I know why."

Brynn shoves her tablet into my hand, tapping the screen to show me the news headline.

"Sav's going to be in a movie," she squeals. "The movie that's filming *here* next month! Oh my *god*, Dad, I can't even believe it. This is prodigious. This is…this is…immaculate!"

Brynn continues to chatter excitedly, but her voice fades into the background as I focus on the tablet screen. The headline confirms what Brynn said.

*Sav Loveless, frontwoman for rock band The Hometown Heartless, has been cast as the lead actress in a new movie.* I don't scroll to read the rest of the article. I can't. Instead, my attention is held frozen by the photograph of the woman staring back at me.

It's the same woman whose face taunts me daily from the posters plastered on Brynn's bedroom walls. The same face I avoid in every grocery store checkout, smirking or scowling from the covers of magazines boasting tell-alls about her various rehab stints, numerous Hollywood hookups, and scandalous on-again-off-again relationship with her bassist.

It's the same face I've seen in my dreams. In my nightmares.

Sav Loveless is a lesson in contrasts.

Every detail about her directly contradicts another. Silver hair and soft, pale skin, with swirling, storm gray, depthless eyes. A heart-shaped face. A delicate jaw. Cupid's bow lips. Her angelic features suggest innocence and kindness, but the stories that precede her prove the exact opposite. She projects this façade of fearlessness, as if nothing can hurt her, while her lyrics rage with pain. Her tongue slices as sharp as a jagged piece of glass, but I know from experience how plush the lips are that contain that tongue, and I know how gentle it can be when coaxed.

She's ethereal and untouchable, yet she was so soft under my palms...

I close my eyes quickly, severing the invisible line of tension between myself and the woman in the photograph.

I'll never forget the way I felt the first time I saw her photo in a tabloid. I almost crashed my car the first time I heard her voice on the radio. My gut still twists at the memory.

After years of nothing, she was everywhere overnight. Then, as if her global popularity wasn't enough, my own daughter had to go and become a diehard fan.

It's been a poetic sort of torture. Perhaps deserved.

Most people get to move on from their first love. Heal from their first heartbreak. Learn from their first big mistake.

But me? I can't seem to escape mine.

I take Brynn's tablet and tell her she needs to go back to sleep. She's got school in the morning, and even though there's only two weeks left until summer break, she still needs to be awake for class.

In theory, anyway.

I think Brynn might be a bit more advanced than the average

seven-year-old. I had to download a dictionary app on my phone just to look up the words she uses on a regular basis, and the other day she spent an hour lecturing me on ways to make my business more environmentally friendly.

I'm proud of her intelligence, but it makes me nervous for the years to come. I can barely keep up with her now.

Once Brynn's light is off and her room is quiet, I make my way out onto the back deck. The rhythmic sound of the water flowing from the ocean and the briny scent of the air, usually so relaxing, do little to calm my nerves. I have an early job in the morning, but I'll never get back to sleep. I might as well make some coffee and enjoy the sunrise in a few hours.

I brace my hands on the deck railing, the cool band on my left ring finger glinting in the moonlight and drop my chin to my chest. I close my eyes, focus on the sounds of the water, and take a deep breath, letting reality settle over my skin.

It prickles uncomfortably, and I grit my teeth.

Savannah is coming here. Back into my life.

She's occupied a space in my head for years. A space that I've tried like hell to avoid. To forget. But here, in my town, avoiding her will be impossible. I have to prepare myself for that.

Savannah may be coming here, but I can't let her back into my heart.

And I can't let her upend my life again.

---

**Meet Savannah and Levi in *Between Never and Forever*, a single dad, rockstar, second chance romance.** Read it today in KU

# ACKNOWLEDGMENTS

Book number eight! How bonkers is that? I wonder if this will ever get less surreal...

I want to thank some VIPs who always come in clutch when I need them, and without whom Sam & Casper wouldn't have been possible.

To my elite team of Betas & Alphas, thank you so much for always being willing to read whatever I throw at you, and for always giving me your most honest feedback. **Kara, Caitlin, Brianna, Mickey, Hales, Jessie, Jenna, and Sarah Beth**, thank you SO MUCH for the work you did with this book. It wouldn't have been half of what it is without your suggestions and feedback. You're in valuable to me.

To my editing team, **Rebecca with Fairest Reviews Editing Services, Emily with Lawrence Editing, and Sarah with All Encompassing Books**, thank you for your keen eyes and attention to detail. You whipped Sam and Chris into shape and it's amazing to see what this book has become considering it started as just a blob of an idea.

**Shauna** (aka loml & wind beneath my wings) and **Becca** at **The Author Agency** - I love you ladies so much. Thank you for believing in me even when I don't and for always being ready with a pep talk or a butt kick. I couldn't do this without you.

To my cover designer, **Murphy Rae**, thank you for giving me another wonderous piece of art to decorate my bookshelf. Obsessed doesn't even begin to cover it.

To my **Street Team** — your enthusiasm and support means the absolute world to me. Your encouragement is why I keep writing and I couldn't do this without you. I hope you know how much I appreciate you. Thank you so much.

To the **ARC readers, bloggers, and bookish creators** who took the time to read this book, thank you so much. There are so many amazing books out there. Thank you for making time to read one of mine. Very special thanks to **Cheyenne**, for loaning me your name and encouraging the creation of Puma the hamster, and to **Stephanie** and **Heather** for giving me such great nick names for Claire.

To my **author friends, my emotional support pirates, and my IRL besties** — thank you for putting up with my shit. Thank for making me feel less alone. For believing in me when I don't believe in myself. For listening to my rambling voice notes and always being down to appreciate an unhinged tiktok. Thank you for talking me off many cliffs and being such fantastic sounding boards. You know who you are, and I hope you know how much I fucking love you.

To **my husband**, my real-life love story, I'm obsessed with you. You're my true north. I couldn't imagine doing life with anyone else. Thank you for being you.

Until the next one, my loves.

Love,

-J-Brit

# ALSO FROM BRIT

**Next Life world**
*The Love of My Next Life* (Lennon & Macon, pt. 1)
*This Life and All the Rest* (Lennon & Macon, pt. 2)
*The Love You Fight For* (Sam & Chris)

**The Hometown Heartless Series**
*Between Never and Forever* (Sav & Levi)

**Better Love series**
*Love You Better* (Ivy & Kelley)
*Better With You* (Bailey & Riggs)
*Nothing Feels Better* (Jocelyn & Jesse)
*Better Than The Beach:* A holiday novella (Cassie & Nolan)

To stay updated on future release dates and plans, follow Brit on Instagram, Facebook, or sign up for her newsletter.

## ABOUT THE AUTHOR

Brit Benson writes real, relatable romance.

She likes outspoken, independent heroines, dirty talking, love-struck heroes, and plots that get you right in the feels.

Brit would almost always rather be reading or writing. When she's not dreaming up her next swoony book boyfriend and fierce book bestie, she's getting lost in someone else's fictional world. When she's not doing that, she's probably marathoning a Netflix series or wandering aimlessly up and down the aisles in Homegoods, sniffing candles and touching things she'll never buy.

www.ingramcontent.com/pod-product-compliance
Ingram Content Group UK Ltd.
Pitfield, Milton Keynes, MK11 3LW, UK
UKHW021044040825
7208UKWH00053B/1288